DATE DUE   AUG 0 6

OCT 17 06			

GAYLORD   PRINTED IN U.S.A.

Great Pretenders

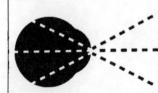

This Large Print Book carries the
Seal of Approval of N.A.V.H.

Great Pretenders

My Strange Love Affair with '50s Pop Music

Karen Schoemer

Thorndike Press • Waterville, Maine

Published in 2006 by arrangement with Free Press, a division of Simon & Schuster, Inc.

Thorndike Press® Large Print Biography.

The tree indicium is a trademark of Thorndike Press.

The text of this Large Print edition is unabridged.
Other aspects of the book may vary from the original edition.

Set in 16 pt. Plantin.

Printed in the United States on permanent paper.

Library of Congress Cataloging-in-Publication Data

Schoemer, Karen.
    Great pretenders : my strange love affair with '50's pop
music / by Karen Schoemer.
        p. cm. — (Thorndike Press large print biography)
    Includes bibliographical references.
    ISBN 0-7862-8712-8 (lg. print : hc : alk. paper)
    1. Popular music — United States — 1951–1960 —
History and criticism.   2. Schoemer, Karen.   3. Large type
books.   I. Title.   II. Thorndike Press large print biography
series.
    ML3477.S36G74 2006b
    781.640973´09045—dc22   2006008364

To Mom

I seem to be what I'm not, you see.

— The Platters

Contents

Introduction

On an early spring day in 1998, I sat in a coach window seat of a descending American Airlines flight, panicking. Below me, the sun-bleached whiteness of the Los Angeles basin loomed closer and closer. I was due to land in twenty-eight minutes, yet I had no idea where I was going. I had no compass, no direction, no guidebook. My destination wasn't on any map; I wasn't even sure if it really existed. I had been to L.A. many times in the past, always with a purpose, always with my expenses paid. I had traveled as a journalist for newspapers and magazines, on assignment to write celebrity profiles and interview musicians. I always knew exactly where to go, and when. Publicists took care of everything. This was different. This time I was writing a book; I was on my own, flying under no prestigious banner, with no one to look out for me. It all seemed like a terrible mistake. I wanted to hit the call button and tell the flight attendant, Help me! I wanted to run up the aisle to the cockpit and instruct the pilots to turn the plane around and put me back on the ground in New York, where I would be safe. I pressed my nose against the window and breathed uneasily. It's not that I've never felt this scared before, I said to myself. It's that I've never felt this stupid.

For my work in L.A., I had a bunch of half-baked ideas. I could drive to Las Vegas and see Steve Lawrence and Eydie Gorme perform at Caesars Palace. Afterward I could head backstage and try to convince them to grant me an interview. Back in L.A., I had an interview tentatively scheduled with Pat Boone. I'd recently interviewed Paul Anka for a *Newsweek* story; I figured he might be willing to talk to me again for the book. I had packets stuffed with clips about each of these performers, and others; I had a travel bag weighted with vintage LPs that I'd picked up at thrift stores and flea markets. But these tools seemed depressingly meager to me. In my computer was a list of more than fifty pop singers, and for all I knew I needed to interview them all. How could I do it? What was my focus? Did I need to know complete biographical and critical histories of every single living fifties pop singer? What was I thinking — that I would write, you know, forty-five words about each of them? I was overwhelmed, clueless. I was afraid I would sit down with these people, who had so generously given their time, and knock around the conversation like a pinball, hoping to bump into something that would light up an idea.

Of course, I did not act so pathetic and aimless when I finally faced these performers. (I don't think I did.) I learned as much as I could about their lives, their music, and the era in which they flourished. I asked questions; I had things I wanted to know. But I was always secretly fearful that someone would find me out. They'd look me in the eye and say, My God, you don't know what you're doing! The worst moments came when people patiently, curiously asked me to tell them a little about my book. I made up something different every time. "My book," I'd say, affecting pomposity, "is about the era between Elvis and the Beatles, when rock and roll was flourishing but old-fashioned pop still held commercial sway." Or I might try, "I'm writing about the teen pop of the fifties, because I feel like no one has ever taken it as seriously as it deserves." If I was feeling particularly uninspired, I'd say, "Nineteen-fifties pop music." I was afraid to tell people the real reasons I was there: that I thought them the most delightfully cheesy performers in pop history; that I saw them as brilliant failures and beautiful also-rans; that I believed that their cheery, Technicolor images covered up something dark and desperate in our cultural past, although I wasn't sure exactly what. I assumed that if I told them this, they would refuse to talk to me.

I had another reason for being there — one that seemed so silly and personal it took me some time to acknowledge it myself. Through meeting these performers and learning about them, I was hoping to get to know my parents better. My mom and dad were both fifties kids. My mom was fifteen in 1956, the year rock and roll exploded onto the charts; I think of her as the archetypal Elvis Girl, the teenager who screamed when she saw him on TV and listened to his records in secret because her parents disapproved. My dad remembers driving around during the summer of 1957 with Paul Anka's "Diana" on the radio, his seventeen-year-old mind enthralled by the song's racy depiction of an older woman and a younger man. I'd chosen the late fifties as the main area of concentration for my book; this was the time my parents came of age. (In my mind, the late fifties spilled over into the early sixties, those three years leading up to the assassination of President Kennedy.) My parents met in the summer of 1958. They started dating a year or two later and married in July 1962, right after my mom finished college. I knew so little about my parents' marriage. I knew plenty about their divorce in 1981 when I was sixteen; I was intimately acquainted with the gruesome details that drove them apart. But the forces that drew them together were a mystery to me. What made them like each other? What did they have in common? In my mind I pasted their faces on those goofy retro postcards you see everywhere: teenagers twisting in front of jukeboxes, sitting with ankles crossed at soda fountain counters, laughing in convertibles as a roller-skated burgerhop wheels up with a tray. Were my parents like that? Were they that happy, that clichéd?

The funny thing was, I didn't feel like I could ask them about their early years together. Nearly twenty years after their divorce, my parents kept a hostile distance from one another, and my relationship with both of them seemed predicated on convincing each that I had as little interest in their former spouse as they did. Both were remarried, both had moved on, yet their mutual loathing persevered; like a lot of kids, I felt caught in the middle. I could remember an eight-year stretch when, living less than thirty miles apart, they went without any communication whatsoever, except alimony checks. It was as if they wanted to erase their past and all that went with it, except for my brother and me. Lately I'd begun to wonder: What is with these people? What expectation of their youth could have been so great that its disappointment left them so angry? Just what on earth happened back there in 1962?

All I had to go on were a few sketchy details, the kind of nuggets parents repeat endlessly to their kids. For me, these details had expanded into myths. I thought of my mom in the fifties as a bit of a rebel, and my dad as a bit of a geek. She was an Italian-Irish girl, tough on the outside, tender within, raised in a typical middle-class neighborhood; her father worked for the phone company, and before she met my dad she used to run around with the local Italian boys. My dad was more upper-crust. His father was a corporate lawyer who once argued a case in front of the Supreme Court; my dad was white collar through and through, an aspiring square. When my mom hooked up with my dad, her parents must have heaved a sigh of relief. My dad was stable, a future accountant, a breadwinner. He'd keep my mom on track, give her a good life. When I was young, my mother showed my brother and me her wedding album. The picture that struck me the most wasn't of my parents

— it was of my mother's parents, dancing gaily, my grandmother kicking up her heels as if it were the best day of her life. And there was another significant photograph that hung on the wall of our house when I was growing up. It was a studio portrait of my mother in her wedding gown. She looked awesomely beautiful: milk-white skin, careful brunet coif, satin gloves coming up past her elbows, dress train spread royally around her. Her expression haunts me still. It wasn't joy, or uncontrolled happiness, or nervous excitement. It was something prouder, more aloof. I think it was triumph.

In 1995, three years before that flight to L.A., I myself had gotten engaged. The event triggered a bitter upheaval in my relationship with my mother. She was unhappy with my choice of a husband; moreover, she was aghast that I seemed to be disregarding her wishes and going ahead with my wedding anyway. We embarked upon our own cold war: weeks or months of stony silence, broken by strings of hideous phone conversations in which hate tried to hide beneath decorum. "I would never have married someone my parents didn't approve of," she hissed at one point. "Yeah, and look where it got you," I snapped back. It didn't occur to me until later to wonder how much control she had

had over her own marriage, her own destiny.

I couldn't turn to her, that much was clear. But in the midst of our fighting, I found an unexpected new ally: her music. Maybe it would tell me things my mother would not.

One day in 1996, as I was going about my job as the pop music critic for *Newsweek*, I received a package from Mercury Records. It was a four-CD box set called *Connie Francis: Souvenirs*. I stared in amazement at the picture of the singer on the cover. Connie Francis looked just like my mom. Same pouf of dark hair. Same Italianate features. I flipped through the booklet. Her gowns looked like something you'd wear to a debutante ball, or a wedding. I scanned the track listing and found the title that was most familiar to me: "Where the Boys Are," a Top 10 hit from 1961, written by Neil Sedaka and Howard Greenfield and released as the title track to the teen movie starring Dolores Hart and Paula Prentiss. I put the CD in the stereo and pressed play.

"Where the Boys Are" began on a startling crescendo of choral voices and insistent drums, then mellowed into a gently swinging rock-and-roll waltz. Pianos plinked in three-quarter time; strings *ahhhed* in the

16

background. The lyric practically had me standing on my chair: it described a netherworld where every girl's perfect mate awaits and told of how, in a world of strangers, the right boy will step forward with arms outstretched, ready to make his girl's dreams come true. Men in this song weren't fully fleshed-out creatures with their own needs and desires; they were ciphers, mere handmaidens to the passions of each particular girl. And women, for their part, were bereft and incomplete until that right boy claimed them. Then, once they'd made their match, they became all-powerful. "I'll climb to the highest steeple," Connie bragged, "and tell the world he's mine."

The words grabbed me, but it was Connie's voice that captivated me the most. It was drenched with emotion yet eerily detached, with the most perfect pitch and throbbing vibrato I'd ever heard. She threw herself into the song as if it were church hymn and opera rolled into one: hitting each note square in the eye, rounding each vowel, draping a bow on each consonant, drawing out each line until her breath left her. The simultaneous power and prettiness of her voice reminded me of Patsy Cline, but there was something different about Connie — something more passive, less modern. She sang impersonally, without meaning, almost obsequiously, as if the song controlled her and she was subservient to it. She didn't interpret the words; they interpreted her.

The critic in me knew that this song was completely ridiculous. It was archaic, unenlightened, antifeminist. But my mother's daughter fell for it right away. I heard in it the sound of every teenage girl in every bedroom on every lonely Saturday going back a thousand years, as she waited for the right boy, praying for him to save her from her shadow-life of misery. I recognized myself in the song; more importantly, I recognized my mom, the elusive teenager I wanted so badly to go back in time to meet. I could picture her in all her radiant whiteness, holding herself back until she met the man who would make her complete, waiting patiently for him to transform her life of unwomanly solitude into one of resplendency. I saw her perched atop that steeple, telling the world, He's mine, exulting in the fulfillment of a longing, as if the struggles of her life were now behind her.

I realized then that the values and themes of the era's pop music brilliantly mirrored the concerns of people's everyday lives. These jukebox hits and chart-toppers, so sugary and disposable on the surface, are actually potent little vessels that allow us to glimpse the world as it existed back then. Or rather, as its participants — both audience and performers — wanted it to exist; these songs were their idealized world, small crystal globes of romantic respite. Love, in reality so impossible and flawed, became attainable and containable in these songs. It wasn't messy or painful; it was celestial and comforting, a balm to soothe aching hearts. Love was perfect. And it was lustless; no earthy realities interfered. The images in these songs were so transfixing and intoxicating that people began to believe them. Girls especially: they dreamed they'd find that ideal boy, and climb that steeple, and then their lives would be set. They'd have everything they needed. They'd get married, raise children, cook nice meals for hard-working husbands. Nobody thought times would change; they figured the future would be just like the present — knowable, orderly, controlled. Love that perfect would, by definition, last forever.

For many years, the music industry and the public collaborated in this fantasy. Everyone got carried away. The listeners thought their icons really were polite, chaste, well-brought-up boys and girls next door who answered their own fan mail, went home to normal families, and upheld solid moral values. The performers, meanwhile, thought it was their job to live up to the images they projected. One slip — a cigarette caught on camera, a caustic word to a fan, an illicit dalliance leaked to the papers — and their entire careers could come crashing down. Behind the scenes, of course, there were clear-eyed cynics who knew that a buck was just a buck, and they exploited the situation for all it was worth. But a surprising number of managers, agents, and executives believed the myths just as ardently as anyone. They viewed themselves as father figures — or mother figures — whose charges were vulnerable children badly in need of discipline and protection. And the performers, for the most part, were happy to let others take care of them. They were young, inexperienced, and financially inept. So they sang the songs they were told to sing, showed up for their recording sessions on time, smiled on cue, and shook the right hands. They performed, no matter where they went. They were a good product, and they sold millions: sonic All-Temperature Cheer, musical $100,000 Bars.

It was a risky enterprise, though, and the pressures were intense. What if these performers were found out? What if they revealed themselves to be flawed and human?

Audiences would be angry. It would be as if they'd gotten home, unwrapped the candy bar, and discovered it was chalky and tasteless. They'd feel betrayed. They'd want their money back. They'd never buy that product again.

On February 8, 1964, a group of mop-haired Brits stepped off a plane at JFK, making so much noise that the country awoke out of its sugar-induced coma. Almost overnight, the old values were overturned and new, wilder, sexually charged ones took their place. Beat poets, lefties, and the publishers of juvenile-delinquent paperbacks had been banging this drum for years, but it wasn't until early 1964, just a few months after President Kennedy's assassination, that the country at large seemed willing to listen. And once people got hip to how square they'd been, they tried to distance themselves as much as possible from the old ways. In a fit of irrationality, they blamed the music, as if it had brainwashed them, as if they hadn't participated in its popularity. "The teen idol era was a product of the assumption that kids were endlessly gullible, utterly tasteless and dependably aroused by a comely face or a gratuitous mention of 'high school' or 'bobby sox,'" Greg Shaw writes in *The Rolling Stone Illustrated History of Rock &*

Roll. Whereas once the music had mirrored the times, now it was somehow culpable, a scam perpetrated on unsuspecting ears. The songs had lied; the performers were fakes. Suddenly, sweet romantic pop was persona non grata. It virtually disappeared off the charts. Careers were leveled; bookings dried up. Some performers, like Patti Page, took refuge in the dwindling nightclub circuit and kept releasing the same old type of material. Some, like Paul Anka and Tommy Sands, packed up and headed to Europe or Hawaii, hoping to find a warmer reception elsewhere. Still others, like Georgia Gibbs, dropped out of the business altogether. Pat Boone temporarily lost his religion to drinking and gambling in Las Vegas. A few, like Bobby Darin, tried to "get real" and change with the times — he threw off his toupee and picked up an acoustic guitar, trying to cut it as a protest singer. The fans who clung on through that phase are the kind every entertainer prays for.

As hard as it was for the performers to adapt, I think it must have been even harder for the audience. The people who came of age in that era didn't just lose a career — they saw their moral foundation crumble, their belief system rot. Year after year, the blunt realities of daily life stratified on top of their youthful ideals, and eventually people had to shoulder out from under the load. I used to believe that my parents' divorce in 1981 was due to the fact that my mother, at the age of forty, had finally discovered women's liberation. She chose to free herself, after nineteen years, from a marriage that crushed and suffocated her. Lately, though, I've begun to wonder. I'm not sure she ever freed herself from those vows of perfect love she pledged in 1962. The shame and disappointment of her failure are with her still. She may have directed her anger at my dad, but it really wasn't about my dad. She was angry at herself for being stupid enough to believe in values that proved collapsible and inadequate. She climbed that steeple, and it dissolved and eroded under her touch. She had a long way to fall.

When I first conceived of this book, I imagined it as an homage to the great rock books I'd read in my early twenties: *Lost Highway* and *Feel Like Going Home* by Peter Guralnick, *Deep Blues* by Robert Palmer, *Unsung Heroes of Rock 'n' Roll* by Nick Tosches, *Mystery Train* by Greil Marcus. These books had shaped my understanding of rock history, and inspired in me a love of roots music, from country to blues to early R&B. I wanted to take their basic structure — critical profiles — and apply it to a genre these writers had studiously avoided: the pop of the fifties. When I was a nascent critic, reading the great books, sending myself to rock school, trying to put together an idea of the way rock history had shaped the music of my own times, I never learned anything about the pop of the fifties. If anything, I had a vague sense that the ascendance of rock and roll had vanquished crummy, stuffy, grown-up pop. Electric guitars rang out, black performers wop-bop-a-lu-bopped, white kids got loose and sent Perry Como packing. But in 1990, a friend suggested that I write an article about Frank Sinatra. I was living in Hoboken, New Jersey, at the time — Frank's hometown — and I'd developed an interest in what I called "Rockefeller Center ice-skating music": drippy, old-fashioned romantic pop. My friend thought I should discuss Sinatra from a young person's perspective, talk about what it was like to discover him. Growing up, I'd never heard Sinatra in my household. He was my parents' parents' music; in our house, we heard the Beatles, Carole King, the Beach Boys, the sound track to *American Grafitti*. Sinatra, rebelled against by my parents' generation, had now almost disappeared. So I wrote a piece for a magazine called *L.A. Style* on the occasion of Sinatra's seventy-fifth birthday. And as I did my research, I learned something funny. The album generally acknowledged as Sinatra's finest, *Frank Sinatra Sings for Only the Lonely*, had been released in 1958. At the height of the rock explosion! Not only that, it had gone to Number 1 on the album charts. But how could that be? I didn't know that old people made records after 1956!

That's how naive I was. But that naiveté had its roots in the way rock critics presented the music of the fifties. It was always us versus them, a face-off, a high-noon showdown in which the youth of America wildly triumphed. In 1995, PBS aired a much-ballyhooed ten-part documentary series, *Rock & Roll*. Its curator was none other than Robert Palmer, one of my writer-heroes. Here's how the documentary opens: with a quote from Robbie Robertson of the Band. Frankly, I've always thought he was a bit of a stuffed shirt, *Basement Tapes* or no *Basement Tapes*. He stares smugly into the camera and says, "It seemed like on Monday, there was Patti Page and Perry Como and whoever these people were. And then on Tuesday, it was like all these people were just waiting in the chute." The film cut to a rapid-fire montage of rock and roll exploding: machine-gun images of

Elvis, Little Richard, Jerry Lee Lewis, Buddy Holly, the Beatles, Janis Joplin, Jimi Hendrix, etc. The idea was that pop music and rock and roll had no relationship to each other whatsoever. They were like James Dean and his dad in *Rebel Without a Cause*: an unbridgeable generation gap, with no overlap, no room for mutual understanding. Rock and roll, in rebelling against pop, allegedly took no lessons from it. It was a wholesale rejection of pop's values. Rock derived from blues, R&B, and outlaw country, borrowing not an ounce of the mainstream complacency that pop represented.

After Connie Francis piqued my interest, I looked more closely at the charts. And what I began to discover was that, at best, this idea was an exaggeration of the truth. In fact, pop and rock coexisted — if not peacefully, then at least side by side for several years after the first wave of rock and rollers arrived. The charts of the late fifties are loaded with hits by the early-fifties superstars. Between 1955 and 1960 Patti Page had more than a dozen Top 40 hits, including two Top 10s: "Allegheny Moon" (Number 2) and "Old Cape Cod" (Number 3). Perry Como had nearly two dozen major hits, including "Hot Diggity (Dog Ziggity Boom)," "Round and Round," and "Catch a Falling Star," all of which lodged at Number 1. Nat "King" Cole had a song in the Top 40 practically every week between 1955 and 1958. But the more I thought about it, the more I began to realize that this idea that fifties pop had nothing in common with rock was worse than an exaggeration. In fact, it looked to me like an actual lie. I mean, you don't need to be a genius to figure out that rock and pop were influencing each other from the get-go. Just look at Elvis. He was a Dean Martin fan. One of his all-time greatest hits was "Love Me Tender." He didn't learn those suave romantic inflections from Big Joe Turner. Many of the great doo-wop acts were covering pop standards from the thirties and forties: the Platters' "Smoke Gets in Your Eyes" was a Paul Whiteman hit from 1934; the Flamingos' "I Only Have Eyes for You" was a Ben Selvin hit that same year.

It's true that by the end of the decade, the predominance of the early-fifties stars like Perry Como and Patti Page had waned. But what replaced it wasn't screech-and-yowl outsider rockabilly. With the notable exception of Elvis, most of the artists lauded as rock-and-roll's greatest pioneers didn't have a huge chart presence in the fifties. Jerry Lee Lewis had only four Top 40 hits during that decade. Johnny Cash had six. Little

Richard had nine. (And of those three, only Cash charted major pop hits after the fifties.) Performers with a more accessible sound, like Fats Domino and the Everly Brothers, scored more consistently. But what replaced those mighty pop stars was a new generation of crooners who combined the beat of rock and roll with the romantic preoccupations of pop. These singers were hybrids of Sinatra and Elvis, well-groomed kids who donned tuxedos and slicked their hair but wiggled and directed their sentiments at the emerging market of teenagers. They were the teen idols, and in the late fifties they were huge. Pat Boone, Connie Francis, Frankie Avalon, Paul Anka, and Bobby Darin remain, to this day, among the most popular artists in the history of rock. Their dominance was unquestionable. Pat Boone was second only to Elvis on the charts. Until Aretha Franklin came along in the late sixties, Connie Francis reigned as the biggest female singer in the world.

If rock critics have always gone for a silent assassination of the early-fifties pop stars, they reserved an even worse fate for the late-fifties teen idols. No group of singers in rock history has been more consistently denigrated and maligned. "Played by bored, middle-aged studio musicians, the music, despite an occasionally tasty saxophone break, at best had an ersatz vivacity," says *The Rolling Stone Illustrated History of Rock & Roll*, in a chapter titled "The Teen Idols"; "More often, it flaunted the cloying, string-laden blandness that the first rockers had revolted against." Nik Cohn, in his 1969 book *Rock From the Beginning*, dubs teen-idol music "highschool": "Where Southern rock introduced something new to popular music — noise, violence, the mixing of R&B and country, gibberish, semi-anarchy — highschool was basically a continuation of existing white traditions. The solo singers were pretty boys, very much in the tradition of Sinatra, Eddie Fisher, or Vic Damone . . . All that changed was that highschool catered solely for a teenage market and that it had no conception of quality whatsoever." These dismissals were part of the larger prevailing theory that, sometime around 1958 or so, rock and roll "died." Elvis got drafted. Jerry Lee Lewis torpedoed his career by marrying his thirteen-year-old cousin. Little Richard left R&B for the church. In early 1959, a plane crash killed Buddy Holly, Ritchie Valens, and the Big Bopper. Soon Chuck Berry was on trial for transporting a minor across state lines. Eddie Cochran died in a car wreck. Except for a couple of minor flutterings of quality — some girl groups, black pop like the Drifters, songwriting teams like Leiber/Stoller and Goffin/King — the body of rock lay in state until the Beatles arrived in 1964, saving humanity once again from the deadening beat of pop ballads, awakening the nation from its teen-idol stupor.

From the sound of "Where the Boys Are" alone, it was clear that the teen idols had gotten an unfair shafting. There had to be more songs like it: moments where the very limitations of romantic pop unlocked pristine confessions of unspecified longings. Other rock critics heard bland, empty industry fodder; I heard unconsciously personal expressions of tension and anxiety. Underneath the well-groomed surfaces, teen-idol music contained seeds of the same explosive passions and aggressions that fueled early rock and roll; the interesting thing about teen-idol music was that it desperately tried to suppress those passions, even as it acknowledged them. I had a sense that reactionary, deeply ingrained critical biases had worked against these singers. Rock criticism hadn't even come into its own until the late sixties. Up until then, pop-music writing was the province of dry-minded newspaper gumshoes or, at the other end of the journalistic spectrum, hysteria-driven fan-

zines. (There was, in addition, a tradition of jazz criticism going back to the forties and early fifties in magazines like *Down Beat* and *Metronome*; popular singers like Patti Page and Georgia Gibbs, interestingly enough, often fared well in these critics' assessments.) Writers began taking rock seriously around the time the music began taking itself seriously. Pioneering rock critics like Robert Christgau, writing in *Esquire* and then *The Village Voice*, and Greil Marcus, writing in *Rolling Stone*, were erstwhile academics seeking to illuminate the sociopolitical radicalism defining every squawk of Jimi Hendrix's guitar. *Rolling Stone* itself had been founded in 1967 in order to gonzoically document the cultural mayhem in its hometown of San Francisco. Rock critics' backward glances at teen pop sounded like the musings of guys who had hated it as kids and couldn't wait to be old enough to grind their ax in print. The fact that teen idols sang of love instead of lust, of conforming instead of breaking out, of behaving instead of transgressing put them at odds with everything the late sixties supposedly stood for; the sentiment of waiting till we're married didn't have a place in a rock planbook that strove toward sexual liberation and loosening morals. No late-sixties critic in his right mind aspired to be a polite nerd who kept his dick in his pants until his wedding day.

I thought I was fairly well qualified to study teen-idol pop. I knew the crush well. I'd been boy-crazy since I was five years old, when my kindergarten class photo captured me sneaking a glance at cute Michael Dayton three heads away. Crushy girls, of course, were the audience for whom fifties pop had been primarily designed. So I figured that it had never been taken seriously because a girl had never bothered to examine it.

I actually liked the idea of taking on a subject loathed by critics. It appealed to one of my decidedly more contemporary sides: the punk contrarian. I felt connected to the music through my parents, but my sensibility had been shaped in the eighties and nineties, when my infatuation had been postpunk and independent rock. I would rescue this music, rehabilitate it, introduce it to new generations. Underneath my critical agenda, though, was that hidden, more personal one: inside, I was pining for my mother, whose rejection I still felt deeply. The book, culminating in my portrait of Connie Francis, would be a secret gift to her. She would clearly see, in the love I expressed for these singers, the thinly veiled love I felt for her. The magnitude of my gift would so move her

that she would forgive my supposed trans-
gressions. When I finished it, I would nudge
her and say, "Mom, every time I say the
name Connie Francis, just know that I am
really talking about you." She would love me
again. Everything would be all right. Happily
ever after and all that rot.

I felt a little weird about this hidden
agenda. It seemed vaguely unprofessional.
If I was writing about music, I should really
be writing about music, right? But I didn't
worry about it too much. I was on a mission.
I wanted my mother not to feel so alone. I
wanted to make right by her failure, to put
what was broken back together. I wanted
her once again to remember those feelings
of being soothed, whispered to, innocently
caressed. Remember, Mom? I wanted to say.
For a few short years, the world made music
just for you.

So I got to work. I was prepared to take on
critics, but very quickly I realized that the
bias against fifties singers wasn't limited to
people whose professional duty it was to
have an opinion about music. Out on the
street, too, these performers had a bad reputation. The first indication that everything
was not all right came in the form of a rejection letter from an editor at a publishing

house, who said something to the effect of, I love Karen Schoemer's writing, but I would never publish a book about this crap.

I didn't get much enthusiasm from friends and acquaintances in the music business, either. I called up the deejay and Sinatraologist Jonathan Schwartz to pick his brain. "You're going to have to explain the numbing mediocrity with which you've chosen to surround yourself," he said. The singer-songwriter John Wesley Harding tried to put a cheerful spin on my choice of a topic. "That sounds great, because you want to read about these people but you don't actually want to listen to the music," he said. I thought I had a sympathetic ear in Kathleen Hanna, the punk-rock riot grrrl, after she told me she'd attended a Connie Francis book signing with her mother. But when I explained the book, she just said, "That's some of the worst music ever made."

Apparently I had a bit of a mountain to climb here, winning all these people over. Well, I was up to the challenge. I began my research. I compiled clippings, breezed through books, scoured video archives. I bought some CD reissues, but my big indulgence was vintage LPs. I loved them as artifacts. They were doorways into the past, talismen of the passions and preoccupations of the era. The old LPs taught me how different the sensibility of the fifties was from my own. Back then, albums were still relatively new and unproven in the marketplace. Singles were the currency: on jukeboxes, on the radio, and in stores, the single-song format established performers and earned the most money. Albums hadn't been established yet as vehicles for auteurism — that would happen later in the sixties, around the time of *Sgt. Pepper's Lonely Hearts Club Band* and the Beach Boys' *Pet Sounds*. In the Connie Francis era, albums were just themed collections of popular songs. They weren't attempts to introduce new material; rather, the thinking was that audiences would want to hear a beloved singer interpret songs that were already familiar. Countless fifties singers recorded albums with the title *Songs Everybody Knows*. They recorded collections of swing tunes, country tunes, old-timey Americana songs. Connie herself covered a staggering variety of styles on her albums: *Country & Western Golden Hits. Rock 'n' Roll Million Sellers. Songs to a Swinging Band. Greatest American Waltzes. Do the Twist. Connie Francis Sings "Never on Sunday" and Other Title Songs from Motion Pictures. Connie Francis Sings Italian Favorites. Connie Francis Sings Spanish and Latin American Favorites. Connie Francis Sings Jewish Favorites. Connie*

Francis Sings German Favorites. Connie Francis Sings Irish Favorites. Connie at the Copa. Hawaii Connie.

The LPs of the era represented an optimism that I coveted. They captured America at an extraordinarily confident moment. Singers could march into foreign territories and conquer them within fifteen minutes per side. The possibilities were endless. It wasn't that I agreed with cultural imperialism. I just liked the idea that people felt so uncomplicated about themselves and their place in the universe. The LPs also demonstrated the way new media were beginning to change the country. With the rise of television and radio, middle-class folks in the suburbs suddenly had access to rural lifestyles, urban lifestyles, ethnic traditions they might not encounter on their own block. An enormous amount of cross-pollination was going on. Yet the weight of the music industry was still behind popular music — stuff that would appeal to as many people as possible. I loved the idea that Connie Francis could take listeners on an aural cruise to the Mediterranean, or that Patti Page would lead a wagon train into the Appalachian hills. The notions themselves, of course, were preposterous. But I was touched by the innocence that allowed people to buy into them.

I learned a lot just by looking at these old LP covers. But eventually, as I started lining up interviews, the time came when I needed to actually listen to them. I'd sit down for an afternoon with a stack of Pat Boones or Patti Pages grinning at me. And then, one by one, I'd try to work my way through them. What I encountered on those listening excursions devastated me. As predicted, the music, more often than not, was terrible. The albums, with extremely rare exceptions, were dull, samey, uninspired, repetitive. It soon became evident that this had a lot to do with the recording conventions of the times. Sessions were often completed in a day or two, with the same musicians and arrangers present; and once a producer or record company executive hit upon a formula that worked, they tended to stick with it. So even if a singer covered a broad stylistic range, the actual feel of the music was notably unadventurous. Rock and roll favors performers who are raw, spontaneous, amateurish — people with no experience can stumble into a recording studio and come out with a hit record. But in the old pop days, professionalism was a virtue. Musicians and singers were expected to hit the right notes, to follow what was written down before them, to obey the producer or Artist and Repertoire director's instructions to the letter. The goal wasn't to shock or jolt or break new ground; it was to soothe and coddle — to placate listeners with reassuring and familiar sounds. Today, a singer like Madonna reinvents herself at every turn. Back then, singers were like offshoots of a new philosophy that was hitting restaurants and hotels: they became recognizable brands as their albums propagated like franchises in a chain. Connie Francis was expected to be Connie Francis, whether she was singing "God Bless America" or "Havah Negilah." Homogeneity ruled.

Understanding why the music was terrible, though, didn't take away from the central fact that it was terrible. I had a major problem on my hands. At first, I tried to deny to myself that it was terrible. I tried to put a positive spin on Patti Page's oeuvre, hunting out the songs that were less awful, identifying the things that she did reasonably well. I wondered if Frankie Laine's "Mule Train" wasn't actually sort of fabulous in its awfulness. I wanted to believe that a few of Pat Boone's delectable crooner nuggets compensated for his mountain of embarrassing R&B covers. I found that I actually liked Georgia Gibbs's much-maligned versions of LaVern Baker and Etta James originals. I tried to believe that these rare gems justified an entire book. But I never quite did. And the more fifties music I listened to, the more nervous I became that I was digging myself into a very deep critical hole.

How was I going to reconcile my desire to rescue teen idol music with my honest critical assessment that the music wasn't very good? The skepticism of my colleagues and peers fed into my already-rampant doubts about the subject of this book. It seemed impossible that every single smart person I knew was wrong and I was right. It seemed a lot more logical to think that I was wrong. I buckled under the weight of conventional wisdom. I did not feel able to turn this massive tide of opinion. I got stomach aches and migraines. I suffered extended bouts of writer's block. The year 1998 was a strange one for me. On sabbatical from *Newsweek*, I traipsed around the country, collecting interviews with pop singers, exuberantly living my lifelong dream of writing a book. But I was also intermittently crippled by anxiety over what my book would eventually say. I had the vain notion that writing a book would deliver me to the inner circle of writers whom I had long worshipped — Peter Guralnick, Nick Tosches, Robert Palmer, and Greil Marcus, among others. I thought that was all I had to do: write a book. Then

I'd be like them. At the same time I feared that my ideas would forever locate me outside that circle. My God, I was nothing like them. I was in direct opposition to them. I even hated them, in an Oedipal sort of way! How did I ever get this fucked up?

In 1999, after my year of interviews, I quit my job at *Newsweek* in order to work on the book full time. But I found myself unable to make any progress. I lost all faith in what I was doing. I psyched myself out. Finally, out of intense frustration, I began writing about what was holding me up. I began to focus on the quandaries and insecurities that were causing me to panic. Two central questions emerged: Why was I attracted to this music, if it was, indeed, awful? And why was I feeling all this anxiety? In early 2001, I began writing in earnest, with these questions in mind and with a determination to be honest with myself. I no longer thought about emulating the writers who had inspired me. I thought only about saving myself the ignominy of going up in personal and professional flames.

So I wrote. And in the writing process, the book changed. The question of what it was about the music that appealed to me became almost more important to me than the singers themselves. The book started to take on strange issues that hadn't previously concerned me: What is the true nature of criticism? Can it be objective, or is it necessarily subjective? Isn't it true that all critics, all the time, bring their own biases and personal histories to bear when they write about music? Is it possible to say that a piece of music is bad or good, in any absolute sense? Or is a critic merely saying at any given moment that he likes or dislikes it?

I knew from the start that my own history and personality were tied up in my interest in fifties music. At some point, it seemed only fair to explore that history, in order to illuminate that interest. So as the writing went on, the book became increasingly personal. Early drafts had been structured more like magazine journalism. I had still been striving toward objectivity, trying to call this music good. By the end, objectivity was out the window. I was only trying to understand what part of me this music called out to.

Thinking big at the outset, I'd interviewed close to thirty singers in 1998. My list of whom to include and whom to leave out was a bit idiosyncratic. I was looking for singers who fit my general hybrid description, those who had adapted the swagger of the Sinatra generation to the rocking beat and teen obsessions of the Elvis era. But then I expanded the description to include a few of the early-fifties singers who had served as models to the idols who came later. One quality seemed particularly important: I wanted singers who had been commercial successes, and it helped if critics loathed them. But I soon found out that my criteria mystified others. Apparently the term "fifties pop singer" wasn't as clear a catch-all as "hillbilly legend" or "obscure R&B pioneer." People were constantly asking me, Is Peggy Lee in your book? It took me a while to figure out a satisfactory answer to this one: No, she's too good. They'd say, Is Johnnie Ray in your book? No, he's dead — can't interview him. What about Roy Orbison? No, he recorded for Sun Records — too rock and roll. A black friend complained that I was concentrating on white singers. And it's true: in the fifties, mainstream audiences were open to black singers who sang in a pop style instead of a renegade R&B style. Nat "King" Cole, Johnny Mathis, Tommy Edwards, and Sam Cooke all scored on the pop charts. R&B singers like Jackie Wilson and Etta James crossed over to pop by interpreting standards. Vocal groups like the Mills Brothers and the Platters mined the pop catalog for their hits. Black pop is its own story, full of nuance. But for my purposes, I was more interested in my own roots as a square white person. This particular tradition of repression and alienation was my preoccupation.

In the end, I found that I was able to tell the story I wanted to tell with only seven singers. And their inclusion — let me be clear about this — is strictly arbitrary. So please don't write me letters complaining that I left out Paul Anka or Frankie Avalon or Bobby Darin or Jo Stafford or Gogi Grant or Teresa Brewer or Joni James or Perry Como or Eddie Fisher or Steve and Eydie. I've heard of them. I know I left them out. You want an encyclopedia of fifties music? Buy *The Virgin Encyclopedia of Fifties Music*.

This book is an odyssey of personal discovery. My lack of direction, and the anxiety it caused me, became the fuel that propelled me forward. Not until I got to the end could I find out where I was going.

One
PATTI

PATTI PAGE, NEW YORKER HOTEL, NYC

... Last time Patti played New York was more than a year ago at Café Society. At that time she was a chubby, awkward kid whose appearance almost obscured the fact that she had a lot of voice. Those deficiencies have now been corrected. She is slimmed down, becomingly gowned, and handles herself with a modest certainty which is in keeping with her clean-cut appearance ...

The young Oklahoman has a forthright, full-throated approach with a definite insistence on beat which makes even a weak-kneed ballad stand up and walk with some assurance. But she seems at her best, and her happiest, when she is belting out a blues, which she gives lyrical shouting treatment.

She was jamming a lot of numbers into her brief spot in the New Yorker show and in the process showing off the virtuosity which gives her a jump on most of her competitors. With her impressive delivery of ballads, novelties, and blues, she seems to be standing right on the fringe of the big time.

—Down Beat, *February 24, 1950*

Hooray! I'm off to discover the fifties! On a hot July afternoon in 1998, I loaded up my tiny red Subaru and hit the road. I was excited about this particular stop on my fifties tour: Patti Page's New England maple-sugar farm. I was packing *Patti Page: A Golden Celebration*, a four-CD box set released by Mercury Records in 1997, plus newspaper clippings, a tape recorder, and my overnight bag. The fifties were approximately six hours away: the New Jersey Turnpike to I-95 north, then I-91 from New Haven through Hartford, Springfield, Brattleboro, and White River Junction, until I reached a tiny town called Wells River, Vermont. It was not an easy trip. The summer weather was hot and my car was not air-conditioned. The heat off the highway blasted through my open windows with an unkindly whoosh, drowning out Patti's softly swinging tunes on the car stereo. I couldn't hear the music. So after Brattleboro, I took a back road instead of the interstate, to better use my time for research. I was so engrossed in an eerie folk number called "Who's Gonna Shoe My Pretty Little

Feet" that a cop pulled me over for going 40 in a 25 zone. Patti's voice warbled sweetly as his shadow darkened my window.

I pulled into Wells River around nightfall, checked into the Wells River Motel, and grabbed dinner at the last open restaurant in town, the Happy Hour. The waitress was polite, unobtrusive — she expressed no curiosity about what in hell I was doing in Wells River, alone, on a Monday night, thank God. After dinner I checked out the Rexall drugstore across the street. This was the site of my meeting the next morning with Patti. Her third husband, Jerry Filiciotto, had described it to me on the phone: he said it was an old-fashioned place with a soda fountain and counter service. Perfect! I could practically see teenagers jitterbugging in the aisles.

The next morning I arrived early to take some notes. Disappointingly, the Rexall felt less like a pristine artifact from a bygone era than just a dusty old drugstore, with seventies faux-wood paneling and creaky greeting-card racks. The only notable detail was that the elderly lady behind the counter served up greasy homemade donuts with the Munchkin hole perched on top. I parked at the counter, got coffee, and contemplated ordering a donut. Suddenly the nineties didn't look so bad.

They must not have looked too bad to Patti, either, because as soon as she walked in with Jerry it became clear that the last thing she wanted to do was soak up the atmosphere in downtown Wells River. She seemed a teeny bit incongruous here — she was too glittery for this place. She had frosted hair, very pink lipstick, and gold-rimmed glasses with brown tinted lenses. She wore slacks and a black-and-white tunic with spangley safari animal designs appliquéd on the pockets. I slurped my coffee, climbed in the backseat of their SUV, and we took off. It was a funny feeling — I was a kid again, riding around in my parents' car. We crossed the state line, and Jerry said they lived near the oldest covered bridge in New Hampshire. We chatted about the 1950s — Patti called the music of her era "passive." Then we were on the private road that led through Hilltop Farm. We weaved among shady maple groves and sun-drenched fields. "If you go down here and turn the motor off," Jerry said, "it's real quiet and you can hear the corn grow." He chuckled. "That's something we tell the kids."

At a bend in the road, Jerry pulled up at a massive barn that he'd converted to a maple sugar refinery. They gave me a tour of coolers and vats and freshly renovated offices. Jerry had started selling syrup several years ago under the name Filiciotto's Hilltop Farm, but no one was buying. Finally Patti said, "Well, if it'll help at all, we can put my name on it." It did. Now consumers can purchase a whole range of "Patti Page's Pure Maple Products from New England." The brochure features a homey illustration of Patti in a strappy evening gown in front of a snow-covered farm scene. Musical notes are sprinkled schematically among the maple leaves. Items for sale include pancake mixes, recipe books, tote bags, and gift baskets like "The Syrup That Sings," which comes with a pint jug of syrup (light, medium, or amber) and a Patti Page Christmas CD. Jerry deposited a free sample in my hand, and I gazed at it fondly, thinking of celebrity souvenirs I've treasured in the past — George Jones cat food, Graceland floatie pens, a Dean Martin wine bottle. I felt warm and fuzzy inside.

The main house looked like a Currier & Ives print sprung to life: it was robin's-egg blue and perched on a gentle rise with a view of the distant White Mountains. Inside, the kitchen bustled with activity; in an old-fashioned mud room, one of Jerry's grandkids was cleaning and organizing coats and boots into neat rows — chores for cash, part of the Filiciotto regimen for teaching respect and family values. Patti ushered me into a quiet living room done up in formal Colonial decor: ornate drapes swooping over roughhewn Indian shutters, fancy upholstered chairs, and a rustic hardwood floor. She paused in front of an antique piano. "It's called a something grand," she said. "Jerry will remember what kind of grand it's called. It's kind of a rare piece. We had it redone, but that's the original wood and strings."

It was becoming clear that Patti Page had it made. We sat down to talk, and I told her that I had described her life to a friend of mine, a struggling singer-songwriter, who quipped, "I should be so lucky."

Patti chuckled. "Well, we do have the best of two worlds," she said. "In California, I have all my material things that women have. When we left for this trip, I said, I don't think I'm going to have to work while I'm here, but what if I was offered a billion dollars for something? I better leave my gown in a particular place where I can tell someone to get it, just in case."

I was starting to feel darn comfortable. I was kind of wondering if they had a spare bedroom, so that I could take up residence as an honorary niece twice removed. But Patti had something weightier on her mind. She told me that she had recently split from her longtime manager, Jack Rael, a musician and bandleader who had steered her career for nearly fifty years. He had discovered her when she was just nineteen, singing pop and Western fare on an Oklahoma radio station, and chauffered her to dream-come-true stardom, helping her score more than sixty hit singles between the years 1948 and 1965 and achieving career sales of over 100 million records. Patti had agreed at the start of their relationship to give him fifty cents of every dollar she made. It's an unusually high fee, but Rael held an exceptional degree of responsibility: he chose her songs, did her arrangements, led the band, produced her TV shows, and even did her lighting on the road. After forty-eight years together, she decided that she was overpaying him, and cut him loose. The way she described it, the split sounded like a brutal divorce. "He was just greedy, it came right down to that," she said, shifting uncomfortably on the sofa. "We couldn't agree on what's going to happen to my royalties when we're no longer here. Are they to be divided between your children and my children? There's got to be a stopping point somewhere. He insisted that he had a right to fifty percent of everything that I would ever do as long as I live and beyond."

Patti's anger was building. The dovelike

timbre in her voice became just a teensy bit more edgy; her hands, which tended to trace the air gracefully as she talked, came to rest in helpless fists at her sides. She complained about other decisions of Rael's. Why, for example, didn't he get her into more movies? She had a supporting part in the 1960 Burt Lancaster film *Elmer Gantry*; why hadn't there been more? "Jack had no vision for now — let's say, fifty years later," she said. "Money was the important thing. I was probably considered for many movies, but maybe no money. And if it didn't have money connected, in his mind I wasn't even up for the part. He was not one that had any sense of, 'You should do a movie even if you don't get any money for it, because someday it will be remembered.' The longevity thing was not in his mind at all."

But what really burned her up were his musical choices. Rael had a knack for hits: it was his idea to add barks to her big hit "(How Much Is) That Doggie in the Window," his idea to overdub her vocals on chart-toppers like "Mockin' Bird Hill" and "Tennessee Waltz," at a time when multitrack recording was cutting-edge in the music industry and "singing with yourself" was a jaw-dropping technological feat. Back then, those nifty gimmicks set her apart from the legions of girl singers scrambling for a place on the hit parade. But as Patti looked back at her career from an older-and-wiser perspective, she began to worry that these cute novelties and pert ditties didn't add up to much. "I wish I had more hits that were romantic," she said. "I'd rather have something like 'Chances Are.' Or 'People,' that Barbra Streisand did. The same writer who wrote 'Doggie in the Window' wrote 'People,' if you can imagine. That is a beautiful song that you can put some heart into. You're not thinking of holding a phrase for four bars on 'Doggie in the Window.' It doesn't matter if you do or not."

She realized she might be sounding ungrateful, and backed off a bit. "I don't mind doing those songs, I really don't," she says. "Especially when I talk to people whose favorite songs are those. That makes it worthwhile. But I really want people to know that I can sing something other than that. This Mercury box set is the first thing that's given people any awareness that I was able to sing. They'd say, 'Oh, you mean the "Doggie in the Window" girl.' A lot of critics have said just that: 'We didn't know she could sing.'"

As she talked, the pleasant environment — the elegant furnishings and postcard views and rustic-chic rooms refreshingly free of showbiz memorabilia and grimacing celebrity photos — began to melt and blur in the face of her discontent. I admired her candor, but wasn't sure what to say. I couldn't exactly agree with her — I'd never heard "People," and I loathed Barbra Streisand. Yet it wasn't like I could mount a rousing defense of the social and philosophical significance of "Doggie in the Window." Of course it was a silly song. But I had really been enjoying the myth of comfort and serenity that Patti projected. I liked her strange little snow-globe world. And here she was, trying to smash it.

Patti Page didn't just happen. She was a meticulous construction, precision-engineered by a vast team of loyal and nameless builders: her audience. They made her. They had help from a well-entrenched music industry that had been manufacturing idols for their pleasure since the early days of radio and sound recordings in the 1920s. The project's foreman was Jack Rael, but even he didn't have the final say on how events unfolded. The public was in charge. Patti was a little pet, a doggie in the window, and they loved to watch her bark.

Stardom literally found her. She didn't go looking for it. She was born Clara Ann Fowler on November 8, 1927, in Claremore,

Oklahoma, the second-youngest of eleven children in a family headed by a railroad man and strict, no-nonsense mother. Patti's parents were deeply religious, and they ran a tight household. When one of the kids did something wrong, Patti's mother would say, "At four o'clock you're going to get spanked." "She knew nothing about psychology, but she certainly used it," Patti said. "And it worked. We'd be angels all day hoping she'd forget, but she never did." Patti and her siblings did as they were told. "We didn't question," she explains. "When we were told to be quiet, we were quiet. We didn't question why."

Music was a large part of the household. Her father played guitar and sang; her mother played the organ in church. As a child Patti sang in a vocal trio with her sisters, and one day at a school assembly a teacher volunteered her to sing "Frankie and Johnny." When she was sixteen, she went to radio station KTUL in Tulsa looking for a summer job as an illustrator; one of the announcers had heard her sing at the assembly, and he asked her if she would like to perform on air. Within a year or two, she became a fixture in Tulsa. KTUL had a show sponsored by the Page Milk Company and hosted by a character named Patti Page. When the reigning Patti Page quit, Clara Ann inherited the job and the name. Still, she had no thoughts of making singing her career. It was just something to pass the time until she found a husband and settled down, like her sisters had.

In the summer of 1944, a touring band called the Jimmy Joy Orchestra came through Tulsa. Jack Rael, its saxophonist and manager, checked into the Bliss Hotel and saw that his coin-operated radio had some time left in it. He tuned in KTUL and heard Patti Page, and that evening tracked her down at a supper club where she was singing and invited her to join the Jimmy Joy band. Patti felt uneasy about the idea — cross state lines with an older man, a virtual stranger? He could be some kind of sex creep. She didn't go with him. But shortly after that, she found out that her boyfriend was two-timing her, and her plans for her immediate future fell through. Jack Rael called from Dallas, nagging her to send airchecks from her radio show. "I surprised him," Patti said. "I did it. I guess that's the only time my ambition came through. My whole career probably hinged on someone jilting me."

In December Patti left Tulsa to hook up with the Jimmy Joy band in Chicago. She was just nineteen and ill-prepared for the carefree life of a girl singer. "I was getting seventy-five dollars a week and I had to pay for my hotel, my food," she said. "With my first week's salary I bought a gold cigarette case, and I had no money to pay my rent." Rael stepped in and took control. He told her where to be, what to sing, how to carry herself, whom to charm. He also kept her virtuous. "It was well known that girl singers were . . . loose," Patti says. "All the guys in the band were told, 'Hands off — this girl's going to be a star.' I thought something was wrong. Nobody paid any attention to me."

Rael wanted to make sure she got the right kind of attention. What Patti lacked in ambition, he more than made up for: by the spring of 1947, he had cut her loose from the Jimmy Joy band and signed her to Mercury Records as a solo act. Her first recordings got nice notices in the music magazine *Down Beat*, but they failed to chart. Rael thought the material the label was giving them stank. He began to pick the songs himself, and take the reins in the recording studio. He came across a mellow ballad called "Confess," and decided that a gimmick would give it some oomph. Cutting corners at a studio session in December 1947 — they couldn't afford backup singers — Rael came up with the idea of having Patti overdub a backing vocal that would answer the lead part like an echo.

He didn't invent overdubbing: the idea had been in the air at least since 1941, when the jazz coronetist Sidney Bechet made his famous "one-man band" recordings, playing several instruments himself on "The Sheik of Araby" and "Blues for Bechet." By the fall of 1947, guitar legend and engineering whiz Les Paul was messing around in his home studio, coming up with sophisticated new miking techniques to improve the fidelity of multitrack recordings. Paul's novelty hit "Lover," on which he played eight dueling guitar parts, beat "Confess" to the charts in March 1948. But Patti was the first singer to hit with a double-tracked vocal. "Confess" went to Number 12 in June, and that December *Down Beat* featured her on the cover, preening in the mirror. Her next hit, the velvety come-on "With My Eyes Wide Open I'm Dreaming," featured four harmony parts and was attributed to the Patti Page Quartet. It reached Number 11 in 1950.

Gimmicks got Patti noticed, and Rael would return to them again and again throughout her career. In late 1950, Patti recorded a novelty Christmas single called "Boogie Woogie Santa Claus." The flip side was a cover of "Tennessee Waltz," a country hit for Pee Wee King in 1948 and a favorite song of her father's. To both Patti and Rael's surprise, deejays ignored "Boogie Woogie Santa Claus," and "Tennessee Waltz" took off. Maybe it was the way Patti's voice seamlessly integrated pop and country styles: she had a country singer's unfussy directness combined with the emotional restraint of a sweet-band balladeer. The timing was certainly right: "Tennessee Waltz" came along just as rural and urban America were getting to know each other better, thanks to the unifying force of television and the spread of the national media. Maybe the success of "Tennessee Waltz" can't really be explained; people just liked it. It appealed to pop fans, country fans, R&B fans, wistful grandpas, lovelorn housewives, heartsick teens. It would eventually sell 10 million copies, becoming one of the top-selling singles of all time and the first major crossover hit of the twentieth century. Patti's success — she earned the nickname "The Singing Rage" — signaled the fertile cross-pollination between country, pop, and R&B that would explode in the mid-fifties as rock and roll. She proved to the industry that the appeal of "fringe material" like country was by no means limited to a country audience.

Patti's image was a large part of her appeal. Her beauty, like that of any successful

girl singer, was glamorous and confection-
ary: pleated gowns, bejeweled nape, dimpled
cheeks, crimped blonde bangs. But underneath, she conveyed a hint of soul. In the
months after I interviewed Patti, I occasionally encountered industry people who had
known or worked with her during her golden
years. Alan Eichler, a publicist who would
arrange my interview with Tommy Sands,
had grown up admiring Patti and had helped
with her fan club as a kid. "Patti you could
see in a supermarket and never think she
was interested in anything other than being
a housewife," he told me. "And yet as a performer, she comes out in the white chiffon
gown and the big smile like she's Doris Day,
like she hasn't got a problem in the world."
The famed executive Mitch Miller worked
briefly with Patti at Mercury Records before
he moved on to Columbia. "She's a country
girl!" he exclaimed. "Did you notice that?
Oh, she sounded sexy on the records, and
then when you saw her she was like a country girl trying to be sophisticated. But she
learned."

As a singer, Patti was an extremely ef-
fective pitchman. She could sell any song.
Rael looked for material with the broadest
possible appeal: pleasing melodies, straight-
forward story lines, sing-along lyrics, and

uncomplicated emotions. Over the next several years, they scored with saucy, stompy tunes ("Steam Heat"), quasi-religious material ("Croce Di Oro [Cross of Gold]"), langorous travelogues ("Old Cape Cod"), folksy curiosities ("Mister and Mississippi"), and sunny reveries ("Mockin' Bird Hill"). Patti's style was so reliable and unflashy that she made the most exotically flavored tune seem reassuringly familiar. She was not an especially varied or inventive singer — she stuck to the melody line, hit her notes square on the head, held them with minimal vibrato, and rarely budged from the given tempo. Her tone was unwaveringly warm and tender. She sang like she cared, like she wanted to wipe your worries away; she *mothered* her listeners. She buffed the edges off emotions, kept them safe and unthreatening. "Tennessee Waltz" may have told the anguished tale of a lover lost to a best friend, but Patti didn't give it a slit-your-wrists somberness. By the time the song ends, she's practically made you feel like you're over it. You'll move on, find a new dance partner. Everything will be just fine.

When I first started listening to Patti, I have to admit I was underwhelmed. I sat down one afternoon with a stack of albums promising a wide spectrum of kitsch: *Patti Sings*

Golden Hits of the Boys, in which the dulcet mama tried her hand at rock-and-roll hits like "Don't Be Cruel," "I'm Walkin'," and "Big Bad John"; *Romance on the Range,* a country collection ("Tumbling Tumbleweeds," "San Antonio Rose") with a cover image of Patti propped against a split-rail fence in a photographer's studio, wearing a cowboy hat and a belt cinched absurdly tight; and two different albums called *The Waltz Queen,* one comprising songs in three-quarter time, the other a budget-line LP comprising songs in no particular time signature. The strangest was *Manhattan Tower,* Patti's version of a concept album about New York City that had been a hit for the composer and orchestrator Gordon Jenkins in 1956. This one wigged me out. It was a collection of songs — "Happiness Cocktail," "Married I Can Always Get" — meant to evoke the skyscrapery, martini'ed romance of city nightlife. The liner notes described the work as "a thrilling narrative tone poem." The cover resembled a backdrop on the evening news.

The eerie thing, at first, was how emotionally washed out Patti's recordings sounded. After listening to a bunch of her albums, I could hardly remember anything I'd heard: it all blended together in a fog of smooth, professional orchestrations and sonorous tonalities. Least compelling were her versions of standards like "What'll I Do" and "Dancing in the Dark." She lacked the nuance to give the lines the sophisticated readings they deserved; she applied an even coat of regret from beginning to end, without modulating sentiments or building drama. It kind of reminded me of the way Michael Bolton, the eighties middle-of-the-road crooner, overemoted through classics like "When a Man Loves a Woman" and "Dock of the Bay," without having the sense to hold back once in a while. Patti did the opposite: she never let go. And yet, as bland as they were, these renditions were competent. Maybe Patti appealed to people who thought jazz singers like Ella Fitzgerald were too taxing and out-there. Maybe Patti was the K-Tel of the fifties: one-stop shopping for all your pop music needs.

But the more I listened, the more I realized I wasn't giving her enough credit. Patti's even-temperedness may seem like a defect to those of us who came along later and grew up with the raucousness of rock and roll. But if you pay close attention, you realize her equanimity was also the seed of her greatest virtue. Patti made silly songs work because she didn't condescend to them, or us. She applied the same game enthusiasm

to "Mockin' Bird Hill" that she gave to a more interesting song like "Taking a Chance on Love." A more intellectual singer would never have allowed us to believe these ditties; with her signature unpretentiousness, Patti brought them to life. "(How Much Is) That Doggie in the Window" may not have been as massive a hit as "Tennessee Waltz," but for me it ultimately defines her. Who else could sound elegant with a couple of grown men barking in the studio as she sang? She seems genuinely charmed by that ridiculous pup, and in the end — admit it! — we are charmed too. Once you've heard the song, you never forget it. It's the only tune of Patti's I knew before I began work on this book. Where did I hear it? On fifties nostalgia mail-order TV commercials during afternoon *Brady Bunch* reruns in the late seventies? On a car radio as I fell asleep on the drive back from Sunday dinner with my grandparents when I was nine years old? I'll never know. But I heard it, and it stuck for decades.

My snobbery about Patti's music faded completely when I saw some of her vintage TV clips. From 1952 to 1959, she hosted several different variety shows, including a half-hour program on CBS in 1957–1958 called *The Big Record*, which brought together jazz singers, rock and rollers, Broadway stars, and other hit paraders into a come-one-come-all melting pot that would be unheard of today. I watched an episode of *The Patti Page Olds Show,* which aired in the 1958–1959 season. When Patti walked out in front of the camera, smiled, and started to sing, I finally got her. She was pretty, and she sang. She wasn't tightly wired and straining and stressed out; she was relaxed and having a good time. She seemed like the kind of person you'd want to have in your living room: she'd sit on the couch, looking great, laughing and cheering everybody up. No wonder audiences in the fifties were transfixed. She was everyone's ideal of what they wanted to be. For a moment, as I sat there, I forgot all my postmodern cynicism and just wallowed in her. The fantasy she projected was a potent one, and I wanted a piece of it too.

We have this idea of how bland and repressive and unexciting the fifties were, yet watching Patti that day, those qualities suddenly didn't seem so horrible. I've had a whole lifetime of angsty music and clangy guitars and pummeling rhythms. Patti's easygoing simplicity made me want to cry with relief. I'm not saying those extreme emotions don't have an important place in our lives. But how nice, once in a while, to steal away and stop thinking so hard and allow yourself to be soothed.

Patti's personal life could not possibly have been as tranquil as the image she projected. No one's could have. Her first marriage in 1948 was a disaster. Lacking models for how to balance work and family, Patti tried in vain to fit herself into the mold of a conventional wife. "He was a college student, from a rich family — I thought," she said. "He looked sharp. I thought, this is what I should do. We were married in New York. We had a little apartment up on 120th Street or something like that. He would go out every day and look for a job. He would leave with a tie and jacket on, and come back the same way, with no job. I pressed his shirts — he'd go out looking good. Even packed him a lunch once in a while. But he never got a job." When Patti realized her husband was content to let her be the provider, she divorced him. Besides, she already had a man in her life — Jack Rael. And for most of the fifties, that relationship flourished.

By 1956, Patti's career was in enough of a groove that she ventured into marriage again. This time she thought she was choosing more wisely. Charlie O'Curran was a successful choreographer and director. His ex-wife was the actress Betty Hutton; he was outgoing and devilish, a bon vivant. Patti was shy and reticent with people, despite the conviviality she projected onstage; she thought O'Curran's gregariousness would bring her out a little. They adopted two children, and her life coasted smoothly along.

The mid-fifties explosion of rock and roll, with its undercurrents of juvenile delinquency and antipathy toward adults, did not harm Patti and her peers. In fact, in a strange way, it cemented their status. With all the controversy, popular music became big news for the first time since the swing years of World War II; grown-ups appalled by rock's rebelliousness could find refuge in swank steadies like Patti. And the new music, for all its supposed iconoclasm, was really not as different from its demure parentage as it first seemed. It was all showbiz. The first wave of rock and rollers had been raised with singers like Patti dominating the culture. One of Elvis's first recordings for Sun Records in 1954 was a cover of Patti's dapper hit "I Don't Care If the Sun Don't Shine"; Patti claims she was his mother's favorite singer, and that he used to bring Gladys to see Patti perform at the Desert Inn in Las Vegas. "He'd sit in the back and no one would notice him," she said. "It was really in the beginning, so he wasn't as huge as he became later." O'Curran would work on Elvis films like *King Creole* and *Blue Hawaii.* "I went on location a couple of times," she added. "It was always really nice. You'd go into the dining room, and then after the dining room you'd meet in the bar, and Elvis would have his guitar, and everybody would be singing."

But in November 1963, the unthinkable happened: President John F. Kennedy was assassinated. The country went into mourning. Three months later, the Beatles arrived to cheer everyone up. A new generation of singers arose, and they were truly a different breed. The Beatles and Bob Dylan were autonomous performers who wrote their own songs, played their own instruments, and actually had a say in the direction of their careers. They talked back to reporters instead of mouthing scripted pleasantries. And they urged kids to get out from under the status quo and take culture into their own hands. Meanwhile, the civil rights movement bloomed, challenging the homogeneity of America's social and political life. Suddenly Patti and her peers seemed as hoary and outdated as a plate-spinning act. After investing in these performers so dearly for so long, Americans turned our backs. For all audiences cared, these relics could never sing another song as long as they lived.

When the Beatles hysteria kicked in, Patti sensed immediately that the world she knew was tumbling down. "The whole complexion of the industry changed," she said. "You would never have seen the Beatles work a club in Vegas, for example. It was the beginning of working arenas and ballparks. I went to a concert in Vegas in the afternoon. I don't remember how big the place was. It must have been fifteen or twenty thousand people. And I was scared to death. I took my daughter, who was probably only four years old. She was standing up on her seat, and I was frightened for her. I mean, it was bedlam. The kids were just in tears. You couldn't hear. There was no way you could tell what they were singing. There were guards everywhere, at every aisle. I couldn't wait to get out."

Patti remained her same stable, secure old self, singing the same hits to an aging coterie of fans who longed for the world that had been left behind. She continued to record and play nightclubs; in 1965 she had her last Top 40 pop hit, "Hush, Hush, Sweet Charlotte," the theme song from the Joan Crawford–Bette Davis film. In the late sixties and seventies, she went to Nashville and made a series of country albums. In the eighties, Rael booked her on cruise ships. In the early nineties, he took her to the Far East. His motto: keep working, keep the money flowing.

For his part, Rael remains proud of what they accomplished. I called him at his home in Rancho Mirage, California, in the fall of 1998; he was nearing eighty then. He spoke about the partnership with bravado. "We made a deal and she honored it and I honored it," he said. "She would do the singing, and nothing else. I picked the songs and produced the records. And if I didn't like a song I changed it. I rewrote 'Doggie in the Window.' Because it was a love song, and I said, 'We have to make it cute.'"

As for the split, he thinks Patti had no use for him once she settled down with Jerry. "I gave her away at their wedding in '91," Rael quips, "and they gave me away in '95." Unlike Patti, he has no regrets about the way her career unfolded. "Nobody touched us in the fifties," he said. "Our success was unheard of. We were never multimillionaires, but we lived very well. I was shooting for her fiftieth anniversary, and they blew the whistle on me and I stopped dead in my tracks. It was sad, but I have no ill feelings."

Patti, ever so sensitive about what her audience wanted from her, felt the rejection more acutely. When I met her, I got the sense that she was trying to revamp her legacy. She wanted to send out the message that her career had been more than just novelties and barks. And, at least in Nashville, she was getting lots of help. In 1999 a glamorous young singer named Mandy Barnett paid tribute to Patti's pioneering countrypolitan side, covering her 1950 hit "With My Eyes Wide Open I'm Dreaming" in high fifties style, with drenching notes of pedal steel guitar and a crooning backup chorus. In 2000, relative whippersnappers like Trisha Yearwood and Alison Krauss joined Patti on *Brand New Tennessee Waltz*, an album that reaffirmed her contribution to country music. However subtly, she was asserting her position in the modern world. She didn't want to be the "Doggie in the Window" lady anymore.

After our interview, Patti and Jerry coddled me some more. They packed me back into the SUV, drove me back to Wells River, and bought me a nice, relaxed lunch at the Happy Hour. The same waitress was working. She gave Patti and Jerry a warm greeting, and me a friendly wink.

I was distraught when they dropped me off at my little red Subaru and drove away. I didn't want them to leave me. I wanted to tell Patti that she didn't need to change. She could keep being Patti Page, the Singing Rage, on and on into eternity for all I cared. And I wanted to tell her that the image of confident autonomy projected by the singers that usurped her was a myth, just as surely as her image ever was. Bob Dylan can pretend he's running the show, but deep inside we know we're still in charge. Without us, he's nothing. He needs our cooperation and approval to survive, just like Patti.

Instead of saying these things, I left something behind. That cute little jug of maple syrup sat forgotten on their backseat as they sped away. It felt like a magical little bottle of my own spirit. And as they drove that pretty countryside and talked unhurriedly about the vicissitudes of their day, I imagined that the part of myself I left behind in that jug looked out the windows eagerly and listened intently, an invisible child, unseen and unheard.

Two
Me

Throughout my work on this book, questions dogged me: Why am I writing about these people? Why am I wasting my time on mediocre commercial singers instead of great artists? Why Frankie Laine and not Frank Sinatra? Why Pat Boone and not Elvis? Why am I attracted to this crappy music? I kept looking for answers in the music, because it was the music, after all, that I was writing about. Yet the answers yielded up by the music never seemed totally satisfying. I'd find little pockets of greatness, but not enough to justify the extent of my infatuation. At some point it began to occur to me that maybe it was time to look for these answers elsewhere. Instead of the music, I needed to look at myself. Maybe there was something about me that heard in these singers a luster that other people didn't. Maybe their greatness was in my ears — a subjective truth, not an objective one. And maybe the only way to understand that truth was to understand the subject that created it.

Perhaps my parents were just beginning to doubt pop's promises of perfect love when I was born in 1965. Both had grown up in Westchester County, New York. My mother was a second-generation child of immigrants: her father's family had emigrated from Ireland in the late nineteenth century, her mother's family from Italy. Her mother, Rose Cribari, was the third of ten children and the first born in the United States. My mother always seemed Italian to me; I never knew the Irish side of the family, and her father died of leukemia before I was born. But my grandmother's family was vast, and we were close. They were loud and funny and demonstrative and gossipy, and they loved fame. My grandmother was friends with the singer Julius La Rosa — Uncle Julie, my mother called him. An uncle, Guido, covered sports and entertainment for a Westchester newspaper. A picture of Guido with Frank Sinatra hung on the wall of my grandmother's apartment, among close-placed photos of family and clergy. My mom's family was deeply middle-class: her father worked for AT&T, and after he died his pension supported my grandmother for the rest of her life.

My father's family was different. German and Irish, they had arrived in this country earlier than my mother's family, and advanced further. My dad's father was a prominent corporate lawyer whose clients included Jaguar and British Petroleum. When I was a kid, my grandparents showed slides on a home projector of their travels to Kenya and Machu Picchu. They lived on top of a hill in Briarcliff Manor, in a mini-mansion with a sunken living room, an ornate dining room with a maid's buzzer hidden under the carpet, two kitchens, a formal staircase with broad landings, and guest rooms with mahogany bedposts topped by carved pineapples.

My mom, needless to say, married up. She was a gorgeous, bright, sassy girl who loved cruising in Italian boys' tricked-out Fords and Chevys with the radio on, but when the time came to settle down she thought big. John Schoemer was good-looking but stable, smart but not stuck up, with a head for numbers — he could multiply or add huge sums in his head, really fast. (He was great to have around when restaurant checks showed up, often catching errors.) My mom never admitted this, but I imagine that her parents had worried about her, wondering if she'd straighten out. She was a free-thinker, a bit of a rebel, a flouter of conventions. When she landed my dad, they must have been mighty impressed.

Once my parents decided on each other, they did everything *right*. They got married in July 1962, immediately following my mom's college graduation. My brother was born ten months later. Dad got his MBA and passed the CPA. They both sacrificed: Dad worked long hours in the accounting industry to support his new family, and Mom, all of twenty-four, stayed home with two tiny kids. My mom's mother used to drive a Buick the color of Silly Putty to our apartment, to help out. When I was three, she dipped into her pension fund for a down payment on their first house; it was in suburban New Rochelle, New York, although I was always told we lived in neighboring Scarsdale — a tonier address.

The tumult of the sixties didn't touch us. My parents were preoccupied with their responsibilities. Neither one of them ever tried so much as a hit of pot; hippies, war, the walk on the moon were pictures on the television set. We have the sense now that culture is central to the way we live, shaping us, overcoming our individuality; we are products of our era. But I don't think my parents saw it that way. Family was the important thing, impregnable to outside forces. Culture was just background noise, wallpaper designs that changed from house to house. You took care of the kids, you strove for a better life; those values didn't change.

And they passed those values down. Even though I was living in the late sixties and seventies, I pretty much grew up in a fifties household. My brother and I came home from school, grabbed Toll House cookies out of the cookie jar, and plopped down in front of the TV. We watched *My Three Sons* and *Father Knows Best* reruns and *Godzilla* features on *The 4:30 Movie*. Mom was always there, hanging out with us. She cooked a lot: meatloaf with mashed potatoes, roasted chicken with crispy skin, an occasional Italian staple like ratatouille. She walked the dog and drew happy pictures on our lunch bags, and she was pretty: walnut-brown eyes, thick black hair pulled into a fat silver barrette. I loved her hair. When I was little, she'd let me comb my fingers through it.

My dad was Mr. A-OK. He woke up to the news and weather on WINS, took the train to New York City wearing wing tips and charcoal suits, never missed a square in the *New York Times* crossword puzzle. Every year he earned a little more money. We got new cars, bigger houses, wider lawns. Sure, my parents yelled at us. They pushed us to excel in school. They punished. But *no way* can I complain. Life was a bike ride on a quiet suburban street as leaves wrinkled in the summer heat. Stability reigned.

But around the time I hit puberty, something changed. I can't say exactly what, or how. It was gradual. Dad traveled more for business, came home grumpier, talked less. He never wanted to do family things anymore. We'd cajole him to take us to the movies and he'd shrug it off. His fun meter had hit empty. On weekends he turned on the tube, settled into the La-Z-Boy, and watched sports with my brother; family Saturdays became marathons of tiny pixilated balls lobbing over courts, courses, fields, and rinks. Anonymous crowds cheered. Mom hated sports. She was outraged by my father and brother's couch drama of uncommunicativeness. Battle lines appeared.

I wasn't sure which side to take. My hormones were raging, and sports offered a convenient parade of men, a flip book of masculine styles. Football players — too fat. Basketball players — too tall. Hockey players — too violent. Tennis players — too exhausting, like mortal combatants. Golfers — too much like my dad. Baseball players — *bingo.* In an effort to bond with the male side of the family, I became an avid Yankees fan, learning box-score terminology and boning up on strategic basics like pickoffs and force-outs. But my dad and brother never took me seriously. I could be as smart but never smarter than they were about the game. Eventually I gave up, and joined ranks with my mom. If war was going to break out, it might as well be a fair fight.

The first shots were fired one night at dinner. By that point we were living in New Canaan, Connecticut, the uptight town portrayed in the novel and then the movie *The Ice Storm* (I remember that ice storm; I was eight years old). Amid what had become our regular nightly performance of silence and sarcasm, Mom or Dad said something that especially pissed off the other. Mom, standing at the stove, pinged my dad with a green bean. He had been picking over a chicken carcass — a gross habit that annoyed the hell out of her — and, face contorting, he grasped the bones with greasy, slipping fingers and hurled the whole thing at her. My brother and I looked at each other, like, *Oh, fuuuuuu . . .* the word that came to mind was one we weren't allowed to finish. We were doomed; we knew it. Our shoulders slumped. We practically waved good-bye to the lives we'd known.

It was the eighties now. The earth spun ten

thousand times in a day. The fifties were gone forever. Mom began going out by herself in the afternoons and sometimes even at night. It was shocking behavior for a woman who'd spent eighteen years without an unexplained absence. She retreated from the affluence my dad represented, making friends with a clique of artist-moms on the west side of town. I trotted along behind her. I'd never fit in with the field-club crowd, anyway; I had poor depth perception, couldn't hit a tennis ball, and regularly came in last in status-defining exercises like round robins. In 1981, Mom went off to a family party — I begged to go, and she said no — and an amazing thing happened. She ran into a guy from the old neighborhood, Eno DePasquale, the best friend of her cousin Jimmy DiMarzo. Eno was divorced and devastatingly handsome. He restored race cars for a living, and occasionally drove them, wearing a traffic-stopping orange jumpsuit. He had dropped out of college and now lived in an apartment known as "The Closet," with a Murphy bed and a hot plate. For my mother, all those years of living by the book and pleasing her parents just washed away. She fell in love. And she was ready for a love on her own terms.

That fall, my brother started college.

While he was home on his midterm break, my dad moved out. It was a pathetic scene. No one was on his side anymore, not even my brother. Dad couldn't get his bureau down the stairs, so he ended up throwing it out my brother's second-story bedroom window into the driveway below, as my mother shrieked and stormed. I stayed in my room, flipping through *Rolling Stone* until I heard his truck wheels crunch the gravel and disappear down the road. And that was that. Bro went back to school and it was just Mom and me in the big house. Well, we didn't need anybody else. We got along great; we were so much alike — twins practically. I'd answer the phone and our voices were so similar that her friends thought it was her. I'd tag along on her antique-scouting road trips — her side venture, something to fill the school hours, had grown into a real business, and recently our house had been featured in *Country Living* — and we'd yak in the car, sing along to the radio, shack up in prim B&Bs. Then I'd wander docilely behind her through other dealers' barn and basement shops, a quiet, invisible presence in an adult world, a strangely young thing in museumlike environments of ornamental decay. I was her loyal shadow. I knew she had been unhappy in her marriage, and I thought she'd be better off without him. My mother used to say her marriage to my dad couldn't have been all bad because it made me. But she spent a lot of time complaining about the guy — what an asshole he'd been, and how he didn't call me enough. He lived right across town, but in those last two years of high school I'd go months without seeing him.

At first I didn't know about Eno. After the house emptied out, I started waking up late at night and hearing my mom giggling on the telephone. "Who are you talking to?" I'd yell from my bedroom. "Go to sleep!" she'd snap. Then hushed noises, then more laughter.

My mom and I moved to a condo while I finished high school. The wedding portrait stayed packed away, and I never saw it again.

Three
FRANKIE

There are Laine fan clubs in such unlikely and remote points as Cairo, Johannesburg, Malta and Iceland, but the key spots are Hollywood, Chicago, Detroit, Buffalo, Philadelphia and New York. In each American city there is a tough Laine top sergeant — most are married women with children — who rides herd on a unit of 500 or more members, and exhorts each one to slavish devotion to the cause. Members have their radios yowling from eight to sixteen hours a day, keeping a box score on Laine records played and what the announcer said when he spun the platter. If a disk jockey makes a crack that can be interpreted as anti-Laine he is soon floundering in a barrage of protesting phone calls, letters, wires and post cards.

There are 300 such Laine clubs, with an estimated membership of 100,000, and each little cell is apt to have its own bizarre pattern. Some of the Lainettes, as the younger girl members are called, paint Laine's initials on their fingernails; others wear hair ribbons stamped with his name . . .

His fan mail runs 200 letters a day and, for a while, until it got too expensive, he was answering each one with a miniature phonograph record which seductively started off, "Hello, baby" for girl members, and a strong, masculine "Hi-ya, guy" for the men, and then went into six bars of "That's My Desire."

— "The Case of the Screaming Troubadour" by Dean Jennings, The Saturday Evening Post, *December 11, 1954*

Frankie Laine's house was full of papers. Newspapers, magazines, folders, files, statements, reports. They sat on desktops, on shelves, in slightly disheveled piles on the floor. A rifled-through copy of the *Wall Street Journal* rested on a coffee table. As I sat in the airy living room of his home in the San Diego hills, I knew I should have been admiring the view: one entire wall was made up of windows, and outside I could see the clear blue summer sky, the prickly green hillside foliage, the steel gray of the distant bay, the white specks of faraway boats. Yet somehow as we talked, my peripheral vision kept getting distracted by those piles. Frankie was eighty-five years old, and he performed and recorded only sporadically. What was he so busy with? A large-screen TV ran CNBC on low volume with the stock ticker scrolling along the bottom. Frankie, it seemed, was preoccupied, too. He loved music and jazz and could talk blithely about his accomplishments as a singer. But his mind was never far from his money.

I told Frankie that I was curious about an album of his from 1957 called *Rockin'!* I'd never actually heard it, but I loved the cover. The background was triumphal rosy red, with the title written in blocky multicolored letters with a *Romper Room* joviality and innocence. In the picture, Frankie exuded happiness and excitement: he leaned forward slightly, arms outstretched, as if he'd just come to the end of a soft-shoe dance and had landed on one knee, panting. His smile was broad and ingratiating: Hey, folks, lemme sell you a Buick! I'd seen this album in used record shops, and rued my decision not to buy it. I didn't know why I'd held out: it seemed to embody a central theme of my book, the idea that a square, old-school entertainer would market himself to teenagers who'd gotten hip to a different style of music. The cover was a desperate but optimistic, good-natured ploy: it banked on the notion that audiences are patsies who'll believe almost anything. *Rockin'!* sold the concept that Frankie Laine was hip, and anyone alive in

1957 would have known that nothing was further from the truth.

Frankie noted my enthusiasm. He stood up, a tall man with a bald head, enormous eyeglasses, and tiny pot belly over skinny legs. "You sit there," he said. "I'll go get it."

He disappeared into another room and returned not just with the album but with a newsflash. "You'll be glad to know," he said in an aside to his assistant, Mary Jo, "that the market is up forty-seven points."

Mary Jo sat at the fringe of the living room, wistfully waiting for Frankie to need her. "Oh, I am, good," she said in her best Ed McMahon.

Frankie settled onto a sofa and contemplated the artifact in his hands. "Duke Ellington wrote a wonderful instrumental called 'Rockin' in Rhythm,'" he said. "That's where I took the title from. I couldn't say 'Rockin' in Rhythm' because that was his title, so I used the 'Rockin'' part."

"So you weren't thinking of rock and roll?" I asked.

"Not really." He handed me the album, and I turned it over to check out the track listing. Something didn't quite make sense. I was looking at titles like "Rockin' Chair," "On the Sunny Side of the Street," "That's My Desire," and "Shine" — all songs from an earlier point in his career. Frankie had his first hits in the late forties for Mercury Records. Back then he was a straight jazz singer, interpreting standards in a rhythmic, emotive style for sophisticated club audiences that had grown up in the big-band years of World War II. But in 1949, Mitch Miller became Frankie's producer and steered him in a more commercial direction, saddling him with hokey, often Western-themed material like "Mule Train," "That Lucky Old Sun," "Cry of the Wild Goose," and "Do Not Forsake Me," the theme from the film *High Noon*. These songs were huge hits for Frankie, each selling more than a million copies, but they alienated his jazz audience. In 1951, Miller moved to Columbia Records and brought Frankie with him. They continued to collaborate on hits like "Blowing Wild," another Western movie theme, and "Tell Me a Story," a duet with the child star Jimmy Boyd, but his career was in a downturn. *Rockin'!* came at the tail end of his chart years. Why was he redoing his old Mercury hits?

Frankie explained. "Most of the companies had a five-year deadline on their stuff," he said. "You could wait five years after you left the company, and then rerecord anything you recorded before."

I'm a little thick sometimes. I still didn't get why Frankie would dilute his great early jazz material for release on a pop album. Then it sank in: Duh. So you can make money from those songs all over again.

I tried to give the album back to Frankie, but he held his hand up. "You can have it," he said.

"Oh, no, really," I protested.

"I've got other copies," he said. "I cover myself pretty good."

"Gee, wow," I said, trying to muster some appreciation. "Thanks."

We stood up, and Frankie led me outside to take in the view. As we stood in the hot San Diego summer air, he pointed out military ships and other landmarks in the bay. He was touched by his own act of generosity. He put his arm around my shoulder, hugging me close.

The physical contact rubbed me the wrong way. Looking out at the monied vista, I thought, This is the view lousy songs bought. I felt queasy.

I was of two minds about Frankie Laine. The critic in me, the grown-up with educated tastes, wanted to say *yuck!* Frankie is a sellout of epic proportions. He was a promising and talented jazz singer who stifled his creative vision when he realized the business wisdom of pandering to the masses. His slick, studio-crafted inanities were exactly the kind of thing mid-fifties rock and roll was rebelling against. Thank goodness performers like Elvis, Jerry Lee Lewis, and Little Richard came along with their raw talent and homespun integrity to save the world from corporate cheesemeisters like Frankie Laine! They took music away from the contented fat cats and brought it back to life with human passion and emotion. Um, that's the way the story goes, right?

Even among his own pop ilk, Frankie was something of a dork. Compare him, for example, to Sinatra. Both men recorded for Columbia Records under Mitch Miller in the early fifties. Laine was at the peak of his popularity; Sinatra, having fallen hard from the hysterical heights of the World War II bobby-soxer years, was at his nadir. He was an adulterer who had dumped his loyal wife and kids for sexy Ava Gardner, he was getting booed in his hometown of Hoboken, and he was deep in the hole with his label, which had signed him for a massive advance that wasn't paying off. Miller brought Sinatra the same kind of lowbrow tunes he was giving Laine, and Sinatra occasionally felt desperate enough to record them. In 1951 he succumbed to a canine novelty called "Mama Will Bark," a duet with a busty TV comedienne named Dagmar. It bombed, and if you listen back to the tune today you can almost hear the disgust in his voice. Sinatra just couldn't sell a piece of crap. He couldn't disregard the inner voice telling him that he was meant for better. As soon as he got back on his feet with *From Here to Eternity* in 1953, he dumped Columbia and spent the rest of his life villifying Miller. One story says that Miller approached Sinatra decades later at an industry function, wanting to make nice. "Keep movin'," Sinatra sneered.

But Frankie could spin crap into gold. He was the anti-Sinatra. He had an inner voice, too; he just chose to smother it. He knew a great song from sentimental hogwash. But from the moment he first scored with a Miller-chosen tune called "That Lucky Old Sun" in 1949, it was as if he sent his old jazz singer self into a witness protection program and tried to pretend it never existed. He became an ardent, bombastic man-of-the-people singer, offering simplistic religious and patriotic fare that described a world without doubt or ambiguity. He was, in effect, a postwar Western sprung to life, where the heroes wear white hats and the bad guys die sputtering, choking deaths. He was a feel-good guy, a mythmaker, a peddler of reassuring platitudes. I've spent afternoons combing Laine's recorded works, trying to understand why his stuff goes in one ear and out the other. One day I made the mistake of finishing out the session with a small dose of Sinatra. I nearly cried with relief. Listening to Sinatra after a steady diet of Frankie Laine was like gawking at a Michelangelo after being surrounded by corporate art.

But just when I would reach my peak of disdain for Frankie Laine, something would always pull me back. There was a part of me that felt much more forgiving toward him. Maybe it was the lingering fan in me, the still-innocent kid who could respond to a song without the interference of intellect. The absence of sexiness in his voice, the bland bonhomie, the uncomplicated rah-rah razzmatazz with which he delivered a line, held a mysterious sparkle of appeal. It re-minded me of every bad song I liked before I was old enough to "know better," before my older brother insulted my music taste so viciously that I abandoned the AM Top 40 radio of my childhood years for the rock-and-roll sophistication of FM rock. I liked "Tie a Yellow Ribbon" by Tony Orlando and Dawn, and "Rock Me Gently" by Andy Kim, and the theme from *Welcome Back, Kotter*,

"Mule Train," "That Lucky Old Sun," "The Cry of the Wild Goose" — these songs were just the "Welcome Back"s of the fifties. They exist for every generation. They were songs for pleasure seekers and hour idlers, jukebox nickel-stuffers and dashboard dial-spinners. They weren't there to console you in your hour of need or make you weep with regret and longing. They were confetti. And in some sense, it's these dime-a-dozen mundanities that keep pop music ticking. Sinatra's barroom masterworks, for all their beauty and elegance, are luxuries by comparison. Are we really looking for artistry in pop music, or is three minutes of ridiculous distraction enough?

We keep trying to get rid of the Frankie Laines of the world, with their dopey messages of easy optimism. Our culture offers antidotes: the Beats, rock and roll, the British Invasion, Woodstock, punk rock, hip-hop, gangsta rap, grunge. But the Frankie Laines keep coming back. He was to Sinatra what Fabian and Tommy Sands would be to Elvis later in the fifties: more chaste, less threatening, lacking that undercurrent of loner angst and anger. The Monkees and the Archies countered Haight-Ashbury in the late sixties. Look at pop music circa 2000: boy bands, Barbie girls, idols hawking manufactured innocence. It's not just music; in film, Tom Hanks wins two Academy Awards. Critics can erase Frankie Laine out of pop history books, but he comes back to haunt us again and again.

In some sense, Frankie Laine found his perfect destiny. He was born Francesco Paolo LoVecchio on March 30, 1913, the oldest of eight kids in Chicago's Little Italy. His parents were Sicilian immigrants with faint ties to the Mob: his father cut Al Capone's hair, and his maternal grandfather was gunned down in the family grocery store while young Frankie played upstairs. He was a straight-arrow kid: sang in the choir, played stickball in the street, stood tall when his baby sister Rose died of diphtheria. The one thing that could inspire him to break rules was music. One time he cut school to see Al Jolson in *The Singing Fool*, then rushed home to practice the new songs he'd learned. His mother figured out that he'd been a truant, and gave him a smack.

His parents couldn't afford a radio, but there was a wind-up Victrola in their furnished apartment, and mixed in with the classical 78s was a copy of Bessie Smith's "Bleeding Hearted Blues." Frankie loved jazz and blues, but he also had an instinct for crowd-pleasing. "One day a friend of mine named Tom Henahan invited me over to his house for his sister Teresa's eighteenth birthday party," he writes in his 1993 auto-biography, *That Lucky Old Son*. "A group of about thirty people gathered in the living room to sing songs . . . We launched into an Italian-flavored pop song of the day called 'Mia Bella Rosa,' and gradually the other voices in the room dropped out until only mine was left. It was the first time I had sung solo to an audience that didn't consist of my relatives, but I was too caught up in the emotion of that pretty little song to notice. I started to cry, and the tears were rolling down my cheeks when I finished singing to an audience that had grown deathly still."

Frankie and his pals kept up with the latest dance steps, and on weekends they'd hang out at Chicago's Merry Garden Ballroom. Sometimes his friends cajoled him onstage with the house band, which included future legends like the drummer Gene Krupa and the trumpeter Muggsy Spanier. He worked part-time as a dance instructor, and also took a series of clerical jobs to help support his family. But jobs dried up with the arrival of the Depression. In 1930, a dance mara-thon came through the Merry Garden, and Frankie joined up. The marathons were a curious Depression-era phenomenon, a sort of traveling human circus in which couples shuffled around a dance floor for weeks on end (they had bathroom and nap breaks) while orchestras and comics provided sideshow entertainment. At first Frankie was a singer and emcee, but eventually he became a contestant. In 1932 he and his partner, Ruth Smith, set the world's record for marathon dancing at Young's Million Dollar Pier in Atlantic City: 145 days, for a total of 3,501 hours. (The marathons inspired the 1969 movie *They Shoot Horses, Don't They?*) Frankie suffered broken ankles, nausea, and nasty foot infections, and developed permanently slumped shoulders from hauling sleeping dames around, but according to his autobiography the marathon circuit was a decent way to make a living. It was show biz, plus he got laid a lot.

In 1935, Frankie quit the marathons to concentrate on his singing career. Times were tough: he hustled for twelve years without a hit. He made the rounds of New York City jazz clubs, slept on park benches, sang for his supper at spaghetti houses, schmoozed an up-and-coming Perry Como in Cleveland, inhaled young Anita O'Day's secondhand pot smoke in a taxicab, wrote songs while working the graveyard shift at a machine plant, managed a girl trio in Hollywood, and landed a chorus slot in MGM musicals. (A deejay at WINS in New York, where Frankie performed three shows a week for a salary of five dollars, gave him his stage name.) He refused to give up. Then, in 1946, he was guesting with a group called Milton Delugg and his Swing Wing at a Hollywood hangout called Billy Berg's. Delugg recorded a novelty single for Mercury Records called "Pickle in the Middle with the Mustard on Top," and Frankie sang the part of an amusement-park barker: "Peanuts! Popcorn! Get your red hots!" The B-side, "I May Be Wrong But I Think You're Wonderful," showcased a more traditional vocal, and it got some radio play in L.A. Mercury signed him to cut four more sides, and one tune, an obscure 1931 blues ballad called "That's My Desire" that always went over big in his nightclub act, made it to Number 4 on the pop charts. At thirty-four he was finally making it.

For the next year or so, Frankie was hot property on the West Coast jazz scene. He packed clubs like the Morocco in L.A., and revived jazz-age standards like Hoagy Carmichael's "Rockin' Chair" and Louis Armstrong's "Shine." His version of Fats Waller and Andy Razaf's racial lament "Black and Blue" was so sensitive and affecting that radio listeners assumed he was black. Part of his appeal lay in the fact that he was a refreshing change of pace from crooners like Sinatra and Crosby. In person, he was a bit of a geek: his hair was thinning, and one of the first things Mercury did was fit him with a toupee, which had a habit of flying off in strong winds. He couldn't see without his glasses, and he had a friendly, not-over-ly-brainy air, like a pharmacist or football coach. When he sang, he never brooded. He let his emotions flow, and seemed willing to come across like a sap in order to woo the woman of his dreams. "Cherie, I love you so," he pledged in "That's My Desire," and sounded like he meant it. Back when he was barely scraping by, Frankie had written "We'll Be Together Again" with his pianist and arranger, Carl Fischer. It went on to become a standard in its own right, recorded by Sinatra, Ella Fitzgerald, Billie Holiday, and Louis Armstrong, and it perfectly sums up Frankie's sentimental, reassuring nature: "So what if we have to part / We'll be to-gether again."

After all the years of struggle, Frankie had a difficult time adjusting to success. He didn't know how to spend money. "When you take seventeen years to make it, you know what a dollar means," he said to me.

"You know what it takes to make it, and you know what it takes to keep it. The only thing I did that you could call outrageous was, I felt I wanted a great car. Up until then I had an old beat-up 1938 Pontiac convertible, which was falling apart. It was held together by strings and springs. Now all of a sudden I could afford a decent car. I went out and got a 1948 Packard sedan, and I didn't like it. I don't know — I still can't understand it. I got rid of it pretty quick."

He may not have enjoyed spending it, but he loved earning it. In 1949, he met someone who would help him earn a lot more: Mitch Miller, Mercury's new A&R director. Miller had a strange relationship with popular music. He was what was known as a longhair: a classical musician. In the thirties and early forties, he'd been one of New York's preeminent oboists, and he performed on many classical recordings, as well as with the NBC symphony orchestra under director Andre Kostelanetz. The famed music scout John Hammond, who discovered Billie Holiday, Aretha Franklin, Bob Dylan, and Bruce Springsteen, produced some of the recordings Miller played on, and they became friends. Hammond was working for a classical label, Key Note, that got absorbed by Mercury, and he suggested that Miller try his hand in the pop field. Miller took to it immediately; at Mercury and then Columbia starting in 1951, he would launch the careers of Rosemary Clooney, Tony Bennett, Vic Damone, and Johnny Mathis, among others. "All I do is see the unique talent in somebody," Miller said when I interviewed him at his office in midtown Manhattan. "And I know how to judge talent, I say that unashamedly."

Miller thought Laine was a competent jazz singer, but he knew he could make bigger money in the pop field. At a session in June 1949, he brought Laine "That Lucky Old Sun," calling it a cross between "Ol' Man River" and "Black and Blue" — i.e., a redemptive anthem about daily toil. Laine knew the song was a stretch, but he liked it enough to give it a shot. He completely changed his style of singing, dropping the tender intimacy of his jazz crooning for a more strident, authoritative sound that came from the gut. The song was a massive success, inspiring cover versions by not only Sinatra, but Vaughn Monroe, Sarah Vaughan, and Louis Armstrong.

Next Miller brought Laine an even bigger stretch. "Mule Train" was an aural Western, an extension of the culture that was dominating Hollywood in films like *Fort Apache*,

She Wore a Yellow Ribbon, and *Red River*. In fact, the song was meant for inclusion in a motion picture called *The Singing Guns*, a vehicle for singer-turning-actor Vaughn Monroe. Miller got a copy before Monroe could release his own version, and he was hot for Frankie to record it. "Mule Train" was a tale of old-fashioned American gumption and perseverance, hailing a feisty team driver who won't quit till he gets his supplies — a plug of chaw tobacco, rheumatism pills, a Bible — to the cowboys and settlers who requested them. The choruses onomatopoeically evoked the sensation of being aboard: "Clippity clop, clippity clop, clippity clippity clippity clippity clippity clopping along."

Frankie freaked out. He protested that this time he would completely lose his jazz audience. Miller countered by saying he'd pick up a whole new country audience. If Frankie had reservations about "Mule Train," they didn't show up in his performance. He threw himself into it like it was the most exciting tune he'd ever done, bellowing "Hyaa, hyaa!" at the end of every verse. Frankie had discovered his inner salesman. He must have convinced himself that the product was meaningful and valid. Once he convinced himself, convincing listeners was easy.

"Mule Train" was the pop phenomenon of

late 1949. Before Frankie's version even hit the streets Bing Crosby had rush-recorded his own version, and the two "Train"s raced each other to the market. Vaughn Monroe hurried out his version, and Tennessee Ernie Ford and Gordon McRae jumped on it too. Nat "King" Cole and Woody Herman even did a parody version. But Frankie's "Mule Train" had something the others lacked: real whip cracks. Miller had dubbed them in after the session, and Mercury sent thousands of promotional whips to the nation's dee-jays. Frankie's version triumphed, lodging at Number 1 for six weeks in late '49 and early '50.

"Mule Train" made him the biggest male singer on the early-fifties charts. Over the next few years he and Miller collaborated again and again on folksy novelties. "The Cry of the Wild Goose" was a driving number in which a lusty rover compares himself to the honking flyer of the title. "Swamp Girl" and "Jezebel" described the evil ministrations of sepulchral hotties. "High Noon (Do Not Forsake Me)" and "Blowing Wild (The Ballad of Black Gold)" were Western themes. "Sugarbush" was a million-selling duet with Doris Day; for "Tell Me a Story" he partnered with Jimmy Boyd, the child star who had just scored big with "I Saw Mommy

Kissing Santa Claus." One of Frankie's biggest hits was the Sunday-morning testimonial "I Believe," a rundown of inspirational images pointing to the existence of an Almighty (drops of rain, a newborn baby crying). Between 1947 and 1958 he scored 9 million sellers and nearly sixty Top 40 hits. He starred in a 1951 musical, *When You're Smiling*, and hosted a TV variety show in the summers of 1955 and 1956. His personal life was a model of show-biz stability: after a quiet divorce from a first wife in 1949, he wed actress Nan Grey in 1950. (She had two daughters from a previous marriage; they had no children of their own.) He and Nan remained married until her death in 1994.

Success did have its downside. Frankie's esteem among critics plummeted. The press coined nicknames for him like "Steel Tonsils" and "Leather Lungs," making fun of his unrelenting vocal boom. In a 1954 profile called "The Case of the Screaming Troubadour," *The Saturday Evening Post* took some good-natured jibes at his performance style: "When he is really gone on a song he shakes the floor, mangles vowels, sings against the tempo and finishes on an offbeat tone that doesn't fade, but just dies. 'St. Vitus with a flatted fifth,' one reviewer called him." Frankie didn't mind the digs. He was laughing all the way to the stockbroker's office. "I guess I looked like a windmill salesman," he quipped to the *Post*, "but at least they knew I was there."

By 1955 the hits were coming a little slower, and Frankie turned back to jazz. He recorded *Jazz Spectacular*, an album with trumpeter Buck Clayton's orchestra; *Torchin'*, a collection of wee-small-hours standards, was released in 1958. His most ambitious album was *Foreign Affair*, a survey of French, Italian, Spanish, and Portuguese ballads arranged by pianist Michel Legrand. But these albums didn't sell. Frankie was like a sitcom actor who couldn't escape his most popular character. When he ventured toward serious material, audiences lost interest.

Thus his career was already on the wane when rock and roll hit. "I loved some of it," he said. "I loved the rhythm, because basically I'm a jazz rhythm singer to begin with." He was role model to second-wave rock-and-roll idols like Paul Anka, Bobby Darin, and Frankie Avalon, who admired his all-around showmanship and ability to sell a tune. Miller, however, encouraged Columbia artists to stay away from rock and roll. He disliked the music on creative grounds, but he was also wary of the payola it took to get on Top 40 stations. "I knew what was going on — everybody in the business knew what was going on," Miller said. "You had to pay to play." Columbia's parent company, CBS, owned radio and TV stations with licenses that needed to be periodically renewed, he said, and the label brass didn't want their hands dirty. (Independent labels, which flourished during the early rock era, were small companies with less at risk; in addition to passing cash to deejays, they would often trade pressing or distribution rights to local power barons in order to break into a radio market.)

In the early sixties Miller got caught up in his *Sing Along with Mitch* album and TV series, a kind of early karaoke that provided symphonic backdrops to popular hits. Frankie left Columbia and recorded an album for Capitol in 1964, then moved to ABC-Paramount, where for several years he retread familiar country, pop, and gospel terrain. In 1974, director Mel Brooks signed him up to record the theme song to his Western parody, *Blazing Saddles*. Frankie also did commercial jingles, like the Amtrak theme. Throughout the eighties and nineties, he stayed on the road, performing his old hits. He felt no need to reinvent himelf or reach out to younger audiences. He was happy being the "Mule Train" man. And he was never broke again.

Unlike Patti Page, Frankie claimed to have no regrets about the arc of his career. He could recall only one instance when his faith in Miller wavered. "I hate to talk about this, but it's a cute story," Frankie said. "Mitch brought me a song called 'Ticky Tick Tick.' That's the sound a maître d' makes when he wants a waiter. It's a little frog, and it makes a ticky tick tick sound. Now, what would you do with that ordinarily? You'd throw it out right away. I said, 'Mitch, "Mule Train," all right, but "Ticky Tick Tick"?' He said, 'Frank, I brought you "I Believe." I brought you "High Noon." I brought you "Lucky Old Sun." Trust me.' I said, 'Okay, Mitch. My instinct tells me that this is not one I should do, but as a favor, all right.' I was right."

Miller, in turn, had no remorse for the way he guided Frankie's career. "People are not going to accept you as a jazz singer unless you've sold them on yourself for other things," he said. "If a magazine put jazz on the front page, how many people would buy it?"

I found it curious that neither Frankie nor Mitch, with all their combined musical expertise, would cop to the fact that the songs they recorded together weren't built to last. In 1951 *Time* magazine put Miller on the spot about the jouncy fluff he produced. Miller admitted, "I wouldn't buy that stuff for myself. There's no real artistic satisfaction in this job. I satisfy my musical ego elsewhere."

I read the quote to Miller, and he looked sheepish. "There is a kernel of truth to that," he said. "Actually, the stuff I buy for myself is great jazz."

One afternoon my friend Robert and I drove south from Los Angeles to see the "Mule Train" man in action. He was performing in front of an audience of prosperous retirees at the Rancho Bernardo Country Club in the San Diego suburbs. From the moment we walked through the clubhouse atrium to the outdoor dinner patio, it was clear that we were outsiders. For one thing, we weren't dressed properly. Robert was wearing a rumpled dinner jacket over a tieless white shirt, black jeans, and black sneakers; I was wearing a Gap dress, ankle socks, and clunky black shoes. Everyone else wore plaid. We encountered an ocean of madras and polo shirts and visors and trim gray hair and thin brown skin. The members were seated at white-clothed tables, clinking silverware on fancy plates and tossing back cocktails as the sun set. We stood at the patio fringe, unsure of what to do. Golf carts whizzed by, almost knocking us over.

An officious-looking man in a bright red vest scrambled over. "Can I help you?" he said suspiciously.

"I'm looking for Marvin Himmel," I said, trying to seem perky.

"Oh," he said, seemingly disappointed. "I'm Marvin Himmel."

"I'm a writer," I explained. "I interviewed Frankie. Mary Jo invited us."

"Oh, right," Marvin said. "I set up a bench for you back here by the spotlight. You're kind of early." He led us to a hard wooden bench on the grass behind the patio, the country-club version of a nosebleed seat. Then he left us to deal with other things.

Robert and I were aghast. In the rock world, promoters give press people *good* seats. And maybe food. We had seen a Denny's at the freeway interchange, and passed it by because this was a *dinner* show.

We settled down and griped to one another. We felt like Commies crashing a Reagan convention. A voice over the P.A. system said, "Ladies and gentlemen, the show will begin promptly at eight-forty-five, right after dessert." My stomach grumbled. I didn't even have a saltine in my pocket.

The sky turned to evening, and the air

became chilly. In the twilight we noticed Marvin's red-vested figure toying with a giant contraption that looked like a truncated World War II cannon. A beam of light began to bounce jaggedly across the patio. "Look," Robert whispered, "Marvin's on the spotlight." As he spoke, Marvin suddenly swerved the thing in our direction, and we both instinctively ducked. "He's shining it right on us!" Robert gasped. "I feel like I'm escaping from a concentration camp."

The spotlight swerved away again, and we waited some more. Finally the band arrived on stage and started up a snazzy intro. Frankie sauntered into view, looking like a very different man than I had encountered at his home. His hair was a golden mass of synthetic curls, and he wore a black tuxedo and a royal blue shirt with a collar winging majestically over his shoulders. He smiled that timeless, unctuous smile, waved at the crowd, and launched into a boisterous, Latin-flavored tune called "Come Back to Me" that reminded me of the theme from *The Love Boat*. Horns blurped, tom-toms rolled. The mini-orchestra lacked a string section, so a keyboard filled them in. Frankie was exhorting his fans all over the globe to return to his fold: "Take a train, steal a car / Hop a freight, grab a star / Come back to me."

The song ended, and the crowd let out a holler like a *Happy Days* pep rally. The decades were falling off these folks. Frankie slow danced through "Makin' Whoopee," and I was impressed at how robust and supple his voice was. I had seen Sinatra in his last decade, and his voice, though still gloriously affecting, was cracked and dry as an old shoe. Clean living had paid off handsome dividends for Frankie. He sang like a man half his age.

He did a couple more quiet numbers, including "That's My Desire," and filled up the space between songs with old-age banter. "It's good to be here," he said at one point. "It's good to be anywhere." Then he pointed to his head and said, "Before we go any further, I want you to know, so you don't sit there wondering all night: it *is* a hairpiece."

Each song got a long-winded explanation about who wrote it and how Frankie came to record it. Sometimes the intros went on way longer than the actual performance. The crowd began to get impatient. Frankie started blathering about his 1953 cover of Hank Williams's "Your Cheatin' Heart," and the crowd began screaming over him. Shouts of "Mule Train!" and "Jezebel!" rose up. Frankie stopped his intro and laughed. "'Jezebel' closes the show," he said. "If we do that we're done." "Mule Train!" demanded the crowd. "Okay, okay!" said Frankie. "But I want to hear you yell!"

The band began the show's signature galloping rhythm. "Muuuuuule traaaaaaain!" hollered Frankie.

"Whooooo!" yelled the crowd.

"Hyaa, hyaa!" called Frankie.

"Whooooo!" answered the crowd.

The old-timers in their plaids were nearly falling out of their seats. They were slapping the air, driving those mules. With every verse, their enthusiasm pitched up a notch.

Something started to come over me. All evening I'd been feeling so cynical and above it all, yet the energy in the place was impossible to resist. I'd been to hundreds of rock shows in my life, and I couldn't remember the last time I'd seen a crowd hang their hearts out quite like this. I'd go to see a favorite band like Sonic Youth, and at the end of a song the cooler-than-thou punks would flap their hands listlessly together, determined not to seem excited, no matter how great the performance. Suddenly my generation's desire always to be smarter than the culture we're fed seemed like a bad trip, a hangup. What made us so special, that we couldn't enjoy an innocent melody, a silly lyric? Why were we so afraid to fall for a song like a bunch of stupid schoolkids?

Frankie's exuberance and the crowd's dedication mingled in a gorgeous wash of untempered joy, and the critic in me was toppled by its force. I was a kid again, swept along with a crowd, taking part instead of standing separate. As Frankie let out his final *hyaa*'s and the crowd erupted into thundering applause, I gave myself up to the moment. I jumped to my feet, put my hands together, and hollered "Whoooooo!" along with everyone else.

Four
PAT

PAT BOONE SAYS: YOU DON'T HAVE TO WIGGLE

... Do I think performers have a moral obligation to their fans? Well, I do. I have had considerable success in the rock-and-roll field, but I think that some of its exponents, usually the instrumentalists, are giving it a black eye. They are way off-base with their onstage contortions. I don't think anything excuses the suggestive gyrations that some rock-and-rollers go in for. ... I like rhythm, too. But the human body consists of about 200 separate bones and I don't think it's necessary to call all of them into play even on a jittery ditty like, "Long, Tall Sally." I belong to the finger-snapping school myself. That, and a little tapping of the feet, is enough to satisfy my soul. And it seems to satisfy my audiences, too.

—Pat Boone, This Week Magazine, *July 7, 1957*

Pat Boone is rock and roll's favorite whipping boy. People love to kick him around. It's an extreme sport for unathletic, hard-living liberals. Boone's white buckskin shoes, milkfed complexion, neatly combed hair, and croony baritone make him an ideal villain for a genre that glorifies emaciation, bedhead, screeching guitars, and raw-throated yowlers. Boone has helped his detractors' case by broadcasting his conservative Christian values and aligning himself with right-wing politicians like Nixon and Reagan. But his greatest sin is a musical one: in the mid-fifties, he recorded tidy, buttoned-up versions of R&B hits like Little Richard's "Tutti Frutti" and Fats Domino's "Ain't It a Shame" (he tweaked the title's grammar to make it "Ain't That a Shame"). Little Richard loves to beef about Boone: in films like *Chuck Berry: Hail! Hail! Rock 'n' Roll* and the PBS documentary *Rock & Roll*, he railed about how Boone's temperate covers shut Richard's raunchier originals out of the pop mainstream. "The white kids wanted [my version] 'cause it was real rough and raw, and Pat Boone had this smooth version," he said in *Hail! Hail! Rock 'n' Roll*. "And so the white kids would take mine and put it in the drawer and put his on top of the dresser." Fats Domino also grumbled. In the liner notes to the 1991 box set *The Legendary Imperial Masters*, he complained, "That hurt. It took me two months to write 'Ain't It a Shame,' and his record comes out around the same time mine did." White guys like to join the fray, too. Upon his induction to the Rock and Roll Hall of Fame in 1999, Billy Joel made a de rigueur sideswipe: "I was into the originators, the real R&B — not stuff like Pat Boone and Frankie Avalon."

Boone is aware of these criticisms, and in his unerringly polite, love-thy-enemy way, he enjoys telling his accusers to *eff off*. "This revisionist idea has sprung up, somehow, that when pop artists covered an R&B record we were inhibiting the progress, instead of enhancing the progress, of the original artists. But in those early days, R&B music did not get played on pop radio. It was too raw, rough, unfinished sounding, garbled — you couldn't understand all the words. People were used to big bands and polished production. Deejays weren't ready to play it and people weren't ready to receive it. But when we would do a more polished pop version of a song it had a chance, and it began to catch on. People don't understand the necessary role the cover versions played. It was pop artists doing R&B music that focused the spotlight on the original artists and opened the door."

We were sitting in the offices of Pat Boone Productions on Sunset Boulevard in L.A., not far from rock-and-roll landmarks like the Whisky a Go-Go, where Jim Morrison dangled off the roof during a Doors performance, and the Hyatt Hotel, where members of Led Zeppelin dumped a TV set off a balcony. Pat's location on the Sunset Strip seemed meaningful: it was as if he were saying that clean-cut, letter-sweater propriety had its rightful place alongside debauchery in rock history. The offices were decked with enough Gold and Platinum records to blind the eye; there were also stage photos, posters from Pat's films (*April Love*, *Bernadine*, *State Fair*) and assorted memorabilia. An L.A. Rams football helmet sat on a cabinet beneath a framed letter from Frank Sinatra, written after Pat broke his jaw in a motorcycle accident. The letter said, "Dummy! Next time use this. Love ya, Frank."

Boone wore a red sweatshirt, jeans, and a baseball cap. His face was lined, but handsome. His disposition was so predictably upbeat and accommodating that at first I kind of felt like I was talking to a hologram: he smiled constantly, apologized profusely for arriving late, held doors open, waited for me to sit down before he seated himself. But it didn't take long to figure out that a human being lurked beneath that epic sunniness. My first clue was his teeth. They were klieg-light white, just as I expected, but also somewhat crooked. I found this reassuring.

He was also a compulsive gabber. Pat discloses information about himself so avidly and uncontrollably that you wonder if he should join a twelve-step program for it. Within moments after I turned on my tape recorder, he had related a dizzying array of salient and not-so-salient facts. He had promised his wife of forty-four years, Shirley, that he would retire in fourteen months, when he reached the age of sixty-five. He was the Number 8-selling singles artist of the rock era — look, it says so right here in this official pop-chart history book. He was watching a documentary about Jim Croce the other night, and he teared up remembering how Shirley used to sing "Time in a Bottle" during their seventies family stage shows. All four of his daughters (Cherry, Lindy, Debby, and Laury, born in rapid-fire succession between 1955 and 1958) had grown up without grounding upon the Hollywood ignominies of drug addiction, rehab, out-of-wedlock pregnancy, or divorce. "In the early part of my career I had about a hundred products with my name or likeness on them," he said, moving right along. "Perfume, bobby socks, lampshades, pillow cases, watches, all kinds of stuff. The proceeds went into trust funds for the girls for their educations and their weddings. I told each of the girls when she was old enough to understand, 'Your college education is provided for. You can go to any Christian college that will admit you, as long as you can be home for dinner.'" Pat, does the phrase *Let's not go there* mean anything to you?

This motormouth tendency hasn't always been to his advantage. One result was that after more than four decades in show business, he had zero mystique. "I'm long-winded," he said cheerfully. "Tom Parker was very smart in keeping Elvis away from the press most of the time. He let his movies and music speak for him, and let there be an air of mystery as much as possible. Me, I was too open and I had a PR guy and I would grant interviews and talk like I'm talking now. So people got to know me very well."

But the upside was that once you got to know him, it was harder to judge him negatively. Pat was like a neighbor whose house you dropped by to borrow a cup of sugar, and you ended up yammering all afternoon, hitting a few balls on his paddle tennis court, and offering to buy stock in his startup company. He killed your disdain with conviviality. He also boasted a quality that was usually missing from far righties: tolerance. "You know, it's only in recent years in all of human history that women left home and got jobs and left the family before they were married," he said at one point, veering off on one of his wackier conservative tangents. "For ninety-eight percent of human history families protected the women until they were married, then they went to the husband and he protected them. As a father I just didn't subscribe to the idea of my daughters going away at eighteen or nineteen, living in maybe a co-ed dorm, and being exposed to all kinds of stuff that they'd been protected from at home." Then he stopped short. "I realize I'm talking to somebody who probably did it, and did it fine."

Pat's relaxation helped me lighten up. I felt like I could ask him anything. Was it true that he shoplifted as a kid? "Oh, yeah," he said. "And I was good at it. Daring. I'd put on clothes under other clothes and walk out blithely. I was never caught, but my conscience began to eat at me. I went to my high school principal and told him what I'd done. He went to the various store owners and said that I was going to get an after-school job and pay for what I stole. And I did." What about the thing I kept reading in old press clips about him brushing his teeth twenty times a day? "Nooooo," he said, laughing. "I might have brushed them eighteen, twenty times when I brushed them — I mean, like, strokes. Now, I did, even in dating days, have a toothbrush over the visor in the car. Shirley should have known how cluttered and hectic our lives would be, because I'd pick her up for a date and maybe I hadn't finished eating dinner, so I'd have a plate of food on the seat. She'd slide in and help feed me while we went to the basketball game or the movie. And when I finished eating I had a toothbrush over the visor, and I'd brush my teeth. So I was always conscientious about personal hygiene."

For me, interviews are like little romances — safe, intellectual ones. Sometimes the chemistry's not right, but sometimes you hit it off. As I sat with Pat, I felt myself falling. And as I fell, I had a vision of the legions of fifties girls who fell too, alone in their rooms or clustered around record players or screaming and weeping in television studios. They were not so foolish. It was easy to fall for Pat.

I reached into my bag and, flicking away any professional embarrassment, pulled out my totems: a handful of his vintage LPs. I had *Star Dust*, a collection of swing-era classics; *Side by Side*, country duets with Shirley; and *Howdy!*, full of whispery versions of thirties ballads. Pat came around his desk and sat down next to me, examining them. "Oh, you've got some of the originals," he said kindly. "They look like they're in good shape. *Star Dust* was a big album, particularly overseas. That was one of my first big-band albums — perhaps the first. Boy, I loved that album."

I gazed at him, dissolving. I had the urge to ask him to sign them. I had the urge to climb into his lap.

When I started work on this chapter, I had no intention of developing a crush on Pat. Please believe that. I thought Pat was icky, just like any normal person does. I arrived at this opinion mostly by osmosis. You spend enough time listening to rock music, and talking to people about rock music, and reading books by people who know about rock music, and pretty soon you can take it for granted that he's awful without ever actually having to ask why. My own exposure to Pat was limited. I'd seen a famous clip that always surfaces in rock documentaries to illustrate the forces of white stodginess that were repressing fifties teenagers: Pat sings "Tutti Frutti" on some unspecified black-

and-white TV show in front of a stylized jukebox stage set, intoning the words with a croony formality that totally contradicts their exultory intent, jerking his body in an uncomfortable approximation of dancing, one set of fingers snapping in an up-and-down motion while the other spazzes from side to side. Other than fifteen seconds of "Tutti Frutti," I can't say I'd heard much else. I spend a lot of time listening to oldies radio, but in my lifetime Pat has calcified into a strata of unhip so unshakable that even oldies radio hardly touches him.

I had made a quick, dutiful run through some of his recorded works the day before my interview, but maybe I was jetlagged, because nothing stuck. I remember I kept falling asleep during his Irving Berlin album, stretched out on the foldaway bed in my friend Robert's L.A. apartment. Months after the interview, when I got ready to write this chapter, I tried again. My little crush had faded. I had low expectations. I had a pot of coffee ready.

For some reason, I started with a 1961 religious album called *My God and I* that Pat had recorded with the Abilene Christian College A Cappella Chorus. Pat was conducting the choir and singing lead, something he had been doing in church services since he was a teenager. I think I had the idea that the Church of Christ was a holy-roller sect with people shouting and clapping and praising to the moon, but these recordings showed that they were a serious, devotional bunch. To my surprise, I liked *My God and I*: it was restrained and elegant, offering stately chant arrangements of big-name hymns like "A Mighty Fortress" in which the vocal tones of the chorus built upon one another like stones in a gothic cathedral. It reminded me of the Roman Catholic high masses of my own youth, where the sound of voices climbing upward was supposed to transport you to a higher spiritual plane. Pat's voice was a flawless lead: he would hit upper-register notes and hold them without wavering, then swoop downward in beautiful baritone arcs.

Then I skipped backward and listened to his 1956 debut album, *Pat Boone*, which collected his early R&B covers: "Ain't That a Shame" and "Tutti Frutti," plus "Two Hearts," a million-seller in 1955, taken from an original by the Charms; "Tra-La-La," a 1951 hit for the Griffin Brothers; and "I'll Be Home," a hit for the Flamingos in 1956. And, okay, the stuff was pretty goofy. In "Two Hearts," Pat tried to adapt a bouncy "doo-de-doo-woo" from the Charms, and wound up sounding like he had the hiccups; in "Tra-

La-La," he tried to fake his way through a barrel-chested blues shout on the line, "They call me a blues singer, because I sing them both night and day." "I'll Be Home" had a pillow-soft prettiness, but it felt remote and emotionally disembodied compared to the original. The Flamingos' version had a depth of feeling Pat just couldn't replicate. It came from a real place, a particular experience: you could hear dark city street corners in its grooves, furtive promises, secrets begging to be revealed. You could hear lives lived. In Pat's, you heard lives merely imagined.

But on his next album, *Howdy!*, also released in '56, he found his *own* groove. The material suited him better: he was interpreting pop classics of the thirties, forties, and fifties with an insouciance that was pure rock and roll. "All I Do Is Dream of You" dated from 1934, although it was more familiar to fifties audiences from Debbie Reynolds's performance of it in *Singin' in the Rain*; Pat's version kicked up the tempo with a rollicking bass line and insistent shuffle rhythm. "Chattanooga Shoe Shine Boy" was a Number 1 hit in 1940 for Red Foley, the Grand Ole Opry star who would later become Pat's father-in-law; Bing Crosby and Frank Sinatra also recorded it that year. Pat's saucy homage had a percussive rag-snap sound effect and a vocal that could teach his father-in-law a thing or two about in-the-pocket phrasing. "Would You Like to Take a Walk?," a hit for Rudy Vallee in 1931, really killed me. The lyrics were hilariously old-fashioned, and Pat delivered them with a sly, light touch. "Ain't you tired of the talkies?" he sang. "I prefer the walkies / Something good'll come from that."

My favorite was "Harbor Lights," a ballad from prewar Britain that became one of the biggest hits of 1950, with covers by Crosby, Guy Lombardo, and Sammy Kaye. Pat, though, claimed it as his own. The detachment that worked against him in "I'll Be Home" dovetailed beautifully with the sentiment in "Harbor Lights": the song is a reverie of lost love, with the title image representing the warmth the couple used to share. Pat's vocal restraint accentuated the longing. He conveyed vulnerability without mushiness, loneliness untainted by self-pity. "Goodbye to tender nights beside the silv'ry sea," he sang. Out of curiosity, I dug up my copy of Elvis's Sun sessions — he had sung an unreleased version of the song in 1954. Granted, Elvis was younger than Pat when he recorded it, and he was uneasy with the song's delicate melodic shifts. But it just goes to show that great singers find their own

metier. At least where this ballad was concerned, Pat kicked Elvis's ass.

After I discovered "Harbor Lights," my
crush just got worse. I started listening to Pat
around the house all the time. I started to
enjoy hokier tunes like "Friendly Persuasion
(Thee I Love)," the theme from a 1956 Gary
Cooper movie about Quakers struggling
through the Civil War. "Put on your bonnet,
your cape and your glove," warbled Pat as
flutes trilled and harp strings glissaded. It
was the rare romantic ballad that implores
a woman to put her clothes *on*. I thought
fondly about that spazzy finger-snapping in
the "Tutti Frutti" TV clip, and wondered if
it weren't actually sort of cute.

There was just one thing to do: interview
him again. So I called Pat on the phone, and
we gabbed a bit, and I worked myself up
to a declaration of ardor. "Pat, I, um, came
in sort of skeptical . . . I'm from a different
background . . . punk rock and all . . . " I was
mumbling. Finally I blurted out, "I think
I'm becoming a real fan!" He laughed, and
then said something that got at the heart of
what I had come to appreciate about him as
a singer. "I grew up loving Bing Crosby," he
replied. "And Perry Como as well. So I considered myself a balladeer. I could do rhythm
tunes, and of course I did those rock-and-roll

124

things. But I was grateful — hungry — to get to some of those pop songs and ballads. And my approach was to be totally honest, totally sincere. I had no gimmick, I had no developed style. I can carry a tune, but many singers can do that. I just wanted people to feel a heartbeat and a pulse and an emotion when I sang. So if you like 'Harbor Lights' and some of the other songs in that album, I think it's because I generally just learned the words, closed my eyes, and sang with my heart on my sleeve."

Of course, all this is a girl's perspective. I can understand why guys loathe Pat. Even before he was famous, many a pimply fifteen-year-old male probably wanted to stick a pencil in his ear. Here's Pat's résumé from David Lipscomb High, a Church of Christ–affiliated school in Nashville, from which he graduated in 1953: he was student body president, and served on Nashville's Inter-High student council. He was captain of the baseball team, and had additional letters in football, basketball, and tennis. He drew cartoons for the school newspaper. He palled around with the principal. He was dating Shirley Foley, the daughter of country star Red Foley. He was voted most popular in his class. He even had a pedigree: he was descended from Kentucky pioneer Daniel Boone. No wonder authorities got so wound up over Elvis; he was practically Malcolm X by comparison.

Pat was always a big achiever. Born June 1, 1934, he was the oldest of four kids delivered to Archie Boone, a building contractor, and Margaret Boone, a nurse. He and his younger brother Nick, who would record under the name Nick Todd in the late fifties, loved to harmonize with pop tunes on the radio. But Pat loved sports even more, and he played hard. He broke so many bones that his mother asked the family doctor if he had soft bones. "No, it's the way he plays the game," the doctor explained. "When he comes up against an immovable object, something has to give." He also loved religion. He planned to be a teacher or a preacher, and though he flirted with rebellion — he smoked, snuck beers into his room at night, went through the brief shoplifting period — for the most part he strove to keep his soul blemish-free. He can blame religion for the fact that he's a lousy dancer: the Church of Christ forbade dancing between unwed couples. "Some of my convictions have ameliorated a little bit," he said in 1998. "I love the joke that Baptists and other Southern religious groups absolutely forbid sex standing up, because it might lead to dancing."

The Boones weren't well off — "lower middle income," Pat said — and one summer he helped out on his father's construction crew. It was a mixed group, black and white. "I was expected to work just as hard and carry just as many wheelbarrows full of concrete," he said. He preferred the perks that came with another of his hobbies, singing. At ten, he had sung on the radio and won a model plane. By the time he was a teenager he was entertaining at Kiwanis clubs and ladies' luncheons, and getting paid in his favorite currency: free meals. Soon he was hosting his own show, *Youth on Parade*, for WSIX in Nashville. In 1953 he won a city-wide talent contest; first prize was a trip to New York to audition for Ted Mack's *The Original Amateur Hour*. He was picked to be on the show and won three weeks in a row, singing earnest renditions of hit-parade fare like Eddie Fisher's "I'm Walking Behind You" and Frankie Laine's "I Believe." But his parents discouraged singing as a career. They wanted him to finish his studies and go to college. They also thought he and Shirley were too young to get married. Thankfully Pat didn't *always* obey. In the fall of 1953 he and Shirley eloped. The following year he recorded a handful of sides for a Nashville independent label, Republic, but nothing came of them. By the end of 1954, Pat and Shirley had moved to Texas, where he enrolled in a teacher's college and got very busy starting a family.

Then, in February 1955, a Nashville entrepreneur named Randy Wood tracked Pat down. They had met back in Tennessee and agreed over a handshake to work together, when the right song came along. Pat and Randy would prove to be a brilliant match. Both were smart, enthusiastic Southern gentlemen with a passion for music. Based in Gallatin, Tennessee, Wood ran a mail-order record business called Randy's Record Shop, selling bundles of old and new hit records over late-night radio. In 1950 he'd started Dot Records, recording gospel groups like the Fairfield Four, the country singer Johnny Maddox, and R&B acts like the Counts, Brownie McGhee, and the Griffin Brothers (whose Dot hit "Tra La La" was one of Pat's first covers). Wood was a master of anecdotal learning. He paid close attention to the titles that sold big: for example, he found that any time he put Bing Crosby's recording of "Love Letters in the Sand" in a record package, buyers snapped it up. He also noticed that R&B was gaining in popularity. Since pop and R&B were segregated on the radio, he knew that a smash R&B song would be virtually unknown to pop listeners. And since pop artists rarely wrote their own songs, they were always in search of good material. Like Sam Phillips over at Sun in Memphis, Wood figured that a nice white boy singing R&B to a white audience would go through the roof. Raw R&B, so frightening to pop audiences, would seem less daunting when softened and sung by a white singer. Pop plus R&B would equal rock and roll. Phillips, edgier by nature, found a soulful misfit named Elvis. Wood found Mr. Popularity, Pat Boone.

By early 1955, when Wood sent Pat into the recording studio for the first time, the concept of covering R&B for white audiences was catching on fast. Covers themselves, of course, were standard practice in the industry. Pop singers frequently covered hit songs by other pop singers. And by the early fifties, pop singers were regularly covering "hillbilly" material, which, like R&B, was segregated from pop on the radio. In 1951, Mitch Miller at Columbia scored Top 10 hits with Frankie Laine covering Hank Williams's "Hey, Good Lookin'" and Tony Bennett singing Williams's "Cold, Cold Heart." And Patti Page at Mercury had sold an astounding 6 million copies of "Tennessee Waltz." The industry was still functioning on an antiquated business model where songs were the standard of currency, not recordings. Way, way back in the day, recordings hadn't even existed — the industry made its money off sheet music, sold for a penny or a nickel. By the thirties and forties, radio had boosted the popularity of recordings, but in their primitive form — ten-inch 78s — they were still bulky, inconvenient things that scratched easily and delivered low fidelity. In the mid-1950s, the arrival of affordable, compact 45 r.p.m. singles would revolutionize record ownership, making it more of a populist enterprise. Still, even in the fifties, a song was more valuable to the industry than a recording. A song could be cut again and again a hundred different ways, earning cash for its publisher each time; a record might come and go overnight. Writers wrote; singers sang. That business model wouldn't really change until the coming of the Beatles, Bob Dylan, and other performers whose self-penned material was indelibly linked with their own voices.

Cover versions like Pat's have been demonized, and they were, indeed, an attempt to rob black performers of their material — in the same way that a Frankie Laine cover of "Mule Train" was an attempt to rob Vaughn Monroe. It was a cutthroat tactic, but it wasn't race-specific. At the same time, cover versions were evidence of the industry's growing acceptance of black artists in the mainstream pop marketplace. In the latter part of 1954, Bill Haley hit the Top 10 with a toned-down version of Big Joe Turner's "Shake, Rattle and Roll." The Crew Cuts reached Number 1 with the Chords' "Sh-Boom" (the Chords' original, by the way, covered Patti Page's "Cross Over the Bridge" on the A-side). In January 1955 the former big-band singer Georgia Gibbs broke with LaVern Baker's "Tweedle Dee." Elvis was causing a stir, although he wouldn't crack the pop charts until early '56 on RCA. The race was on: pop had discovered R&B. Black performers were on the bus, even if the industry was still confining them to the backseat.

Wood called Pat in Texas and told him to hop a train to Chicago. He had a song for him: "Two Hearts" by an R&B group called the Charms. Pat assumed from the title that it would be a romantic ballad, the kind of thing Eddie Fisher would sing. When Wood played it over the phone, Pat thought the turntable was on the wrong speed. "I had only the vaguest idea what R&B meant," he admitted. In Chicago, he spent hours listening to the Charms's version over and over, trying to master the unfamiliar inflections. He recorded it that same night, along with "Tra La La." Wood knew that other pop artists were jumping on "Two Hearts" — Frank Sinatra, Doris Day, and the vocal group the Lancers all recorded versions — and he flogged deejays and distributors with Pat's record. It was palatable to pop listeners, yet it had more rock-and-roll energy than Sinatra's or Day's. Soon it had trumped the competitors, and Pat was on his way to his first million-seller.

For the next year and a half, Wood fed Pat an exclusive diet of R&B: Domino's "Ain't That a Shame," the El Dorados' "At My Front Door (Crazy Little Mama)," Ivory Joe Hunter's "I Almost Lost My Mind." But by mid-1956, Elvis's incendiary style was creating mass hysteria, and a few brave deejays, led by Alan Freed, were breaking the color barrier on radio. A new, integrated radio format was fermenting: Top 40, which played the most popular hits regardless of genre. Freed brought black performers like Chuck Berry and LaVern Baker directly to white audiences in live shows and in films like *Rock, Rock, Rock*. Pat had learned R&B like a student studying for a test, and he began to get the sense that he didn't really fit in. "Alan Freed booked me into a rock-

and-roll night at the Paramount Theater in Brooklyn," he recalled. "Chuck Berry, Bo Diddley — I can't remember who else, but real R&B artists were on. The audience was, like, half black and half white — very with-it, aware young kids. They were really into Bo Diddley and Chuck, and now I come out and I'm snapping my finger, got a button-down collar on my shirt and a thin knit tie, every hair in place, tapping my white buck shoe. I was doing my best to be as exciting as those guys were, and the young kids screamed. But I did feel out of my element, like this is not who I am. I'm getting away with it and I've had a couple of hit records, but I'm not sure I belong on the stage with these guys. This is music they originated, and I'm just picking up on it."

Of all the early rock and rollers, Pat was best poised to graduate to adult pop. And in 1957, adult pop was still huge business. Perry Como kicked off the year with a Number 1 hit, "Round and Round"; Patti Page was relaxing in "Old Cape Cod." For all its revolutionary fervor, rock and roll hadn't displaced the establishment. Quite the opposite: mainstream pop was absorbing rock and roll, softening it to make it appealing to a broader range of listeners beyond just renegade teens. In late '56, Pat scored his first nonrock hit, the orchestral movie theme "Friendly Persuasion (Thee I Love)." In '57, he starred in his first movie, the collegiate morality play *Bernadine*, with a title song written by Johnny Mercer. Its flip, a cover of Crosby's "Love Letters in the Sand," would become the biggest hit of his career, lodging at Number 1 for seven weeks. Old-guard singers like Sinatra, who famously denigrated rock and roll as music made by "cretinous goons," went out of their way to praise Pat. "Boone is better than Elvis," Frank opined. "He has a better technique and can sing several types of songs. He's the one who will last longer."

At the time, it certainly seemed that way. Pat's spotless character led Wood to dub him "the first teenage idol that Grandma can dig, too." By 1957, he had transferred to Columbia University in New York, determined to honor his parents' wish that he finish college. He studied speech, earned an A average, and graduated magna cum laude. At the same time, he was hosting *The Pat Boone–Chevy Showroom* on ABC-TV; it debuted in the fall of '57 and ran for three successful seasons. In 1959, he published a book of advice for teens, *'Twixt Twelve and Twenty*, which became the top-selling nonfiction book of the year. After Elvis, he was the second-most-popular singer of the early rock era: he logged in six Number 1 records, and placed more than three dozen singles in the Top 40. Between July 2, 1955, and June 1, 1959, not a *single week* went by without a Pat Boone song in the charts.

His image certainly contributed to his success, yet it wasn't quite as monochromatic as detractors have made it out to be. He was clean-cut, yet not insufferable. He constantly entertained journalists with his idiosyncratic worldviews and odd habits. He told reporters that he hated wasting time, and liked to study while driving, with a book propped on the steering wheel. "I don't recommend it," he cheerfully added. He told *Cosmopolitan* magazine that when *Bernadine* finished filming, he purchased gifts for cast and crew — jewelry items like cufflinks and watches. "While I was at it, I picked out a watch for myself. The jeweler said he'd engrave it for free, and what did I want on it?" He chose an inscription that read, "To Pat — from one who has followed your career closely." He liked to start *and* end his meals with a banana split. On records, he did all his own whistling.

When times began to change in the sixties he made halfhearted attempts to change with them. In 1962 he took what was for him a racy role in a picture called *The Main Attraction*, in which he smoked and had sex with an older woman. In 1964, Bruce Johnston of the Beach Boys and producer Terry Melcher recorded a surf song with him, "Beach Girl," but it stiffed. By the mid-sixties he was hopelessly out of date. He was ill-prepared for people to dislike him. Up until that point in his life, hardly anyone had.

The late sixties were a cruel time for Pat. Randy Wood exited Dot, and Pat was left without a label home. Business investments went sour; he nearly went bankrupt trying to support a basketball team, the Oakland Oaks. His marriage to Shirley got shaky. He drank and gambled. Religion saved him: he became born-again, and started speaking in tongues and baptizing converts in his Beverly Hills swimming pool, for which he and Shirley were defellowshipped from the Church of Christ. But by the mid-seventies, things were looking up. He started his own Christian label, Lamb & Lion, and took to the road with his wife and four daughters in tow. *Rolling Stone* ran a recantatory cover story called "The Great White Buck," in which the reporter, John Anderson, admitted liking Pat in spite of himself. In 1977, twenty-year-old Debby hit Number 1 with "You Light Up My Life." By 1980, with Reagan's election, the country's values seemed to be swinging back in his direction.

Through all the ups and downs, Pat found that he did best when he remained just Pat. He discovered his own bizarre form of authenticity: times would change, but he could stay the same square, straitlaced, smiling guy. When I met him in 1998, he was still coming down off the high of his 1997 album, *In a Metal Mood: No More Mr. Nice Guy*. This tongue-in-cheek collection of metal standards sung with big-band arrangements was the pop year's ultimate party joke; snazzing his way through Guns N' Roses's "Paradise City" and Metallica's "Enter Sandman" as if they were tunes in a Vegas revue, Pat managed to poke fun at headbangers and himself, and along the way proved that the most disparate of genres can be reconciled, given the right light treatment. Evangelicals didn't approve of him appearing on the *American Music Awards* clad in black leather, but metal fans, hipsters with an ear for lounge, and anyone who remembered *Happy Days* got the gag. The album became his first chart hit in thirty-five years.

But it was the pop standards that interested me. As the interview was winding down, he told me one last story — a long-winded, entertaining, poignant tale that was pure Pat.

I'll tell you, I had the most goose-bumpy, wonderful moment about five years ago. It was an epiphany, really. I'd been inveigled into a tour of England and Europe. I hadn't appeared there in seventeen years. I thought, this promoter is nuts. He thinks people still want to hear these songs. Just because he remembers them, he thinks everybody else does. He's going to lose his shirt, and I'm going to feel bad. And I tried not to do it, but he wouldn't take no for an answer. He kept beseeching me to come. I figured he must know what he's doing — he's experienced. So I let him talk me into it.

The first night was at the Victoria Theater in London. I really took it seriously. I rehearsed and vocalized, I really wanted to be my best. I was nervous that if this tour didn't start out well, word might get around. And I was nervous that the poor guy was wrong about my appeal. Well, that night was fabulous. The tickets sold out, and it was completely jammed. I looked out and saw a theater filled main-

ly with well-dressed, middle-aged people. There were men in three-piece suits and women with fur stoles. It could have been a command performance or something. You half expected to see the queen. The show went really well, and I did a long show. Well-to-do women would come to the foot of the stage with four, five, six albums in their arms. They'd want me to sign them in the middle of the show. I did it once or twice, and then I said, "Look, I'm flattered, but I'll do this afterward. Let's not stop the show while I scribble my name." Then they'd name a song and ask me to sing it. I'd say, "Gee, I don't remember that. I didn't sing that, did I?" And they'd hold up the album and point to it. You know, I've done over a hundred albums. In many cases I would learn a song for an album, and then I'd never sing it again. I would literally forget that I ever did it. But they loved this particular song, and it was incomprehensible that I couldn't immediately sing it.

Well, it was a friendly, happy time. I finished the show and did a couple of encores, and I came off feeling great. The musicians were all buzzed, saying, "That was really terrific. Listen, they're still cheering, the lights are up, the show's over and they're still standing out there stomping." I went out and took a couple of bows, and it was obvious they weren't planning to go home. I scratched my head, because we'd done everything we rehearsed. I said to the guys, "Why don't you get out 'Star Dust.' I hope I remember all the words." Now, remember, the lights are all up, there's nothing romantic in the place. No production, just the stage, which looks sort of drab with the lights up. The audience is standing all jammed toward the front of the theater. So I started singing: "Sometimes I wonder why I spend the lonely night / Dreaming of a song . . ."

I tell you, there were many tears in the crowd. I got choked up, too. And I thought, that's what this music is all about. There's something magical in pop ballads. They worm their way into your heart and your memories and associations and life. It's the one way, except maybe a beautiful picture or some old film that you find, that you can go back and revisit a time that's long gone. For that four minutes — and I stretched that version of "Star Dust" out, I didn't want it to end myself — we were all transported back thirty-five years to a time we thought was gone forever, and now suddenly we were all living it again in the context of the song. And if you look at the lyrics, that's what the song says. It's about how that melody helps the person relive that vanished time.

I think that's the appeal of songs like "Harbor Lights" and "Dream" and "Good Night, Sweetheart." They've ended so many high school dances. "Dream, when you're feeling blue / Dream, that's the thing to do." Those songs were the ones that everyone did the last romantic slow dance to. They have tremendous emotional meaning to millions of people.

Just then Pat looked at his watch, and realized we'd been talking for over two hours. "I've got to get home!" he exclaimed. "I haven't wished Shirley happy birthday. This is her birthday, and she wasn't up when I came over." He told me that Shirley had been fighting clinical depression. The lifelong demands of his career had drained her; she had realized that he would never slow down, and they would never have the quiet, intimate life together that she had envisioned when they married so long ago. That was why he told her he would semiretire at sixty-five. "She was saying things like,

'I know now that as long as I live, I'll never have the life I once thought I might have — just you and me together, me being Mrs. Pat Boone and you being my husband, and us going where we want to go and doing what we want to do.'"

We shook hands and said good-bye. I wanted to ride the elevator with him, but I forced myself to sit in the lobby and wait for him to go down by himself. He deserved a little peace, after giving me so much. As I waited, I thought about his wife. I wanted to tell her, Shirley, you're not alone. None of us can get enough of him.

Five

ME AGAIN

By the age of sixteen I had already decided to be a rock critic. Maybe I was young to be so directed, but the choice seemed logical. I'd been a musichead for as long as I could remember. When I was four, I loved listening to the radio as we drove to Sunday dinners at my grandparents' house. I loved the hits from Carole King's *Tapestry*; "Don't Pull Your Love" by Hamilton, Joe Frank & Reynolds; and "Raindrops Keep Fallin' on My Head" by B. J. Thomas. By the mid-seventies, when I was eight, I was spending my weekly seventy-five-cent allowance on 45s at the Gramophone Shop in New Canaan. I bought "Feelings" by Morris Albert, Glen Campbell's "Rhinestone Cowboy," and "Seasons in the Sun" by Terry Jacks. I kept them in a red vinyl 45s box and, like a junior Casey Kasem, made new Top 10 lists every week; the most common Number 1 was "Beach Baby" by the First Class, which I did not then recognize to be a hollow knockoff of the Beach Boys. I went through my prepubescent poster stage (Donny Osmond) and my pubescent poster stage (the Bee Gees, with their weird hairy chests). The emotions in pop songs seemed so much more meaningful than anything in my real life. The Bee Gees asking "How deep is your love?" was like *Wuthering Heights* to a soul whose days consisted of book reports about badgers and an older brother's nougies.

My brother skidded into adolescence a couple of years before me, and he began making fun of me for still listening to AM radio. So, at around the age of thirteen, I switched to FM. My real-life romances were getting more complex, too. There was Eric, a Holden Caulfield–esque misanthrope who yammered about his ideals in the hallway during our freshman-year free periods. On the night of the dance, he brought me to his garage to see the black VW Beetle that he'd bought for eight hundred dollars and would soon fix up, even though he was two years away from legally driving it. I thought he'd kiss me but he blew the chance, so I broke up with him. He sent a series of irate letters written on blue-lined paper in minuscule, spindley longhand with faint gray pencil. I could barely read them, but the epic nature of his distress made it all seem very important. That spring, I began dating Jeff, a senior. He took me to the prom; I was one of only two freshman girls who attended. We rode in a limo and sucked face happily while his best friend and date looked on in disgust. One evening, locked in my bedroom with my parents downstairs, he took me to third base — and I mean, he *really* took me to third base, with bells ringing and fireworks exploding. Then he packed up and headed to his parents' Swiss château for the summer. At first the missives were passionate: he inserted "Gee, I really miss you" over a caret between the first and second sentences of his first letter. But as the months wore by, the letters trickled off. I got mono that summer, and gained weight. Jeff was a gentleman. He came home and sat me down in the formal living room my parents never used, and dumped me in person before heading off to college.

I was lost, bereft, cruelly abandoned on the threshold of sexual knowledge. Luckily he left behind a token. One splendorous afternoon before summer set in, we had sprawled on the grass in my backyard, talking about music. "You've never heard Bruce Springsteen's *Born to Run*?" he asked. "Oh, you gotta hear it. There's a song called 'She's the One'" — and he wiggled his eyebrows suggestively at me. With Jeff gone, I held the dutifully purchased LP in my hands and took a deep breath, preparing for a plunge. I had heard Springsteen on WPLJ-FM, and I didn't like his harsh bleat of a voice; the *No Nukes* concert album was current, and his live version of Mitch Ryder and the Detroit Wheels' "Devil in a Blue Dress / C. C. Ryder" was in heavy rotation, an assiduously unromantic introduction to the man's oeuvre. But the moment the needle dropped on *Born to Run*, I was a goner. The soft pling of piano at the opening of "Thunder Road," the twangy, dawnlike rays of harmonica, the enigmatic and evocative lines "The screen door slams / Mary's dress waves"; the street-corner bravado of "Tenth Avenue Freeze-Out," the unrelenting acceleration of "Born to Run"; the midnight showdown between the hero and his girl, Terry, in "Backstreets," and the dissipative wanderings of the Rat and his compatriots in "Jungleland" — this was rock and roll as I had never heard it before, sensual yet forceful, invigorating yet reassuring, telling stories of loss and redemption that eerily mimicked the wreckage and rebuilding of my first broken heart. I became totally obsessed. I listened to the album every day, several times a day. My family, listening through the floorboards, turned my obsession into a joke. Mom, the former Elvis Girl, seemed to understand better than the others, but even she burned out on the noisome repetition of the "Backstreets" coda.

I didn't care. *Born to Run* was mending me. My feelings about it weren't, you know, gross — it wasn't like I jacked off to it. Rather it became a refuge, a roadmap to a place where romance might not be so cruel. I submerged myself in the characters, the muscle-car rhythms, the mantra of escape. Sequestered in leafy suburbia, I stumbled upon a world I'd never imagined: scarred highways, crumbling stoops, twilight waterfront vistas. New Jersey. I wanted to go there. I couldn't wait to grow up, get out of sheltered, phony New Canaan, and bask in a tough, real world.

My fever for *Born to Run* spread to other albums, other singers. On WPLJ I heard Tom Petty, the Kinks, Bob Seger, Stevie Nicks. From my brother's room I overheard a different strain of rock: the Who, Led Zeppelin, Aerosmith, Journey, Foreigner. That stuff was okay, but it was storytellers who interested me the most, and no one came close to Springsteen. He was my shining icon. I read interviews with him in *Rolling Stone* and *Musician* and taped the covers to my wall. I loved his sincerity, his morality, his true-blue unpretentiousness. *Rolling Stone*'s 1980 cover story "Bruce Springsteen and the Secret of the World" featured a photo of him ice skating, huddled in a dark coat. I was there with him, skating through an emotional winter, hell-bent for salvation. One day, browsing with my mom in the New Canaan Book Shop, I came across a copy of *The Bruce Springsteen Story* by Dave Marsh, and held it up to my mother in mute appeal. She bought it for me, and as I devoured every word and photo caption I made a discovery. Journalists had access. They could meet their idols without having to wait around the arena door at two in the morning. They could have long conversations about meaningful topics like lyrics and recording studios, and the relationship was legitimate. I wore a Springsteen button pinned to my jean jacket, and a cousin had asked me, with a smirk, "Are you a groupie?" "I don't know what that is," I said warily, although I didn't like the sound of it. Clearly Dave Marsh was no groupie. He was a welcome gazer at the foot of the pedestal. That's where I wanted to be.

So, at sixteen, I embarked upon a career. I reviewed albums in my high-school newspaper, aping opinions I'd read in *Musician* and *Rolling Stone*; John Cougar "oozes insincerity with every bark," I wrote in a year-end roundup. And I began firing off little diatribes to the big magazines, two of which got published. A screed against Nick Lowe — he had insulted Creedence Clearwater Revival! What a jerk! — made it to the letters page in *Musician*. While I was away that summer as a mother's helper, Nick Lowe actually *called my house* and asked my brother why I hated him so much. My brother couldn't believe it was him, and quizzed him about *Rockpile* to be sure. A more general screed against critics made it to the letters page in *Rolling Stone*:

> *I'm really sick of all the critics putting down today's rock audience. I happen to be sixteen and love rock. I listen to what I like, not what gets shoved down my throat. I enjoy Stevie Nicks and Tom Petty, and apparently many others do, too, but as far as the critics are concerned, the American teens of today are mindless, brainless idiots — because we like someone saying "Don't stop believing."*
>
> Karen Schoemer
> *New Canaan, Connecticut*

I actually got a date out of that letter. A couple of college guys from Long Island, one of them an intern at WPLJ, tracked me down and we met at the station's mailroom while my mom waited outside in the car. I think they were expecting some halter-topped fury with a frosted blond perm and PETTY FOREVER tattooed on her torso, and I could see the disappointment in their faces when I turned out to be a pudgy suburbanite in pleated dress pants and teardrop eyeglasses. Oh, well. My name in print was reward enough. I'd been in *Rolling Stone.* I was part of something, practically a member of the press.

In college I discovered indie rock and interviewed bands for my campus radio station. The high point was ten minutes at the feet of Pete Buck following an R.E.M. show at a local arena; the low point was me drunk outside the band's bus, begging Buck to come to a dorm party. I applied for a college internship at *Rolling Stone* and got rejected, but then it turned out that Eno De Pasquale, Mr. Uneducated-Blue-Collar-Man-of-the-People, rode horseback at the same Westchester stable as *Rolling Stone*'s general manager, and he got me in. I was deliriously happy. I got research bylines. When the editors heard about my letter of yore, they republished it in a twentieth-anniversary issue. I was set to devote my life to the magazine, and on the eve of my graduation toodled to New York City to discuss a job as an editorial assistant. The music editor stared me down. "You want to be a writer, don't you?" he asked. "This job isn't right for you. There's no writing involved." Then I was offered a position at a sister publication, *US* — a *women's* magazine — take it or leave it. I knew damn well that male interns had risen through the ranks at *Rolling Stone*. I spent a year at *US*, answering phones and fuming.

In the late eighties, though, *Rolling Stone* was the only boys' club left in rock journalism. I spread like a fungus. I wrote for *Spin*, *Creem*, *New York*, and *Interview*; I covered indie rock in fanzines like *Option* and *Jersey Beat*. My favorite outlet was an exuberant rag called *The Bob*, scorned by ultra-hipsters for never giving a bad review. By 1990 I was a stringer for the *New York Times*, writing reviews, previews, and features and tallying, at my peak, more than two hundred bylines in a year. Most of the time I was content to be my fannish self. Writing, for me, was a way to give back: I really did *love* rock, and I tried to replicate my experience for readers, so that they might be inspired to buy the record and experience those joyfully transcendent feelings themselves. I promoted the cause of unheralded bands that I thought deserved a chance, and worshipped heroes like Paul Westerberg, Nick Cave, and Robyn Hitchcock without apology. Interviews were my forte. I loved meeting musicians, talking with them. I thought they were the most thoughtful, original, fascinating people on the planet. The good ones were so true to themselves; they were never in it for the money. I never went into an interview with a list of questions. I'd just fish around until I found a topic that appealed to the person and put him at ease, and then pursue it to any end. My goal was intimacy. I looked for the moment of revelation, where the person forgot he was speaking to the press and simply became himself and said what was on his mind. That moment of trust was like a drug to me. I craved it, and if I didn't get it out of an interview, I felt cranky and unsatisfied, like I'd engaged in a dry hump. But I almost always got it. Then I built my stories around those moments, collapsing after my deadlines into an exhausted, spent heap.

My heart and intentions seemed so pure that I found myself stunned whenever someone turned out not to be a fan of *me*. A magazine called *New York Woman* ran an item called "Critiquing the Critics"; next to my name, an anonymous snoot wrote, "She may not have many insights of her own, but she'll write" — I can't remember the exact adverb, something like *gushingly* — "about the unsatisfied boys in rock who do." When a friend suggested me for an assignment at the *Village Voice*, word get back to me that the music editor had shrugged me off. "Great profile writer. Not a thinker." It didn't matter that I was in the *Times* six days a week, that my phone rang off the hook with offers for work; these slights got under my skin. I felt like a lightweight, a teenybop Oriana Fallaci. Sure, put me in a room with some crusty rock guy and the wacky quotes flew, but put me in a room with just an album playing on a stereo, and not a single original thought would pop into my head. Apparently colleagues could see through me. I wasn't a real journalist; I was just a cheerleader, chanting cute nonsense while the *guy* critics did the intellectual grunt work on the field.

Still, my career progressed rapidly. By 1992, even *Rolling Stone* was giving me features. My research became more in-depth; I'd spend up to three days with a band, hanging out in their hometown, sightseeing, eating with them, drinking with them, passing out with them. Alcohol was my friend and ally; I loved to drink, and the habit endeared me to besotted musicians. But there was a point where all this unresolved hothouse intimacy began to take a toll on me. I'd get so close to people, so fast, and then never speak to them again. It really was like falling in love, and when it was good it seemed reciprocal, as if the person trusted and cared about me in return. Sometimes we'd swear to keep in touch after the story came out, but friendships rarely evolved, especially as my subjects' level of fame increased. The withdrawal was like the crash from a drug high. Recovering and moving on became painful and confusing. Was the love real or fake? I was losing track.

In 1993, *Rolling Stone* sent me to interview the country singer Dwight Yoakam. We hit it off big-time; the interview included a ride on his Harley through the Hollywood Hills down to Melrose, where he shopped for a Mother's Day card. We hung out in his kitchen listening to his jukebox as his hound dogs gazed at me with quiet, wondering eyes. I arranged for a follow-up when he came through New York; I couldn't stand not seeing him again. The following day he left a long message on my answering machine about what an honest and sincere person I was. Then he invited me to fly to Arizona and meet him at a concert.

My story was due. What was I supposed to do? Blow my deadline? Run off and join the proverbial circus? But I was in love. This time it felt really, really real. My mom happened to be with me that day. My twin, my best friend, my confidante. She listened to the message, and then she made the decision for me. "What I don't understand," she said sternly, "is why someone who dated Sharon Stone would be interested in you."

Well, I didn't go to Arizona. And I lay in bed at night for weeks, writhing in agony and regret. I thought, I just can't do this anymore. I needed a real boyfriend. I needed to take myself out of circulation, before I did something stupid that ruined my career and my reputation.

Two months later, I met my husband.

Six
GEORGIA

In September [1958] the country was suddenly in the grip of the Hula Hoop craze ... The impact on the music business was violent. The first to cut a Hoop disc was Atlantic. Over a weekend Trinity Music publisher-songwriter Charlie Grean wrote "Hoopla Hoola" with Bob Davie. On Tuesday, September 2, Grean flew to Chicago where he recorded Betty Johnson ... Atlantic rushed out deejay acetates the following day while a pretty Trinity secretary visited New York disk jockeys to demonstrate Hoop swinging ...

Meanwhile, Georgia Gibbs recorded a ditty titled "The Hula Hoop Song." La Gibbs beat Betty Johnson to the TV tube, introducing her Roulette disk on The Ed Sullivan Show *on September 6 and on [Dick] Clark's daytime show on September 9. Roulette followed the Atlantic pattern of cutting one day (Friday, September 5) and having copies in the hands of deejays and distributors by Monday, September 8.*

On the same day that Gibbs was recording at Roulette, Teresa Brewer was cutting the same song at Coral. The Decca subsidiary did not wait until Monday, but had copies on the turntables of New York disk jockeys the same afternoon. While Gibbs was lip-syncing her record on American Bandstand, *Steve Allen was in a Dot studio recording a Hula Hoop song he had written . . . "Hula Hoop" was the title not only of Allen's opus, but of another Hoop song cut by Imperial Records. That made four different songs and five different disks racing in breakneck competition to cash in on the craze. Who picked up the money? The manufacturers of Hula Hoops.*

—*Arnold Shaw,* The Rockin' '50s

I was full of doubt as I rode the elevator to Georgia Gibbs's ninth-floor apartment on upper Fifth Avenue. Why was I doing this? What was wrong with me? I was seeking out one of the most disdained figures in rock history. In 1955, just as rock and roll was starting to take hold, Georgia, a white big-band singer, released a cover of LaVern Baker's joyous blues rollick "Tweedle Dee." The basic arrangement was lifted almost note for note from Baker's Atlantic original, but Georgia's Mercury version had cleaner enunciation and more polished production, with peppy horn blasts and humming boy singers in the background. Radio was segregated at the time, and only Georgia's version was picked up by pop stations. It scooted to Number 2 on the charts and sold over a million copies, while LaVern's stalled on the charts at Number 14. Three months later, Georgia covered Etta James's "The Wallflower," remaking it as the cheerfully titled "Dance with Me, Henry (Wallflower)." Etta's record never cracked the pop charts, while Georgia's soared to Number 1 and sold another million copies.

History caught up with her, though. In the late sixties, rockers like the Rolling Stones and Janis Joplin hailed the contributions of Baker and James, while Georgia's name faded. Rock critics, when writing about these R&B pioneers, never fail to point out the miserable turn done to them by the evil Miss Gibbs. The liner notes to a LaVern Baker compilation LP on Charly Records refers to Georgia as LaVern's "nemesis." And Etta had her say in her 1995 autobiography, *Rage to Survive*: "Suddenly Georgia Gibbs came out with her Suzy Creamcheese version . . . Georgia's cutesy-pie do-over went over big. My version went underground and continued to sell while Georgia's whitewash went through the roof. Her Henry became a million seller. I was happy to have any success, but I was enraged to see Georgia singing the song on *The Ed Sullivan Show* while I was singing it in some funky dive in Watts. It was an early lesson and a painful one: Like green cash or flashy diamonds, songs get stolen."

In other words, justice had been served; a sentence had been delivered. So why was I trying to rehabilitate Georgia? Why was I trying to *un*do history? I figured that if I were attracted to the story of Georgia Gibbs, I must be, deep inside, a corrupt person. Maybe I was a racist. At the very least I must be a masochist, because I had spoken to Georgia on the phone before our interview and she did not seem very friendly. First of all, she was trying to find a publisher for her own autobiography, and she kept hustling me for information about the book industry. Did I know many editors? What kind of proposal did I write? Did I have an agent? Could I arrange a meeting between her and my agent? Georgia's way of forcing her agenda made my head spin. I was barely coping with the demands of my own book. Then she tested my knowledge of the fifties and flaunted her own. "I think I know pretty much all there is to know about the record business," she said. She started on a rant against one of her record labels. "They were big crooks — they

159

never paid me. Oh, of course. You know that's true. All the singers — everybody's suing. They haven't paid us hundreds of thousands of dollars. Did you know that? This is something you should look into, because I think it would be an important fact for you to write about."

I was caught off guard. This was not an area I had looked into at all. "You're talking about performance royalties?" I asked a bit stupidly. If I'd been thinking straight, I would have remembered that performance royalties go to songwriters, not singers.

An exasperated hiss came over the phone. "*Record* royalties," Georgia said. "You make a record, you're supposed to get your percentages. They haven't paid. Everybody knows that."

In the elevator on my way to the interview, I carried a big pot of flowers. They were my shield. I'd knock on her door and hold them in front of me, and if she had her claws bared she'd shred a few stems instead of me.

To my surprise, the woman who greeted me wasn't fierce and gargantuan and scowling at all. She was a trim, elderly lady standing barely five feet tall, wearing a navy blue sweater and slacks, strappy high heels, and reading glasses on a chain. She oohed over the flowers, and then ushered me into a sunny, comfortable apartment that looked as though it had been tastefully decorated circa 1962 and not messed with since. There was a heavy round table and chairs in one corner, an iron chandelier, French windows, a grand piano, paintings with lights on them, and walls and walls of books. The TV was a giant old console job, and it had videotapes piled on top of it, as if the room had been designed without the storage of such items in mind. Fake lilies sprung from a vase. Georgia seated me on a beautiful vintage green velvet couch, and I complimented it, even though I could see it was worn in spots. "Darling, don't look," she said. "Everything is so old. I need everything to be slipcovered."

She was unpretentious, almost fragile. She got me a cup of tea and showed me a bandage on her hand. "Look at what happened to me," she said. "I was in the emergency room at nine o'clock this morning. Oh, I had a pot of water and I always move too fast and the whole damn thing —" She trailed off with a self-conscious laugh. She told me that she had moved into the apartment more than twenty-five years before, when she married her husband, Frank Gervasi. He was a journalist and author, and their romance was something of a fairy tale. She met him in Paris when she was still in her

161

teens, then lost touch with him for twelve years; they reconnected late in the fifties, and remained happily together until his death in 1992. Frank had published several books, and they were lined up on a shelf next to a window. "He was a world-renowned foreign correspondent," Georgia said proudly. "He covered seven wars. He finished this book, *The Violent Decade*, shortly before he died. The reviews said it was the most complete picture of the war done from an American correspondent's eyes. It got Book of the Month Club. It broke my heart, because he died before he was able to enjoy it."

Naively, I had thought Georgia was obscure because in some moral sense she deserved to be — she had done things in the fifties that people found abhorrent and now no one talked about her. But as I spoke to her, I realized that her own choices had more to do with the way her career had evolved. After she met Frank, she didn't *want* a career anymore. "See, I took time off when I got married," she said. "Darling, I'd been living in lonely hotel rooms since the age of thirteen. I didn't want to go out. Why would I want a lonely hotel when I had a nice, warm man waiting for me at home?" She had performed only once in New York since Frank's death, at a private theatrical club in

Gramercy Park, with a small jazz combo. "The Players Club is all directors and actors a hundred years old," she said. "And they invited me to do it. After my husband died, I couldn't sing. But I said, what the hell, I'll try it and see. And it was like swimming. You never lose it, really."

I asked her why, if she enjoyed it so much, she didn't perform in public. This is where the feisty Georgia I had encountered on the phone started to reemerge. "First of all, darling, you have agents today who are twenty-two years old and don't know who I am," she said. "They don't know anything about me or the world I lived in. And of course, if you're gone for a little bit they think you weigh three hundred pounds and you're pushing a walker and you can't sing. I'm one of the few that's still the same weight. And I've kept my voice in shape. I rehearse two or three times a week."

"What about cabarets?" I asked. "There are a lot of nice cabarets in New York City."

Georgia harrumphed. "It's all become terribly chic," she said. "You've got to do these unknown songs, and frankly it bores the hell out of me. If you're commercial, they think you're passé. I've seen some [cabaret singers] that are very good, but as a rule I can't tell one from the other. They all sound the same.

They do one song, and then they do another song, just with a piano. It doesn't knock me out. You can't do performance like I grew up doing performance. I do a complete musical show. I do Gershwin, I do rock and roll, I do blues, I do jazz."

"I think it would be great to see you perform," I persisted. "People know so little about you. All they really know about are the R&B covers."

I guess I should have known it would be a sore subject. Georgia didn't waste time being all polite and affable like Pat Boone. She just opened up her lungs, got in my face, and let her feelings fly.

"Oh, I read her book," she snapped. "Was it Emma James? Etta James. Boy, she really took out on me. 'Her cheesecake version of "Dance with Me."' You know, a lot of cover jobs went on. 'Fever' was a cover job for Peggy Lee. Wee Willie Jones [Little Willie John] or somebody like that had it on King records. This was just another cover job. And I had absolutely nothing to do with it. I never heard the records. A&R just came in, gave me the songs, and I did them. I had no say about what I recorded. My arrangements were made up before I came in. All the black artists have really been down on me. Ruth Brown was putting me down. Sarah Vaughan was putting me down. 'Georgia Gibbs did this and that.' I think it's quite unjust."

She was so agitated that her reading glasses, which had been perched on her head, kept sliding off. "And LaVern Baker with her 'Tweedle Dee'!" she went on. "To this day I've never heard her record. Because it was all segregated, sweetie. They had the R&B for the blacks, they had pop which was white, and they had country-and-western, which didn't sell above the Mason-Dixon line. I never heard of any of those black singers. How was I going to know, darling? You never heard them on the radio. If you wanted to buy a black record you had to go to Harlem. I didn't know about LaVern Baker. Oh —!" She was sputtering. "Do you know what she did to me? I was getting ready to go to Monte Carlo, because I used to sing there every summer. As I was leaving I got a Western Union Express." Baker, embarking on a tour of Australia, had taken out a flight insurance policy that named Georgia as the beneficiary. The gag was that, in the event of Baker's death, Georgia wouldn't have a source of material. "That's a pretty lousy thing to do. That's really and truly not nice."

I tried to soothe her. "You and Pat Boone got it the worst," I said. "I think it's because you had the biggest hits. But everybody covered. Teresa Brewer covered Johnny Ace and Sam Cooke. Johnnie Ray covered Clyde McPhatter. Perry Como, Sinatra, Doris Day, the McGuire Sisters, the Fontane Sisters, the Crew Cuts, the Four Lads — all of them did R&B covers."

"How about Elvis Presley's covers?" Georgia demanded. "Hound Dog."

"And Bill Haley covered Big Joe Turner," I said. "But that was different, because those songs really were rock and roll. You were doing pop."

She planted her reading glasses back on her head and grew thoughtful. "We were giving the white version of it," she said. "It was sanitized, to some extent. I never thought of it until this very minute, but I imagine that's what it was. Because we were singing for a larger white audience, and the other was strictly rhythm and blues. A&R wanted the same song, but they wanted to sell it in a different way to white audiences."

Since long before I met Georgia, I had been struggling to understand the cover syndrome. I knew instinctively that singers like Pat Boone and Georgia didn't deserve to be singled out for a phenomenon that was happening throughout the industry, but I found it difficult to exonerate them when so many decades of conventional wisdom said otherwise. As Georgia spoke, the issue became clearer. There was something morally suspect about white covers, but the blame didn't belong to the singers alone. *We* bought the records. *We* liked them. The songs were a reflection of *us*, too: whites with no exposure to or understanding of black culture.

"It wasn't just the music that was segregated," I said.

Georgia nodded solemnly. "The country was segregated," she said. "Civil rights didn't come in until '65. It was terribly unjust, but all America was unjust at that time."

Like Georgia herself, Georgia's music isn't immediately likable. After our interview, I sat down to reassess her work. There isn't much available. *Like a Song*, a Pickwick CD released in 1998, collected recordings made between 1946 and 1948 for the Majestic label. *The Best of Georgia Gibbs: The Mercury Years* surveyed her period of greatest success, 1951 to 1957, when she made the transition from feisty hit-parade belter to bubbly rock bandwagoneer. It included her 1951 breakthrough hit, "Kiss of Fire," as well as her R&B covers and a couple of standards, like "It's the Talk of the Town" and "Happiness Is a Thing Called Joe." While at Mercury,

Georgia also recorded three LPs, which were long out of print by the time I met her. I had one of them, *Swinging with Her Nibs*, a small-band jazz outing from 1956. She left Mercury the following year and recorded her last chart hit, "The Hula Hoop Song," for Roulette in 1958. In the sixties she recorded for Epic and Imperial before releasing her last album, *Call Me*, on Bell in 1966. She had other, earlier work that was out of print. In the late thirties, when she was still in her teens, she recorded with the Hudson-DeLange big band on Brunswick. In 1942, she freelanced a couple of sides with Artie Shaw. After her Majestic stint, and before Mercury, she landed for a while on Coral. And just before Roulette, she was on RCA. Georgia got around.

At first I didn't care much for any of her work. Georgia was a strong, able singer, but her voice had a hard edge that didn't particularly suit the niceties of forties and fifties pop. Mercury handed her plenty of weepers — the jilt anthem "While You Danced, Danced, Danced" in 1951, the operatically forlorn "The Bridge of Sighs" in 1953 — and her tone never quite achieved the doelike vulnerability called for in the lyrics. Just when you thought she was going to throw herself into the abyss, her voice took a turn toward bravado. A similar problem beset standards like "One for My Baby" on *Swinging with Her Nibs*. Georgia just wasn't convincing in ballads. I couldn't help hearing echoes of Sinatra and June Christy, who could communicate both devastation and chin-up resolution in the space of a single line. Georgia handled the fortitude part, but she shied away from expressions of deep vulnerability. Maybe it was a quasi-feminist streak running through her, and that put her at odds with her era; if she had come along a few generations later, she would have kicked ass on a tune like "Love Is a Battlefield."

She fared better on up-tempo tunes. I liked "Seven Lonely Days," a country jaunt that hit the Top 5 in 1953. When Patsy Cline remade it in 1961, her phrasing mimicked Georgia's to the point of homage. And "Kiss of Fire," though corny, was a hell of a performance. Based on an Argentine tango called "El Choclo," it aimed for a kind of tympanic overload, opening with a battalion of trumpets blaring loudly enough to announce royalty, then piling on castanets, flutes, bassoons, and God knows what else — you could practically hear the pounding hoofbeats and clanging armor. The lyric came from the Frankie Laine / "Jezebel" school of sorcerous lovers. "Love me tonight and let the devil take tomorrow [she sang, clipping each consonant so forcefully that she left empty spaces between each word], I know that I must have your kiss although it dooms me." She ended on a glass-breaking high note. "Kiss of Fire" was a monster hit; it held the Number 1 spot for seven weeks in 1952.

What really turned me around, though, were her R&B covers. If LaVern Baker's "Tweedle Dee" was intended as a slice of good-natured, hip-shaking nonsense — "Jiminy crickets, jiminy jack / You make my heart go clickety clack" — then Georgia achieved that on her own terms. She may have been white, but she was no stiff: her infectious vocal grabbed you by the hand and tried to wrest you from your chair. "Dance with Me, Henry (Wallflower)" suffered even less by comparison. Etta James is a brilliant vocal stylist, but "Wallflower" — written as a response to Hank Ballard and the Midnighters' "Work with Me, Annie" — was her first commercial recording, and her immaturity showed; the tempo was sluggish, the vocal hesitant and flat. Georgia, on the other hand, pow'ed it. She put real adrenaline into her singing — it sounded as if, after she was done with the tune, she'd have enough leftover energy to lift a car. The best of her covers was less well-known. "I Want You to Be My Baby," from an original by Lillian Biggs, combined high-speed burlesque banjo strumming with a charging rock-and-roll backbeat. Georgia was the rare fifties canary with a genuine flair for rock and roll. Patti Page couldn't have spat these words out if she'd swallowed a fistful of Dexedrine.

By the time I was through listening to all this, I had a healthy new respect for Georgia, and a sense of indignation over her neglect by critics. In his landmark treatise *The Sound of the City*, Charlie Gillett had delivered a backhanded compliment to Georgia's version of "Wallflower": he called it "spirited compared to most records made for the white market." I'd go a step further: it was spirited for *any* market. It was better than the original. Though Georgia's tunes were clearly descended from the "Doggie in the Window" school of fifties pop, they provided an important break from that tradition: they proved that pop conventions could be stretched to allow plenty of room for rock-style excitement. Rock critics, in their effort to trace the music's evolution directly from blues and R&B (with an occasional nod to country outlaws like Hank Williams), tend to shut pop out of the picture. But rock and roll didn't happen in a vacuum, separate from the most dominant and pervasive music in the country. Covers like Georgia's and Pat Boone's show that rock and pop were intertwined from the outset. They would influence each other throughout the rest of the fifties and into the early sixties, and the resulting hybrids would prove immensely pleasing to audiences. Purists were deeply annoyed. They still are.

It's ironic that Georgia inspired such antipathy among R&B devotees, because she had an upbringing to rival any hard-luck blues singer's. She was born Fredda Gibson in Worcester, Massachusetts, the youngest of four children. She won't confirm her age; the birthdate most commonly given is August 17, 1920. Her father died when she was six months old, and a year later her mother deposited the children in a Jewish charitable orphanage. Georgia was separated from her siblings, and saw her mother only every six or seven weeks. Although she moved back in with her mother when she was seven, she never felt close to her. "She's somebody I called Mama, but I wasn't bonded with her," Georgia said. "There's a world-famous pediatrician, T. Berry Brazleton. He said that if a child in the formative years is not loved or nurtured, that child will grow up with a hole in her heart that will never heal. And he's one hundred percent right."

The bright light in her life was singing. At the orphanage she led yearly musical shows. Back at home, her mother, a midwife, disappeared for weeks at a time, leaving Georgia with just a Philco radio to keep her company. "I was told all my life that I was too short, I wasn't pretty, but I had a hell of a voice," she said. "When you're a kid, you want to be told you're pretty. So you're hardened. But I *listened*. I wasn't even aware of it at the time. I unconsciously found myself listening more to music. All those antennas were working. You don't realize how much you're learning. You're learning about orchestrations, you're learning about arrangements."

When she was thirteen, Georgia began singing in local ballrooms. "The era of ballrooms was marvelous," she said. "Every town had a ballroom — a Danceland, a Stardust. It was the social scene for the young. You went to a ballroom for a dollar, you dressed up, you didn't need a date, and you never had to be lonely. You danced to a fourteen-piece band, you heard Gershwin, you heard all the great music. I learned every song." She wore homemade gowns that helped her pass for sixteen, and within a year a promoter offered her a chance to sing at the Raymor Ballroom in Boston for twenty dollars per week. She wasn't quite through with eighth grade, but the night work was making it difficult for her to stay awake in school. So she quit, caught a bus to Boston, and sent the money home to her family. Soon she received an offer to go on the road with the Hudson-DeLange orchestra. "I did about six months, and it was the most unbelievably hard work in my life," she said. "Every night was two hundred, three hundred miles. We didn't have a bus. It was a broken-down car with the shift between my legs and bleeding, chapped thighs because there was no heater. They didn't have motels then, so you'd see a for-let sign and get yourself a room with a toilet down the hall. It was *marvelously horrible*. A band like Benny Goodman, they traveled in a bus. They were big-time. I wasn't big-time, darling. I was just a little working girl singer, that's all."

Despite the social nature of the music business, Georgia was shy and never hired a manager. "When you come out of an orphanage, you're very distrustful of life," she said. "You're distrustful of the world because you're so unhappy. So I just kept myself away. After all, it's a tough business for a young kid with musicians. You're jailbait, and you're alone twenty-four hours a day. I just said, 'I'm not going to bed with any of these guys.' And I wasn't." It was her own drive to succeed that pushed her every little step forward. She freelanced for bandleaders like Artie Shaw and Frankie Trumbauer, landed a slot on the radio show *Your Hit Parade*, and, in the early forties, changed her name at the suggestion of an agent. From 1943 until 1947 she was a regular on *The Jimmy Durante and Garry Moore Show*, a hugely popular radio program. One day Moore blurted out a nickname that stuck with her throughout her career: "Her Nibs, Miss Georgia Gibbs." "Nibs is an English phrase, darling," she said. "It's someone of authority, but in a sarcastic tone. 'His nibs is sleeping,' meaning the queen or the king is sleeping, with a tongue in the cheek. It's a colloquialism. It's not American. Most people don't know what the hell it means." In other words, she hated it. "I used to get gifts with just 'Her Nibs' written on them, and it used to get to me."

In late 1946 she signed a deal with Majestic, which yielded no hits. Around 1948 she was offered a job supporting Danny Kaye at the Paramount Theater in New York. They did six or seven shows a day, and one afternoon she was instructed to join Danny onstage. She jelled as his comedic sidekick

— she could laugh *really convincingly* on cue at jokes she didn't think were funny — and they spent two years on the road together. In 1950 she had her first hit: a cover of Eileen Barton's pop novelty "If I Knew You Were Comin' I'd've Baked a Cake," on Coral. By the time she signed with Mercury in 1951, she was a dedicated, efficient pro with two decades of show-biz experience. At a session in 1952, a publisher plunked down the sheet music to "Kiss of Fire." Her voice was raw — she'd already been singing for two and a half hours, and she'd worked the night before — and she had to learn it and master it on the spot, with the clock ticking. "It's a tough song to sing, because it's an octave and four notes and I have to hit a top D flat," she said. "I said, 'Look, my voice is awfully tired. Why don't you balance the band and we won't go for a take. If I hit the D flat, we'll leave it in and let it go at that.' So I hit the D flat, and that was it. I just sang it that once."

"Kiss of Fire" was the high she'd been striving for: it sold more than a million copies, sat on the charts for five months, and inspired the deejay Martin Block to call her "the most underrated singer in the business." But without a manager, Georgia was unable to capitalize on its success. A dreary romantic follow-up, "So Madly in Love," lost the momentum, and by 1954 she was floundering again. Georgia lacked the schmooze gene: "I wasn't a drinker, and I was always frightened of people in the business, frankly. I just wasn't interested in how many times this one has gone to bed with that one. It's a bloody bore to me." So she stayed close to home: the Mercury offices. One day she struck up a conversation with a couple of characters named Hugo Peretti and Luigi Creatore, who worked for a subsidiary kiddie label called Child Craft. Hugo and Luigi were hip to the new phenomenon known as rock and roll, and they had bold ideas about material that might suit Georgia. Soon they were ensconced as Mercury's new A&R men, steering her back up the charts with R&B covers like "Tweedle Dee" and "Dance with Me, Henry (Wallflower)." Hugo and Luigi became semilegendary rock-and-roll figures: they would go on to produce classics like the Isley Brothers' "Shout," Buddy Knox's "Party Doll," and Sam Cooke's "Cupid" and "Chain Gang." How does Georgia remember them? "They stuck it to me pretty good," she said. "They made thousands of dollars on me, because they were getting a piece of a lot of the songs."

I knew Georgia was bitter, but I couldn't hold it against her. She was alone in the music business in an era when women barely had careers, much less functioned as their own self-styled management executives. Imagine Patti Page without a manager — she would have ended up a quiet housewife in Tulsa. Georgia's fighting spirit was decades ahead of its time. There is a moment on her album *Swinging with Her Nibs* that sums up the struggles she was facing, and her seemingly endless ability to surmount them. During Cole Porter's "Let's Do It," she twisted her tongue on the line "Cape Cod cold clams against their wish do it," and burst out laughing, then went on. "Every one of those songs was done only once," she said. "They only gave us eight hours to make the whole album. You couldn't go over time. They didn't want to spend the money. I broke up, and they said, 'That's it, let's go to the next one.' 'But I broke up!' 'It's okay, Georgia — you broke up on the beat.'"

Her story had only one hero: Georgia herself. "The agents and the bookers and the accountants — they saw I have vulnerable eyes and, whew, they went right after me," she said. "But I persevered and I made it, which I think is a very big success story in itself."

After she finished talking, both of us were silent for a few moments. The afternoon sunlight was so bright that the tables and vases seemed to sparkle. I asked Georgia if I could see her Gold records, which she said were stored in a side room. "What do you want to look at those for?" she mumbled.

"Come on," I said.

"What, haven't you seen 78s?" she snapped, and I let it drop.

An award shaped like an old-fashioned gramophone sat on a bookshelf. "Is that a Grammy?" I asked.

"Well, no," she said. "My husband got that for me, because he thought I deserved one."

Eventually she decided I deserved to see *something.* So she rummaged around the videotapes on top of the TV console, and loaded one into the VCR. "You have to understand," she said, "this is my *very first* television appearance."

It was a tape of Frank Sinatra's short-lived early fifties TV series, with Georgia as a guest star. Sinatra was singing "It's Almost Like Being in Love," handsomely, in black and white. Georgia and I settled down in front of the set like a couple of kids who'd never seen a TV before. "At this time I was appearing at the Waldorf-Astoria with Sid Caesar," Georgia said. "I had just left Danny Kaye. I hadn't gotten my recording contract with Mercury yet."

"Good evening, ladies and gentlemen, boys and girls. Happy New Year to you all," Frank said with an uncharacteristic pallidness that seemed calibrated for the new medium. "Winter finally caught up with us in the East, you've probably been reading about it." He went into a skit about how he was having a party and had no one to help him serve guests. "If Jack Benny were in town I could use Rochester," he said, a reference that went over my head. "If Jack Benny were in town I could use Jack Benny." "These shows are so awful!" Georgia interjected. "The repartee is not to be believed." But she seemed excited in spite of herself.

The apartment buzzer on the set rang, and Frank opened the door. "Her Nibs, Miss Georgia Gibbs!" Frank exclaimed, to warm audience applause.

The TV Georgia swirled into the room wearing a dark, calf-length gown with a sassy flaring skirt. "A wonderful party you've got going on here," she said in a bubbly, breathless voice.

"Georgia, you look lovely, sweetie. I think you get prettier every day," Frank said.

"Oh, now, Frank," Georgia said with a blush that did not seem at all phony.

"What do you want to sing for us?" Frank said.

"Well, now that I'm trapped — do you have anything planned, Frank?" He backed out of the frame, and Georgia began singing "Taking a Chance on Love." That feisty edge was in her voice, but there was also a fluttery girlishness I had never detected. She seemed nervous and thrilled, like this was some kind of unimaginable childhood dream come true.

I turned to look at the Georgia who was in the room with me, and nearly fifty years later her expression carried that same innocent joy. "Every time I look, I can't believe it's me," she said. "It was *Frank Sinatra*. I was starry-eyed."

I was a little bit starry-eyed too, marveling at real-life Georgia's sudden absence of bitterness. Enough had gone wrong for her that she allowed herself to relish a moment that had gone completely right. As I watched her watch herself, I saw a facet of her personality that I hadn't noticed before. It was a tiny reserve of tenderness, buried deep inside but always clamoring to get out. Maybe that's what has driven her forward for all these years, I thought. The feistiness is there for all the world to see, but the real point of music, or any art, is to release the sides we're afraid to show.

The song ended, and the crowd applauded. I clapped, too, and yelled proudly for her.

Georgia shot me a dirty look, and hurried the tape out of the machine. The moment had passed. But we both knew what we'd seen.

Seven

TOMMY

"I've had to make all kinds of compromises and I haven't liked it. I'm the only person in the world who knows what I want to accomplish and I'm the only one who can accomplish these things for myself. But everyone else has an idea for me. They listen to what I want to do then they come up with their own ideas and the next thing I know, I've compromised. There is always the compromise."

Mr. Sands, who is a slight, wiry young man, laughed when we suggested that most teenagers would consider him very fortunate indeed and would gladly trade places with him.

"I suppose you're right," he admitted, "but they are not with me when I get up in the morning and face that terrible insecurity. I look in the mirror and say to myself, 'You aren't the greatest actor or singer in the world. What are you? Nothing.'"

—New York Herald-Tribune, *August 11, 1958*

When I decided to do a book about the fifties, I had the idea that interviews with former stars would be easy to get. I figured all these people were just, you know, sitting around their houses feeling sad that young people didn't care about them anymore. They were just waiting for someone like myself to come along and rescue them. I'd ring on the phone, and they'd jump for joy. *Karen! Thank God you finally found us! What took you so long?* Then they'd invite me to their homes and make me a nice lunch and spill their darkest and dearest secrets and stories. My book would be the equivalent of a stage upon which they would all parade once more. And audiences, a community of readers, would shout and cheer, welcoming them back, restoring their faded glory.

Well, this did not turn out to be the case. I found that many former stars still kept up active careers, touring casinos and theaters in towns heavily populated by retirees. The crowds may have aged, but they hung in there with impressive loyalty. And even the performers whose careers had slowed often had little interest in the rigamarole of interviews. I dealt with many, many unreturned phone calls from agents, assistants, and managers. I learned to be persistent, exploring many angles of access, trying several different phone numbers per person, sometimes sending multiple packages by FedEx to offices and home addresses. But no matter how avidly I followed up, sometimes I just couldn't get through and I had to give up and move on to someone else. I always felt slightly hurt when someone said no or ignored me. I took my mission so personally. Why didn't they like me? My intentions were so good!

But one person whom I simply could not give up on was Tommy Sands. Like Connie Francis, Tommy connected me to my mother. She had been a fan of his when she was fifteen; her parents had allowed her to see him in concert, whereas they never allowed her to see Elvis. If my book was to be a gift at my mother's feet, asking her to forgive me for marrying someone she didn't like, then I needed to deliver Tommy wrapped up in a bow. Even beyond the connection with my mother, Tommy struck me as an intriguing figure. He was the first Elvis clone. In early 1957, he starred in a TV play called *The Singing Idol*, about a pompadoured rocker who makes the girls go wild. The show spawned a Number 2 hit, "Teen-Age Crush," and a Top 5 album, *Steady Date with Tommy Sands*. Tommy *wuh-huh-huh'ed* when he sang, just like Elvis, and his voice had a raw hillbilly edge; he arrived on the scene just as Elvis was being shipped into the army, a hard-working bench replacement whose job was to keep the team's lead from evaporating while the hero was off the court. Tommy lacked Elvis's visceral energy, but his bashful eyes and placating manner were just the thing to make rock and roll less threatening. He had solid show-biz credentials: he'd been a rising young country singer in the early fifties, signed for a time to RCA, and was even managed by Colonel Tom Parker before Parker hooked up with Elvis. He was a decent kid, a professional, not some hell-raiser who'd do something crazy like marry his thirteen-year-old cousin. Tommy toed the industry line, acting in nice, dumb movies like *Mardi Gras* with Pat Boone in 1958 and inching toward tasteful pop with albums like *Sands at the Sands*, a 1960 concert recording of his splashy Las Vegas debut. That same year, he became an instant member of the pop establishment when he married Frank Sinatra's eldest daughter, Nancy.

But somewhere along the way, his career began to ricochet in the wrong directions. Despite some high-profile movie roles — *Babes in Toyland* with Annette Funicello in 1961, the World War II epic *The Longest Day* in 1962 — he was not taken seriously as an actor. Two albums with Sinatra arranger

Nelson Riddle failed to chart. In 1965 he divorced Nancy, and sank from public view. I borrowed a file of Tommy Sands clippings from *Newsweek*, and the most recent item was a "where are they now"–style piece — from *1973*. Tommy was living in Hawaii, managing hotel showrooms, and claimed only to sing in the shower. After that, silence. I snooped on the Internet but turned up nothing. Of all the singers on my fifties list, Tommy turned out to be the most elusive. How was I going to find him, this rare safari animal? How was I going to add him to my trophy display?

One day, good fortune hit. A researcher friend at *Newsweek* stumbled upon a gossip item about Tommy. The item, from the *New York Post*, said that the *National Enquirer* had recently run an exposé about his battles with drugs. That story caught the attention of two producers from the TV show *Baywatch*, and they'd signed to make a movie about his life, with Tommy playing himself in his later years. With a little hunting I got the number of a publicist named Alan Eichler, and began leaving frantic messages. No answer. I faxed him; no answer. But I couldn't give up. I busied myself with other interviews, other fifties stars, but every once in a while I'd bug Alan again. And one day — I almost fell off my chair — he called back.

Things were happening for Tommy, he said. The death of Frank Sinatra in May of 1998 meant he could speak more openly about his past. Bear Family had released a retrospective CD, *The Worryin' Kind*; Tommy had a new band, the Blue Jets, and was trying to put together a club tour. Alan said I could meet him on my next trip to L.A. "It's time for him to step forward," Alan said. "There's more to him than people know." There was just one catch. Tommy struggled with mental illness. Alan didn't want to go into it — he would leave it up to Tommy to decide how much detail to relay. And one other thing: Tommy was broke. Would I mind buying him lunch at an L.A. coffee shop?

I told him that all of this was fine. I'd be sensitive to Tommy's problems, and of course I didn't mind treating him to lunch. I hung up the phone and whooped. I'd bagged him! I went on the Internet and booked a plane ticket. Then I went to a CD Web site and ordered a reissue called *Steady Date with Tommy Sands*. It included his entire debut album plus a couple of singles and B-sides. The moment the package arrived in the mail, I ripped it open and scanned the track listing. "Teen-Age Crush" was there, and I skipped right to it.

I don't know what I was expecting, but the

sound that came out of my stereo was unlike anything I'd ever heard. It was a version of rock and roll so misshapen, so exaggerated, that it verged on the grotesque. Tommy's vocal was a hiccupy approximation of Elvis that evoked Bill Murray's lounge singer on *Saturday Night Live*. The arrangement didn't gel: there were so many triplets that the piano could have been recorded on the back of a jouncing flatbed truck, yet the bass player plodded and the guitarist kept falling behind the beat. In other words, it was awful. I sat there at my desk, sort of traumatized. Why hadn't it occurred to me to listen to his music *before* I hunted him across the globe? How was I going to rescue him, if his music didn't deserve to be rescued? How was I going to reconcile the rock critic in me with the girl who was her mother's daughter, interested in cute boys, going gaga over distant celebrities? What the hell was wrong with me, anyway? Why had I persisted in a book project that was constantly on the verge of disaster?

I tried, as I had with Patti and Frankie and Pat, to put a positive spin on the Tommy oeuvre. I told myself that it was, so to speak, *good* bad, the kind of bad that warms the heart. I tried to think of it as outsider music — misguided, naive, intensely sincere. These rationalizations helped keep the lid on my anxieties. In the days leading up to the interview, I stopped worrying about the music, and switched to worrying about Tommy himself.

I felt torn about the whole thing. Tommy had plunged lower than any singer I had yet encountered. I was dying to meet someone who could go from being Frank Sinatra's son-in-law to not owning a phone, but underneath my excitement was a twinge of self-disgust. Negative comments could prove more hurtful to him, professionally *and* personally. I knew my intentions were a moral cut above the *National Enquirer*'s, yet I couldn't shake the feeling that I was exploiting him too. The encounter had a sideshow air about it, with me as the barker. I'd be ogling him, and I'd bring others in to ogle him too. Well, I tried not to think about that. I figured I was a pretty nice person, as far as journalists go. I'd be responsible. I wouldn't hurt him.

We met at a coffee shop called Coco's, a clean and cheerful outpost in a seedy stretch of North Hollywood. It reminded me of the kind of place where Tom Waits might hang out: sort of upscale drifter. Tommy came in wearing a black T-shirt and black jeans. His hair was dyed an optimistic shade of sun-god yellow that didn't match the troubled look in his eyes. He was affable, even solicitous, but clearly nervous. I told him that my mom had been a big fan, and instead of looking pleased he seemed worried. He took a long, deep breath. "Is she still here?" he said at last. I told him yes, and he heaved with relief. "Greeeat," he said.

"She went to see you at Radio City Music Hall when she was sixteen," I said.

"I never played Radio City," he corrected. "I played the Roxy, a block down. They looked alike — same marquee. And, oh, they payed huge money. Then I think they sold the building and tore it down. I don't know what's there now."

"Her parents wouldn't let her see Elvis, but they thought you were okay."

"Well, that's because I didn't do anything except stand there in terror," Tommy said. "It terrifies me to go onstage. The week before *The Singing Idol* I couldn't eat. Bites of food — nothing. It would have come up."

He seemed prone to self-incriminating statements. "I'm about twenty pounds overweight," he said at one point. "I can barely get into my clothes." A few minutes later, he blurted out, "I'm not, nor have I ever been, gay. I've had gay friends and I don't look down on them, but I'm not." Finally he put his anxieties on the table. "When I was seven or eight I was diagnosed as an acute chronic depressive," he said. "I fought fear and depression all my life. Coming to see you was a big thing. I had to work through my little things that I do."

I felt guilty as hell. "I'm glad you're here, Tommy," I mumbled.

"I don't know what I should go into and what I shouldn't," he said.

I tried to steer him — and myself — toward the high road. "I'm really more interested in your music than your personal life," I lied.

"So just ask me questions, then, and I'll answer them," he said.

I hesitated. Fabulous Sinatra stories that I would never hear seemed to float out the window into the scrubby parking lot. I couldn't help myself. "Just talk about whatever you want to talk about," I gushed. "Don't hold back."

In a weird way, this was exactly what Tommy wanted to hear. Keeping up a façade takes so much energy; maybe he needed the reassurance that he could be himself. He settled back into the booth with his cup of coffee, and launched into a description of what it was like to be a surrogate Sinatra. "My career was dead as soon as I married Nancy," he said. "I was referred to as Frank Sinatra's son-in-law, instead of my own identity. I got madder and madder. One night, before we went to bed, I packed a bag. The next morning I woke up and said, 'Nancy, I don't love you and I don't want to be married.' And I went out and got in the car. Nobody knew where I went. I went to a hotel that I liked, the Sunset Marquis. And I got a room. I was heading into drugs then. I was sleeping and the phone rang and rang. Finally I staggered over to the phone and said [slurring], 'Hello.' And this unmistakable voice said, 'Tommy, this is Frank. I want to see you.' I said, 'All right. When?' He said, 'Right now.'

"So I drove over to Warner Brothers. At that time he was a producer and an actor in films. He had his own building. I went in, and Dean Martin and Sammy Davis Junior and Joey Bishop were playing pool. 'Hey, Tommaso.' 'Hey, buddy, how you doing?' I walked in and Frank was staring at the wall. He said, 'Sit down over there, please.' He said, 'Tommy, I don't want to pry into your personal business, and I don't want to ask you how the marriage was or get into my daughter's life. I just want to know one thing.' And he turned to me and there were tears in his eyes. He said, 'Do you love my daughter?' And I said, 'No.' He kind of looked down.

Then he got up, put his hand out, and said, 'If there's ever anything I can do for you . . . Take care.' And that's the way it was. No rage, no recriminations, no advice, no nothing."

I was stunned. "I can't believe Frank didn't kill you," I said.

"He was always like that with me," Tommy said. "Always so nice and gentle."

He emptied his coffee cup, and the waitress came by with a refill. I was still staring with my jaw on the table. Tommy laughed at my reaction. Even one-on-one, even after all this time, he took evident pleasure at beating an audience's expectations.

Later, after I'd interviewed Tommy, I decided to listen to his music again. I had the feeling that meeting him might allow me to hear his music more sympathetically. So one day back at home, I settled down with a pile of LPs and CDs. I had the Collectables reissue, plus several of his original albums for Capitol. *Sandstorm*, from 1959, was a collection of R&B covers; *This Thing Called Love*, also from '59, was a mellow assortment of pop ballads. I had *Sands at the Sands* plus the two Nelson Riddle albums: *When I'm Thinking of You* from 1960 and *Dream with Me* from 1961.

The first thing I did was listen to "Teen-Age Crush" again. And it was as if I heard a different song. Before, I'd focused on its ramshackle elements; now, suddenly, I was standing on the inside, and I got it. "Teen-Age Crush" was a love song addressed not to a girl, but to her parents. It picked up on the theme of juvenile rebellion that had been building momentum since *The Blackboard Jungle* and "Rock Around the Clock," and put it in romantic terms. Kids had to be free to love who they wanted, how they wanted. "Please don't try to keep us apart," Tommy sang, asking more nicely — "please" — than Elvis might have. "Don't call it a teen-age crush." It's "Love Me Tender" as a call to action. The simplicity bordered on brilliance. The awkwardness of the performance actually sealed its power. Tommy literally seemed like the kind of person he was singing about: a lovestruck kid, confused and plaintive, stuck under the thumb of authority. He connected with the song, and as soon as I felt that, I connected with it, too.

I listened again and again, and my infatuation didn't diminish. In fact, the more I listened, the more I began to realize that the song hadn't changed; I had changed. I wasn't hearing some facet of the song that I had missed before; I was listening with a different part of my brain. If I tried, I could still sort of hear it the old way. I could acknowledge that, by any objective standard, "Teen-Age Crush" wasn't, you know, *good*. The vocal was bizarre, the musicianship was subpar, and the whole enterprise lacked original-ity. But this new part of my brain overrode those quibbles. I know some people claim that ideas hit quickly, like a thunderbolt. This one came to me very slowly, after much painstaking work. I listened again and again, studying my reaction, and finally, on about the eighth go-round, I figured out what was going on. Sure, in a technical sense, "Teen-Age Crush" sucked. *But I didn't care.* I liked it anyway. I liked bad music! God, it felt like such a relief to finally figure this out. Give me bad music, give me more, more, more! Wheeeeeee!

Then I thought back to the other singers I'd met. I thought about Patti Page's insipid "Doggie in the Window," Frankie Laine's ridiculous "Mule Train," Pat Boone's icky "Tutti Frutti," and Georgia Gibbs's bastard-ized "Dance with Me, Henry." And I realized that I liked them, too. I just hadn't been able to admit it until now. It just had never clicked in my mind that I could be a critic who liked bad music. I thought that critics were only supposed to like good music, like the Velvet

Underground and Jerry Lee Lewis and the Band and Wynonie Harris and Elmore James — music that other critics had already said was good. So my job, as I'd unconsciously laid it out in my own mind, was to go out there and find music that fit in with other critics' definitions, and proclaim it good and suitable for consumption by others. I never thought that being a critic was just saying what you liked, and why. I never permitted myself to be subjective. I was constantly trying to live up to a standard that others had imposed.

But as I listened to "Teen-Age Crush," I began to understand that I could like something that other critics didn't. Now it seemed so obvious. People like bad music, the same way that they like McDonald's hamburgers and sitting on the beach until their skin burns and reading a trashy novel and forging to the multiplex with the throngs on the fourth of July to see the latest ridiculous blockbuster. As a critic, I had lost track of that fundamental principle. "Teen-Age Crush" was bringing it back to me. The song connected me with my mother, with millions of other girls who'd fallen in love with a pop song, not caring whether it was bad or good. The song put me in touch with my own innocence. It helped me resolve the conflicting impulses that had nagged me since I started the book: the objectivity of the critic and the subjectivity of the fan. It allowed me to be critic and fan at the same time. I could love bad music, and then find the words to explain why.

From there, I listened to more of Tommy's work. His debut album, *Steady Date with Tommy Sands*, was "Teen-Age Crush" times twelve: a collection of songs on the theme of adolescent ardor, with an emphasis on slow dances, moonlit walks, inexperienced fumblings, and scribbled love notes. The material came from an intriguing array of sources: Faron Young's "Goin' Steady" was a country classic, while "Walkin' My Baby Back Home" (Ted Weems, 1931), " 'A' You're Adorable (The Alphabet Song)" (Perry Como, 1949), and "Teach Me Tonight" (Jo Stafford, 1954) drew from the pre-rock songbook. Nat "King" Cole's "Too Young" was here, revamped with a slouchy blues backbeat and Scotty Moore–inspired guitar sass. A couple of tracks belonged just to Tommy, like the exquisitely dopey "Ring My Phone," in which guitar blings passed themselves off as the sound effect of the title. Despite the variety, everything sounded like Tommy. There was a fragile sweetness to him, almost a gullibility, that perfectly suited the theme at hand. The lyrics called for a depiction of the starry-eyed, clueless phase of love, and he delivered. It may not seem like much of a compliment to say that Tommy made material like the great Sammy Cahn's "Teach Me Tonight" sound like it was hammered out by an amateur in a garage, but I found it impressive that these songs adapted so easily to a relatively crude rock environment. At the same time, it was becoming clear that Tommy was improving, in a technical sense, as he gained in age and experience. His voice was relaxing into a breathy croon, and the musicians played more by feel than rote. And while the sentiments were uniformly chaste, Tommy's hepped-up energy on the upbeat tracks suggested distant dreams of lust. *Steady Date* was the sound of a guy saying all the right things in order to get into a girl's pants, right up to the pledges of eventual betrothal. It was petting music, an exquisite early example of chick rock. Its words said no, but its heart said yes, yes, yes.

Like Pat Boone, Tommy was clearly being groomed for adult stardom. *This Thing Called Love* was a faux-stodgy rock-pop collection; the cover showed Tommy in a cable-knit sweater, his hair buzzed into a helmet shape, against a backdrop of fuzzily focused flowers. Like Pat, Tommy had a facility with ballads, but his version of "All I Do Is Dream of You," which Pat recorded in '56, shows how different the two singers were. Pat, the Crosby-Como devotee, always seemed calm and satisfied; the lyric is about twenty-four-hour-a-day obsession, but he sang it as if he were kicking back in the Barcalounger with a college-bowl game in the background. Tommy, schooled in country music, yearned. He lacked Pat's light touch with a melody, yet the burr in his voice communicated a knowledge of darker things. That quality made romantic fluff like *This Thing Called Love* unexpectedly rich.

The Nelson Riddle albums had an element of the divine. The arranger must have taken note of that yearning in his voice, that dissatisfaction; it was a junior cousin to the magnificent loneliness of Sinatra. The first album, *When I'm Thinking of You*, re-created the saloon drama of Sinatra albums like *In the Wee Small Hours* and *Only the Lonely*, but with a softer edge. Violins shuddered on high notes, trombones rumbled in the shadows. Tommy brought a spooky sadness to "Hello, Young Lovers" — he was only twenty-three, for God's sake, summoning the regret of one whose best days were behind him. The second Riddle album, *Dream with Me*, threw convention to the wind. It was a surrealist knock-out, a musing on the unreality of love.

Angel voices hovered, tempos drifted like clouds, and the songs didn't seem to start and stop so much as get up, stretch, and lie down again. The effect was practically psychedelic. "The beetle bugs are zooming and the tulip trees are blooming," Tommy sang in "Lazy Afternoon," his voice a haze of bliss.

I couldn't vouch for the objective greatness of these albums, but I could say they moved me wildly. If *I* were writing rock history, instead of all those authoritative guys who came before me, I'd say this: Tommy made a real contribution to it when he sang standards with a rock-and-roll accent. His roots in country and rock brought an emotional immediacy, a paradoxical *un*sophistication, to the melodic bounty of the pop canon. As much as I loved Sinatra, I never quite felt like I could call him my own. His context was too far removed. It was like having a conversation with my erudite lawyer grandfather: we'd be getting along fine, and then I'd blurt out "ohmigod" or use the word "like" six times in a sentence, and he would shake his head with a sad, she'll-never-learn expression.

Tommy spoke my language. I realized this when I heard his version of "I'll Be Seeing You," a minor chart hit from the first Nelson Riddle album. Now, this was one of the great love songs of the twentieth century. Its lyric harbored gentlemanly values that were the antithesis of rock: the singer has been dumped, and he responds not with anger but with a heightened sense of devotion and respect; every time he revisits a place they've been together he promises to cherish the memory, despite the pain it causes him. Tommy nailed every nuance. The rawness of his vibrato signified the depth of his heartbreak, but the way his voice pulled out of it, smoothening and softening, reaffirmed the constancy and persistence of his love. It was like the emotion of "I'm So Lonesome I Could Cry" grafted on to a song constructed of ermines and brandy. I'd heard "I'll Be Seeing You" many times before, performed by singers far more accomplished and revered. But it was Tommy who gave it to me. He allowed me to own it. I loved him for it.

Tommy was born in Chicago on August 27, 1937. He grew up with a variety of musical influences, but pop was in his blood. His mother, Grace Lou Dixon, was a sweet-band singer who had performed with Art Kassel and his Kassels-in-the-Air. His father, Benny Sands, was a tough mug from New York City's Hell's Kitchen; he had a bullet lodged visibly in his forehead. He played piano, and at thirteen he ran away from home to join the Paul Whiteman orchestra. Benny came from a family of Russian immigrants; Grace was of Scotch-Irish-English descent. "I was loaded," said Tommy of his ethnic background. "I have not just one, but several wars going on inside me."

From the time Tommy was two, Grace and Benny would periodically split up and reunite. Parenting was not their strong suit. "He and my mother used to leave me alone and go to the gambling casino, and watch the races," he said. "They'd spend their whole day in there, sometimes into the night, smoking, gambling, drinking." When she and Benny were on the outs, Grace would shuttle Tommy from Chicago to Shreveport, Louisiana, where her uncle had a farm. The uncle wasn't much of a father figure, either. "He had something wrong up here," said Tommy, tapping his skull. "He was a politician at one point, and he had a thousand acres of cotton, but he was vicious. I remember seeing him one night take a pitcher of ice and throw it into my mother's face. There was a rage in him that I'll never understand."

Life down south had its advantages, though. Tommy fell in love with country music, and when he was five his mother bought him a guitar. Within a few years he was singing on the radio and performing at stock shows and in bars. When he was eleven or twelve, with Benny long gone, Grace decided she could support her son better in Houston, where she could get a job as a department store salesgirl. And Tommy, in turn, could help support her. "She said, 'You go down there first and see if you can find work.' So I did. I took a bus and I found who the number-one disc jockey was, a guy named Biff Collie. I went to his station, and he put me on the radio the next day. He was also the producer of shows around Houston, and he started using me on every one of his shows. I worked with George Jones and Slim Whitman and, oh, a lot of them — Kitty Wells and Johnny and Jack and the Tennessee Mountain Boys."

Tommy loved the attention that performing brought him. "I used to stop the show," he said. "I'd go out there and do anything I could to get 'em. It was natural. I'd roll on the ground and jump and do all these gyrations and things." In 1950, a Houston independent label, Freedom, released Tommy's first single. "It was a cute song for a kid," Tommy said. "It went, 'Oh misery, sadness and woe / The size of my troubles no one will ever know.'" One night, after he sang that song in a Houston bar, a man approached him. "He said, 'I'm Colonel Parker, I'm Eddie Arnold's manager, and I think you've got something,'" Tommy recalled. "He said, 'Do you have a manager?' I said, 'No.' He said, 'Well, you do now.'"

Colonel Parker was, at last, the father figure Tommy had craved. "He started taking me in his car following the Eddie Arnold tours, every summer and during any school break," he said. "Talking, talking, talking incessantly. He taught me everything about the business, told me what I was going to run into." The Colonel had a friendly relationship with RCA — it was Eddie Arnold's label — and he got Tommy a deal. RCA released seven of Tommy's singles between '52 and '54. "They didn't sell seven records between them," Tommy said. "My voice sounded like a parakeet. It was real high." Yet as a live attraction, he remained quite popular. Appearing on shows around Houston, he encountered the young Elvis Presley, and claims to have tipped off the Colonel about him. "Colonel Parker called me and said, 'What's going on around there? Anything exciting?' I said, 'Colonel, there's a guy who's the most incredible, phenomenal singer you've ever seen. Women go absolutely insane the minute he walks on the stage.' He said, 'Boy, I have to meet that boy.'" (A biography of Parker, *The Colonel*, by Alanna Nash, says Parker heard about Elvis through a number of sources, including a deejay named Uncle Dudley and a promoter named Oscar Davis.)

On these jaunts through the South, Tommy also saw the business's darker side. "Hank Williams was — is — my all-time country-and-western idol," he said. "I was working in a club about a week before he died. They kept making me do set after set because he was so late. And then he came in with five or six guys around him, and they carried him into the office. As soon as I finished my set I went into the office. They had this big cauldron, like a professional restaurant-size cauldron of hot coffee, and they were holding his mouth open and pouring it down. He was so thin you could see the bones underneath his cowboy shirt. He had his own doctor with him, with a bag, and they were giving him shots in the vein. He staggered out there, finally, with two guys standing on either side of him, holding him up while he sang maybe two or three songs. You couldn't understand a word. I just cried."

Tommy's relationship with the Colonel ended by 1955. "My mother and the Colonel hated each other," he said. "She had been the dominant force in my life, and she saw him as a threat. She worked and worked until she broke that contract." Grace took Tommy out to Hollywood, where they knocked on doors to no avail. In late '56, the Colonel made good on his long-term investment in Tommy. The *Kraft Theater Hour* needed a star for its one-hour TV play, *The Singing Idol*, once Elvis dropped out, and the Colonel recommended Tommy. "He had never stopped believing in me and working for me," Tommy said. He flew to New York, auditioned, and won the role. Capitol Records, which had been scouting him for years, signed him and prepared copies of the movie's featured song, "Teen-Age Crush." The show's impact was enormous. "In one night, I had over a million dollars in offers," he says. "One night."

For the next several months, he rode *The Singing Idol* wave. Twentieth Century-Fox revamped the drama into a full-length motion picture, retitling it *Sing, Boy, Sing*, and in 1958 the theme song became his last Top 40 hit. But once the heat wore off, his lack of an individual style hurt him. As a singer, he emulated Elvis; as an actor, he wanted to be James Dean. "I've always been a follower," he said. "When I saw James Dean, I started watching real closely. It wasn't like I was imitating — it just became a part of me and the way I did things. And when I saw Elvis, it was the same thing. It was a subconscious thing. Like learning to play football. You've got a big brother, and you begin to learn how to play football by watching him. Subconsciously you pick up the moves."

Tommy realized that the industry had him in a box, and he diligently struggled to break out of it. He improved his acting, studying at New York's Actors Studio in the early sixties. And when his rock-and-roll records stopped selling, he welcomed the chance to sing pop ballads. "That's the way I wanted to sing," he said. "But because of my age and my look, and the fact that I had been playing the guitar and doing country music a lot like Elvis when I was a kid, that's the slot they wanted me for. With *The Singing Idol*, my fate was sealed. After I stopped selling and nobody cared, Capitol let me do what I wanted. I said, 'I want Nelson Riddle to be the arranger. I want to do beautiful ballads my way.' We had nothing to lose." Working with Nelson was a revelation. "He helped me a lot," Tommy said. "He told me, 'You're a viola.' And then he arranged around that. He had me singing a bit lower than I normally sing, and it was better."

But those albums didn't sell either. Tommy's marriage to Nancy, whom he met at a Hollywood party, attracted a burst of publicity. But by the mid-sixties, kids like my mother, who had been part of rock-and-roll's first boom, had grown up, settled down, turned to more serious music like folk, or become captivated, along with the rest of the country, by the Beatles. Singers like Tommy, who revered the old-school showmanship and pop palatability of the Sinatra generation, seemed hopelessly old-fashioned. He was among the last of a breed, along with late-fifties idols like Connie Francis and Bobby Darin. Performers like Dylan and the Beatles were *artists:* they followed an inner voice, using music as a vehicle for self-expression. Tommy was an entertainer. He lived to please an audience. He couldn't exist making cool, out-there albums for hipsters and cognoscenti; for him, a record that failed to chart was a dud, no matter its artistic merit. Without the audience's seal of approval, he was useless, an empty vessel, a mirror reflecting nothing.

To this day Tommy intuitively morphs himself, depending on what he thinks an audience wants. His comeback shows emphasize his rock-and-roll material — albums like *Sandstorm* — because that work has retro cachet with the Bear Family, hard-core collector crowd. "Y'know," he said in the liner notes to his Bear Family CD, *The Worryin' Kind*, "Capitol would have gotten a lot more out of me if they let me do what they let Gene Vincent do . . . rockabilly. *Sandstorm* was not a big hit, but it's my favorite album."

He told me a different story. Sensing my interest in his Sinatra connection and his pop excursions, he played up the importance of the Nelson Riddle collaboration. "The albums that I like most that I've ever done are *When I'm Thinking of You* and *Dream with Me*," he said. "Those two albums are my prizes."

After lunch, Tommy wanted a cigarette. He wasn't allowed to smoke inside, so I told him I'd meet him outside. Then his face clouded again. "I didn't bring any money," he said, shame in his eyes. I told him not to worry, I'd pick up the tab. A few minutes later I found him leaning against the cement wall, and his mood was better. "I just watched a plane take off and head out to the ocean," he said gently. "I love to watch planes take off. It's pretty."

At some point that afternoon it occurred to me that Tommy couldn't depend on *any* coterie for his survival. Credibility wasn't going to get him on his feet. He needed the masses. Luckily, he had something in his possession far more valuable than a handful of old records: personal tragedy. If he could market it correctly, his life would change for the better. He told me that he was anxious to see if the *Baywatch* producers could get his movie bio up and running. "I told them my whole life story on a tape recorder," he said. "They wrote it down, and they've got it now. I just pray to God that it really comes off. Because if it does, I'll work until I die, a lot. People haven't seen me nationally in thirty-five years."

After the Nelson Riddle albums tanked, Tommy began cracking up. His marriage to Nancy unraveled. ("As soon as I left, Lee Hazlewood wrote a song for her called 'These Boots Are Made for Walking,'" he said. "And I'm the reason those boots were made for walking.") He was using drugs. Still sympathetic to him, Sinatra cast him in *None But the Brave*, a World War II drama that Sinatra directed and starred in. The film was released in 1965, just as the divorce was coming through. Months later, someone tipped Tommy off about a review in the *L.A. Times* suggesting that Sinatra should have avoided nepotism. "I got so mad," Tommy said. "I drove to the reviewer's office and beat him up. Then I got home and it was all over the papers and my friends were talking about it and people were laughing at me. I got embarrassed and took off for Hawaii. I'd always wanted to live in the tropics. I stayed twenty years."

He and some partners opened a hotel showroom, with Tommy as the featured performer. He tried, unsuccessfully, to clean up. "I worked seven nights a week, from nine p.m. until four in the morning," he said. "And midway through that I started using again. Every night I was terror-stricken. By the way, the only thing I ever used was pills. I've never shot anything. They've got to strap me down to take blood. And I never liked cocaine. The pills that I took would keep you high for eight hours. Then the pills to go to sleep would make you sleep for eight hours. But these other things like crack and meth-amphetamine and heroin, they don't last that long, from what I've heard. No wonder people spend fortunes on them. Every thirty minutes they've got to buy more."

He quit the showroom, and began promoting package tours around Honolulu. "I was making more money than I had made since I was first a star," he says. "I got myself a beautiful, beautiful apartment. Got myself a new Jaguar every year." He also remarried, and eventually divorced. Hotel bosses took a piece of his profits, his tours fell apart, and by the mid-seventies he was broke. "Then I didn't work until I came back over here, and work has been scarce over here. From '75 or '76 until now, it's been lean."

At times, mental illness made work impossible. "I'd be walking around so crazy that my friends would get frightened and commit me," he said. "The kind of places I've been, they put a guy in isolation for mouthing off. Another boy was in there because he was asthmatic, and his vaporizer was empty, and he was calling and then finally screaming for a vaporizer. He couldn't breathe. So they put him in this room where there's wire outside the door and wire on the windows. I was in there with him. He got an attack and I was pounding on the door and yelling and screaming, and he died right there. When they finally came and opened the door, the big guy who was on duty looked and just kind of picked him up with one hand and took him out. He said, 'Sands, you can go.'" A truck blasted past on Lankershim Boulevard, and Tommy waited for the noise to die down before he continued. "That's what these places were like. They're good places to *get* sick."

He leaned over and stubbed out his cigarette in the gravel. We prepared to say good-bye. I felt like I should do something more for him. He had given me so much; I hated to think that he had no one to take care of him. But in the end, I just gave him my phone number. It seemed like such a meager gesture. "You can call me any time," I said. "If there's ever anything I can do for you, please let me know."

Tommy looked thoughtful. "Do you believe in God?" he said at last.

"I don't know" would have been the correct answer, but I'd just offered to help. "Yes," I said, morphing myself just a tiny bit.

"Okay," he said. "Will you say a prayer that this life story happens? Just say a prayer. I don't believe in praying for things that are selfish, but there's nothing bad about this. And I really need it."

I promised him that I would. And I did.

Eight
MORE ME

All through my twenties, my mom and I had remained unusually close. Maybe too close. She and Eno now resided in a homestead called the Ponderosa, a hilltop plot of eight acres overlooking a bird sanctuary in northern Westchester. Eno built the house with his own hands. He had bought the land for next to nothing, bulldozed a road, cleared the trees, and laid the foundations with the help of some buddies. The house was shaped like a large gray shoebox. It had a garage on one side of the ground floor — with a half-painted vintage Ferrari or Porsche usually in residence — and a stable on the other side, where he kept two horses. Upstairs was living space. Mom filled it with antiques: hooked rugs, painted cupboards, cloth dolls. I loved the Ponderosa; they kept a room for me. Mom had taken to saying that despite genetics, I was really her and Eno's daughter, because I was so much like them both. Meanwhile, my relationship with my father had dribbled away. When I was in college he married a woman I didn't like, and we went for eleven months without speaking. We patched up in time for my graduation, but the truce was uneasy. I'd see him a few times a year for dinner in New York, and then report back to my mom the following day: "Yep, still an asshole."

Though my career flourished, I wasn't having too much luck in my own relationships. I didn't know why, but my track record was poor. I was either pining after guys who weren't interested in me or dragging around clingy nerds who dreamed of nothing more than transcribing my concert-review notes into gold-plated three-ring binders written in illuminated script. I guess I had a comparison problem. How could humble earthlings compete with the magnificent demigods I was interviewing? Intimacy was easy to achieve within the space of an hour in a record company conference room, but I ran shrieking any time it reared its head in my personal life. I became a dumping machine, consistently calling off romances after a month or two. My mom, fifties girl that she was, unintentionally fueled this. I often turned to her for advice. She knew I wasn't a virgin — I'd told her about it when I was seventeen, like that lunatic girl in the early Cameron Crowe movie *Say Anything*

— and after that her mantra was simple: *Don't sleep with him!* She was into women playing the pursued, not the pursuer. Her lesser admonishment was, *Don't call him!* Usually I followed her advice, and told her what a good little girl I was. When I didn't, I kept my mouth shut — no sense ruining her image of me. She had only slept with two people: my dad and Eno. She didn't need to know how many of her lifetimes I was living.

I met Dave on my twenty-eighth birthday, and went over the moon for him pretty fast. He had the attributes of a musician, without the fame: he played guitar, held cigarette nubs in a sexy way between strong fingers, was free-spirited, and loved to wander. Raised in New Jersey, he'd spent time in Georgia, Colorado, California, and Nevada, and he spun tales about ne'er-do-wells he'd met along the way with names like the Percodan Kid. He was a carpenter by trade and worked when he felt like it, building little equipment frames for indie-rock recording studios and designing 45s cabinets for the members of Yo La Tengo. We had a lot in common: we both, like, worshipped Kim Gordon and Thurston Moore to the exact same degree. Mom and Eno took an instant dislike to him. He was Jewish, for one thing, and prejudice lurked deep in my family. But they also thought he lacked direction and a work ethic. I remember one conversation where she said icily, "This could be the one." "Well," I said with a nervous laugh, "we passed the two-month mark." I was mystified by their response. He was so much like Eno — a nonconformist! Poor! After we got engaged I brought him to the Ponderosa, with the idea that we would marry there. Dave failed to pay proper fealty to the owners, and my mom later informed me that the space was unavailable. She never came out and told me not to marry him, but she thought I'd get her drift and take her advice. When I ignored it, our relationship fractured. That same exchange from that one particularly long and gruesome phone conversation kept coming back to me: *I would never have married someone my parents didn't approve of,* she had said. I had snorted back: *Yeah, and look where it got you.*

Dave and I married in exile, on a three-week marriage/honeymoon road trip in the West. We bought a house in Jersey City, over Mom's intense protests. This was not long after the first World Trade Center bombing. "How do you know you don't like Jersey City?" I demanded. "You've never seen it." To which she replied, "I've seen it on the news." Her disapproval made me stagger.

She'd always been proud of everything I'd done. When I was twenty-two, she'd flashed a copy of *The Bob* at a dinner party, showing Robyn Hitchcock with a mouthful of dirty British teeth, announcing, "My daughter's a rock critic!" I spent hours on the phone trying to convince her that I had not metamorphosized into a bad, hurtful child. I still wanted to please her. But she didn't buy it, and eventually I gave up trying. I figured she'd come around some day; Dave and I would wear her down with our constant, evident happiness. And we were happy. We held hands at rock shows, shared pints in old-man bars. We had sex every night, at least once. We drove everywhere. We spent hours, days, weeks on the road. We drove the California coast and the Nevada desert and the Blue Ridge Mountains. We even tried to drive the English countryside, although we cursed that country for its backward traffic circles and roads that never seemed to go more than a few miles before grinding to a crawl in some narrow, plinky town. At home, he introduced me to the Jersey roads he'd grown up with, like Route 17, with its Gulf orange and Tool Town red neon. We ate at the Bendix and Tri Boro and Tick Tock diners. And every road trip, even to the airport, started on the Turnpike, with its blinking radio towers and polluted magenta sunsets. I had fulfilled a dream: my life was a Springsteen song. "Beneath the refinery glow, out where the great black rivers flow."

Dave even looked a little bit like Springsteen: solid and rugged, with deep-set eyes and dark curly hair. Once I was hanging out with a colleague when a Springsteen greatest-hits package arrived in the mail. My friend glanced through the booklet and came across a photo of Springsteen from the late seventies, leaning against a muscle car and gazing at the camera with gentle defiance. "No one can say you don't have a type," he said.

Now that I was happily married, it was time to clean up my professional act. I needed to get a little less intense, cast off some of those weird habits I'd fallen into as a freelancer. Conveniently, a job opportunity arose. *Newsweek* was looking for a staff pop critic. The corporate angle wigged me out a bit, but the pay was obscene. And when I stood in the office of one of the top editors for an interview, she greeted me by saying, "I like the way you think." My mind flickered back to my old naysayers, the ones who said I wasn't good for anything but profiles. *This'll show 'em.* For five years I strove to reinvent myself. I tried to think big thoughts instead of small ones; I tried to react objectively instead of personally. I tried to locate the line between *good* music and music I simply liked, figuring that they were not one and the same. And I succeeded. My boss asked me to get the jump on a new Madonna album; I was no fan, but sitting in a vacant office at Warner Bros. Records with *Ray of Light* pumping out of megawatt speakers, I knew it was great, and I was the first national critic to say so in print. A colleague and I were among the first journalists to hear Dylan's *Time Out of Mind*; we immediately recommended him for a cover. I finally felt smart. I was playing on the big field.

But I couldn't give myself a total personality transplant. I still preferred to write about earnest obscure music, instead of crass commercial stuff. The week a new Eric Clapton album came out I pitched a story on the quirky country-rockers Giant Sand and Palace (headline: "Cheatin' Hearts, Flannel Shirts"). I lauded Mike Watt and Jon Spencer. I wheedled a two-page spread on the lounge music revival, centered around an interview with the Mexican cult king Esquivel. For a while I managed to please both my editors and myself, but by the mid-nineties pop music was changing. Indie bands no longer graduated to the mainstream. Women in rock became a hot media topic. The Spice Girls, with their pubescent packaging and girl-power tagline, became one of the biggest acts in the world. Alanis Morissette's album *Jagged Little Pill* sold 13 million copies. Punk badass Courtney Love was readying herself for a Hollywood takeover. Simpery-sweet Lilith Fair became a tour sensation. In *Newsweek*, I griped about all of them. I thought the women-in-rock hooha was too much about gender and image, and not enough about talent. I belittled so many chart chicks that Courtney Love, onstage with her band Hole in New York, accused me of hating women. Her insult was picked up by many of my female colleagues. This was after the Republican takeover in Congress; one writer sent me a letter lambasting my "Newtian" ethics. A music industry conference in Texas convened a panel of critics to discuss my print attack on Courtney Love; the event was nicknamed the Karen Schoemer barbecue.

I was furious. Why, I loved women! Like my friend Cheryl! And Kim Gordon — she was my hero! But underneath, I had to accept the fact that these accusations held a grain of truth. I really was uncomfortable with overt, rage-infused female sexuality. I disliked slut-

tiness as a marketing ploy. I thought these were dangerous messages to flash to girls in their early teens and even preteens; I was reliving my own adolescence, and remembering how vulnerable I felt. Like, what if I had slept with Jeff and gotten pregnant and my whole life had been screwed up? It was implausible but true: rock and roll had delivered me from sex during my adolescence. It had given me a viable alternative, a repository for all that repressed energy. My writing was a veiled attempt to counsel readers to follow my path. Don't get in trouble; funnel your passions into something safe — music. It will give you transcendence; it will set you free. Reality is too painful. Stick to the fantasy.

I didn't know that this was what I was thinking. I was just doing my job, giving opinions. But as time went on, the forum for my psychodramas began to shrink. *Newsweek*'s management changed, and the new regime was less interested in my obsessive compulsions. They wanted me to cleave more amicably to the Top 10. I gave my new boss a passionate pitch for a Tom Waits album, *Mule Variations*, on the punk indie label Epitaph. "Hmm, okay," she said politely. "So . . . what do you think of Andrea Boccelli?" I left her office thinking, Time to get out of here.

★ ★ ★

The day that I came across that Connie Francis box set in my mail pile, I found my escape route. It was one of those weird, unexpected moments when your life changes. I was instantly in love with her. She looked so forlorn, so out of place in the cruel, cynical nineties, a freak of conventionality amid the commodified rebellion of gangsta rap and major-label punk-metal. I was mesmerized by her asexuality; she swept me back into a distant, mythical era of buttoned-down propriety. On some unconscious level I saw her as an antidote to the bitch-goddesses and unredeemed bad girls of my own time. Her smooth presentation belied an anxiety within; she seemed to be screaming, "Help me, I'm going to explode if I have to act perky for one more instant!" So much lurked beneath the plastic façade. She was a stew of conflict, and that conflict was far more interesting to me than the supposedly more authentic rage and transgression of my generation.

By the time I heard "Where the Boys Are" that day, I had already developed an interest in the classic pop of the fifties: Sinatra, Dean Martin, Rosemary Clooney. Now I wanted to combine that interest with an exploration of the pop that came after rock and roll

— the junior crooners and teen idols who adapted the Sinatra style for the new generation. It was a way to get to know my parents. I wanted to know what was in the air when they came of age romantically; the music would be the words I wasn't around to hear them speak. By elevating the music, I could rescue my parents from the shame and disappointment of their divorce. If I could find something worthwhile in the sound track, then I could validate the impulses that led them into marriage.

In my down time at *Newsweek*, I put together a book proposal. I wrote about the late fifties as a forgotten era in pop music, unjustly maligned by critics. I wrote about my parents, and how this exploration was a way of getting to know them. I wrote about my infatuation with Connie, and how she reminded me of my mother. There was just one detail that I left out. I didn't bother to mention the fact that my mom and I were fighting, and that this book was my way of making up to her. I wanted her to forgive me for disobeying her. I still wanted her approval, desperately. The book would be my peace offering, stitching our love for one another back together, making the tattered remnants of my family whole again.

A publisher bought it. I quit *Newsweek*

and spent a year bouncing around the country, collecting interviews with singers. I was writing a book about *them*, and I was writing a book about my parents. Yet I was uneasy. Something didn't add up. The writing went gruelingly slowly. Months went by; years. In all that time, with all that thought and analysis and research, it never occurred to me that I was writing a book about myself.

Nine
FABIAN

Bob [Marcucci] called me to tell me about Fabian. He was excited.

"Dick, you know Elvis and Ricky Nelson are really hot."

I agreed.

"Well, neither of them are doing anything. They're not getting out there where the kids can see them, they won't let the kids touch them. I figured this out and said to myself, I've got to find someone and take him and let him be touched by everybody. I've got this kid named Fabian. He looks like Ricky Nelson. I want to make him into a giant star, then put him out on the road where the kids can get close to him."

"I'm doing a hop on Friday night, why don't you bring him around," I told Bob.

That Friday Bob showed up with Fabian. He had Fabian dressed in a blue sweater, tight-fitting pants, and white bucks. Fabian gave me a smile as I introduced him, pushed back a few strands of his pompadour, and crooned into the mike, lip-syncing to an acetate Bob had brought of his first record, "I'm a Man."

The little girls at the hop went wild. They started screaming and yelling for this guy who didn't do a thing but stand there. I've never seen anything like it.

—*Dick Clark with Richard Robinson,*
Rock, Roll & Remember

I was desperate to hear my mother's recollections of fifties music. She was there when it all happened. She was sixteen in 1957: the precise target audience. Before I began doing interviews, I had called her and timidly asked who her favorite singers were. She overcame her simmering resentment of me enough to speak a few sentences. She said she loved Elvis, of course, and that her parents so strongly disapproved of him that she had to listen to his records in secret up in her room. She said she loved Tommy Sands — "He was so sweet" — and that her parents found him acceptable enough to allow her to see his concert in New York City. Then she mentioned one other singer. "I liked the cute one, what was his name," she said. "The Italian one." I knew exactly who she meant. There were cute singers and there were Italian singers, but those two adjectives together described only one person. Mom dug Fabian. I tried to get her to elaborate, but she told me she had laundry going and hung up. It was the worst interview I did for this book.

Mom's interest in Fabian fascinated and horrified me, because I had such a negative impression of him. Fabian was the world's first synthetic rock star. In 1958, a Philadelphia record executive named Bob Marcucci plucked him off a doorstep because he had that dreamy Elvis–Ricky Nelson look: supple cheeks, pouty lips, ladykiller-blue eyes. Fabiano Forte, just fifteen, couldn't sing, but Marcucci didn't care. He sent his idol-to-be to a succession of voice teachers, found him a racy Doc Pomus–Mort Shuman tune called "I'm a Man," swirled his hair up into a pompadour, and slapped on some tight pants. A few bookings on *American Bandstand* later, and Fabian was the country's newest object of shriek worship. He placed eight songs in the Top 40 between 1959 and 1960, scored a couple of best-selling albums, and landed supporting roles in real movies with real actors (*North to Alaska* with John Wayne, *Mr. Hobbs Takes a Vacation* and *Dear Brigitte* with Jimmy Stewart). But along the way, he became a joke. *Time* magazine dubbed him "Tuneless Tiger." The hormone surge wore off, and Fabian's career ended before his teens. Still, his infamy lives on. Today his name is a sort of code word for music-business phoniness. Whenever cute singers get criticized for too much fluff and not enough singing talent — for example Paula Abdul and the Spice Girls, who sang poorly, or Milli Vanilli, who didn't sing at all — people love to remember that Fabian was there first.

So what did my mom see in this charlatan? She had listed Elvis, Tommy Sands, and Fabian as if they were all somehow equal in her estimation. The degree of her love may have varied — she adored Elvis the most — but the manner in which she loved them was essentially the same. They were all cute boy singers who decorated her youth, fleeting crushes that she had left behind when she moved on to adult pursuits (college, marriage, family). As a critic, I would never equate Elvis with Fabian. In fact, I see them as polar opposites. Elvis was an originator, an avatar, a pioneering hero who broke down racial barriers and loosened restrictive morals by bringing the influence of black music to the masses. He's worthy of weighty biographies, academic seminars, endless gossip. Fabian was just some hapless hunk with a couple of forgettable hits. Who would study *him?* He was a concoction, whereas Elvis was a true artist.

The battle between authenticity and inauthenticity is central to rock criticism, and I've internalized it ever since I started reading *Rolling Stone* and *Musician* as a teenager. Authenticity is one of the fundamental standards that rock critics use to judge records. Does the music express an honest inner truth? Then it's good. Is it escapist fantasy, a manufactured lie designed to take people out of themselves? Then it's disposable crap. Whether you like it or not is almost beside the point. Throwing Elvis into the same subset as Fabian is practically sacrilege. It's like saying there's no qualitative difference between Nirvana and a commercial knockoff band like Bush. And if there is no qualitative difference between Nirvana and Bush, why have I spent my entire career saying that there is?

I tried to rationalize my mother's responses. Maybe she didn't know Fabian was manufactured. But that line of reasoning didn't take me far. She wasn't stupid. It's easy to dismiss the tastes of the general public, but harder to criticize the likes and dislikes of an individual. Maybe she knew he was manufactured and *didn't care*. And maybe most kids didn't care. They didn't care, in the same way that I'd learned not to care about whether Tommy Sands's music was "bad" or "good." The pleasure of the music was what mattered, not the impulses and machinations behind it. A performer was greater than the sum of his parts; what he gave his audience transcended the elements that went into making him. The right singer could turn a trifling song into a momentary masterpiece.

And sometimes, the very element of manufacturedness becomes an unconscious draw. I liked so-called authentic music because it allowed me to feel connected to other people who shared the same feelings and experiences as I did. Listening to Nirvana circa 1992 was exhilarating because it helped me believe that others felt just as alienated as I did. But what if that connection was itself an illusion? Is connecting with a song a substitute for connecting directly with another person? Maybe inauthentic music — pop ephemera — affirms our disconnect from the reality of our lives. In the absence of real connection, it comforts us; it acknowledges the presence of loneliness, and embraces us. The fakeness of the music becomes perversely reassuring, a pillow of safety. We are fakers, too. What we present to the world is, by necessity, fake — sometimes by design, and sometimes simply because we can't possibly communicate all that goes on in our hearts and minds. We are alone, as much as we pretend not to be. The singer who relays that message, whether by accident or intention, becomes our ally.

This question was tremendously important to me. I practically felt as though my life hinged upon it. I couldn't figure it out alone. Since my mom wouldn't help me, I decided to ask Fabian.

A few days after the Tommy Sands interview, while I was still in L.A., I called up Fabian's manager, a sharp, congenial fellow named Oscar Arslanian. I gave him my most passionate sales pitch. I said that the *Rolling Stone* version of rock history was unfairly biased against singers who appealed primarily to women, and that Fabian's contributions deserved serious reconsideration by a critic with a better understanding of his relationship to his audience. I sensed Oscar practically misting up right there on the telephone. He cleared his throat and said gruffly, "I think Fabian should do this." He offered to set up a meeting at the end of the week, as soon as Fabian returned from Montreal, where he was performing the Teen Angel role in a production of *Grease!*

The night before the interview, I unpacked all my Fabian paraphernalia from my travel bag. I had LPs, reissue CDs, newspaper clippings, printouts from Web sites. I spread it all out on the floor, and soaked it in. Hmmm. It was as if I'd suddenly been transported to the layout room at *Teen Beat*. Here was Fabian on the cover of his debut album, *Hold That Tiger!*, lying down on one hip with his shirt collar open, his hand stroking the back of a surprised-looking stuffed cat. Here was his 1959 album *The Fabulous Fabian* (title written in tiki letters), the gatefold sleeve open to reveal black-and-white pictures that the captions described as the "tiger" in his "lair"; two of the seven photos captured him shirtless. And here was a 1961 album called *The Fabian Façade: Young and Wonderful*, with a velveteen cover framing a sultry headshot of the handsome lad. The package originally came with a detachable portrait suitable for wall hanging. My copy was missing that piece, but I paid fifty bucks for it anyway. Oh, and here was something interesting: images from his 1973 *Playgirl* centerfold, which I'd pulled off the Internet. In the most revealing shot, he straddles a massive motorcycle, stomach muscles rippling, eyes squinting into the sun, his pee-pee tapering discreetly out of view behind a tanned thigh. Oooh, I felt dirty.

With all this beefcake ogling me, I briefly wondered if I should pack my bags, cancel the book contract, retreat to the woods near

Big Sur, and promise never again to look for depth and substance in fifties teen idols. But something stopped me. Basically, I got my own little hormone surge. Fabian *was* cute, and there didn't seem to be anything wrong with appreciating his fine physical attributes. Yet the pictures struck an emotional chord, too. Maybe it was the little Catholic cross laid upon that bare, hairy chest in the *Playgirl* photos, but I began to see him as a sort of martyr. Fabian gave himself up to women. The melancholy cast to his eyes, the hesitancy in his smile, made me think that his devotion came at a personal cost, yet he did it anyway. I am so used to seeing women objectify themselves that I rarely think twice about it, but a man who does it evokes powerful feelings in me. It reminded me of Leonardo DiCaprio in the film *Titanic*, sacrificing his life to make the world a better place for his gal. It reminded me of Richard Gere in *American Gigolo* and *Breathless* and a bunch of his other films. It reminded me of Elvis onstage in Las Vegas during the seventies, dispensing kisses to every female in the audience as he sang "Love Me Tender." Women don't just get off on male sacrifice — we empathize and identify with it, because we sacrifice ourselves so much more readily. I didn't feel any disdain for Fabian. I felt gratitude.

Then I put on *The Best of Fabian,* a compilation of his chart hits released by Varèse Sarabande in 1995. The critic in me, who had been sort of wandering around the back yard, snapped to attention. Fabian totally rocked. The music may have lacked the hot-wire snap of Elvis's biggest hits, but it was less pop than anything else I'd covered for the book; the drums pounded and roiled, the guitars skittered and squealed. Fabian's voice was no virtuosic instrument, but it had a visceral urgency that matched the vibrant, racy thump of the music. He sang like a bulldozer, plowing through melodies without much concern for pitch, getting by on feel rather than nuance. I wouldn't entrust him with Gershwin, but so what? I wouldn't want to hear Thurston Moore attempt "Summertime" either, and no one complains when *he* sings. In fact, Fabian's energy was decidedly punk. If he had come along twenty years later, he might have flourished in the Southern California hard-core scene, bleating out Social Distortion–style antagonisms against a ferocious three-chord beat. Maybe if he had seen Johnny Rotten and Patti Smith and Courtney Love coming, he wouldn't have believed his own antihype. Fabian could sing. He just didn't know it.

He was ahead of his time in another respect: his songs' obsession with sex. While other teen idols warbled about the joys of soggy palms pressed together and prayed that someday they'd be able to do it legal-style, Fabian was concerned about the moment at hand. He wanted gratification, *now*, even if he couldn't exactly spell it out in terms acceptable to *The Ed Sullivan Show*. "When I see her home and we kiss good night / Well, turn me loose, turn me loose, turn me loose," he sang in Doc Pomus and Mort Shuman's "Turn Me Loose." He frequently worried that his tender young age would lead females to think he was substandard in the libido department. "Why do you treat me like an overgrown child when you know my kisses drive you wild?" he panted in "I'm a Man." Sometimes animal metaphors were helpful. He was a "Tiger," he was a "Hound Dog Man." Sometimes the complexities of female pursuit required the wiles of a whole wild kingdom menagerie. "I'm buzzin' in circles like a bumblebee / You got me swingin' in the breeze like a monkey in a tree," he sang in "Mighty Cold" (another Pomus-Shuman tune).

Quality control was, admittedly, not always stringent. "And when you kiss me, baby, it's the most / You start me burnin' like a piece of toast," went a couplet in "Got the Feeling." (Songwriters Bob and Dick Sherman went on to better things in the sixties: they wrote the musicals *Mary Poppins* and *Chitty Chitty Bang Bang*, and the Disney perennial "It's a Small, Small World.") And, like most teen idols, Fabian found himself confronting the pop-jazz songbook when it came time to fill out an album. His attempt at Fats Waller's "Ain't Misbehavin'," from *The Fabulous Fabian*, didn't bother me so much — it's a stretch, but you can almost hear the tune as a sixteen-year-old, white, Philly ne'er-do-well's lament. But a fully orchestrated swing version of "All of Me," from *Young and Wonderful*, hit me in my Sinatra spot, and it hurt. The band, arranged by Larry Gordon, aped Nelson Riddle, while poor Fabian stuttered through two quick verses as if his eyes were shut and a train was barreling down the tracks straight at him. It was like a juvenile drag-queen revue, minus the twisted sexuality and camp. It was like William Shatner singing "It Ain't Me, Babe," only not funny.

As painful as these clunkers were, they couldn't really dampen my enthusiasm for the guy. It was weird, but I really was starting to relate to music differently. Tallying Fabian's hits and misses, weighing derivations versus originality, assigning letter grades for musicianship, lyrical content, and vocal prowess seemed boring and beside the point. As I drifted off to sleep that night, I thought about the look of humble supplication in his eyes, and the earnest desire to please that had infused every note. The critic was out to pasture. What remained was a girl with a happy, clandestine thrill.

"YOU JERK!"

Fabian snapped his head around, as if someone had called his name.

An attractive, forty-ish woman with tan, spindly legs was scooting around the sidewalk, trying to collect three bouncy accessory dogs who were off the leash and ignoring her. She saw Fabian looking at her, straightened up, and smoothed her hair. "Hey, how are you!" she said. "Good to see you."

Fabian seemed to know her. "How you doin'," he said warmly. "I thought you were calling me a jerk."

"No, he's a jerk," she said, pointing to the dog furthest away. She tried to affect a commanding voice: "Come here!"

The dog ran to Fabian. "This is Sammy," she said, "a toy poodle I got ripped off for."

Fabian rumpled and petted him. "Yeah, my girl's got one of those," he said. "What a great dog."

"That's Lucy," she said, gesturing at another fluffball. "And that one's Casey."

"We're doing an interview here," Oscar said sternly.

"Imsorrygoodbye," she said, and corralled her dogs elsewhere.

"Nice seeing you!" Fabian called. Then he leaned toward Oscar. "Who is that?"

Oscar identified her as So-and-so's wife. "Too bad," Fabian said, watching her retreat.

I withered as all this went on. We were sitting in the outdoor plaza of Crossroads of the World, a funky mini-mall on Sunset Boulevard. Designed in the 1930s, it had wooden storefronts in various global-themed designs: Mexican haciendas, French cottages. Most were out of use, with battened-down windows and sunworn paint. The place looked like a movie set that someone had forgotten to dismantle and take away. Locals wandered desultorily about; a thespian-aired middle-aged man leafed lazily through a newspaper. In the center of the plaza loomed a giant replica of an ocean liner. Oscar's management office was on the second floor. When I had called ahead to get instructions, he explained this about six times: "It's in a ship. The office is *in* a ship. You can't miss it." I had knocked on a portside door, and an assistant led me upstairs, where Oscar's cluttered desk was wedged into the bow. I fought the urge to call him "Cap'n."

Now we were downstairs at a picnic table, and the interview was bombing. Oscar had decided to sit in, and his presence threw me off. Third parties make me self-conscious; they ruin my illusion of intimacy. And Fabian seemed about as enthusiastic as an adolescent ordered into the principal's office. He fidgeted, fiddled with his hands, blew out his cheeks. He wore an untucked blue polo shirt and a baseball cap pulled so low over his eyes that I could hardly see his face in the shadows. He and Oscar were bringing out the bad boy in one another, chatting about pending deals as if I weren't there. The casual attitude made all my deep thoughts about women and critics and martyrdom seem ludicrous and out of place. Yet I had no other questions prepared. So I stumbled around the conversation, lobbing out dopey small-talk.

ME: How did your thing go?

FABIAN [CONFUSED]: Which thing?

ME: You did *Grease*!

FABIAN: Oh, up in Montreal. Teen Angel

— right. An ex-teen idol playing Teen Angel. It was funny. You mean the response? The response was great. [Long silence]

ME: What have you got there?

FABIAN: It's a pacifier. [He holds up a plastic cigarette, dented and chewed like a pen tip] You've got to break the oral habit. There's menthol in there. [He sticks it in his mouth, gnaws]

OSCAR: He's six weeks now.

FABIAN: I'm on the patch, too.

OSCAR: How is it?

FABIAN: Oh, I still want to smoke.

ME [glancing at watch, realizing it's after two]: You need a sandwich or anything?

FABIAN: Me? No, I'm good. I grabbed something on the way here. [Another silence] Well, what can I do for you?

I mumbled a couple of half-sentences about rock critics glossing over teen idols. Oscar, who was theoretically there to protect his client from the cruel and sarcastic attacks of hardball journalists, sensed that the ship was going down. He switched allegiances and came to my rescue. "Karen believes that people like yourself didn't get the credit you could have gotten for your contribution to the music business."

Fabian perked up. "Oh. That's possible."

"Rock history is written by men, even though girls were such an important part of the audience," I said, grabbing the ball from Oscar and trotting a few steps. "So the things girls were into get shortchanged."

"They were into everything, girls," Fabian said. "They were into all aspects of rock and roll, not just teen idols."

Good point. "Your songs were kind of aggressive," I said. "Were you aware of that at the time?"

"No, I wasn't aware of it," he said. "It just felt good. I remember when Doc Pomus sang 'Turn Me Loose' for me. I said, 'I've got to do that.' The lyrics were a little too mature, so they changed some of the lyrics. I don't remember what had to be changed, but it was dumb, if you think about it today. It wasn't risqué or anything, just a little more mature."

"When you heard a song, did you have a feel for how you wanted to sing it?" I asked.

"Oh, sure," he said. "Absolutely. I rehearsed with a guy named Pete DeAngelis, who was part owner of the company. He would put the band together, because I was fifteen. Al Caiola, Panama Jackson, guys like that were in the band. King Curtis — a famous sax player. These were great studio players. I would rehearse it, and then listen to them play. Then we rehearsed together. In those days you would do it live, meaning you wouldn't stop and start. You did it with the band. Basically it was a live performance. Not like today where you can stop and cut. So it was exciting."

"You did some standards," I said.

"I never should have done those," he said quickly. "That was a management decision that I totally regret. I didn't know what I was doing. Ugh. It was torture. I would have been happy with all the rock and roll they ever gave me. I was comfortable with that, not the other stuff."

"People had a real attitude about you being manufactured," I ventured.

He groaned. "Believe me, I lived through it," he said. He took off his hat and ran his hand through his hair, and I could see his face for the first time. He looked good. His cheeks still had that fullness. Crinkle lines suggested a multitude of smiles. His eyes were so blue and bright, they could have been a paint swatch: Fabian blue. Set designers would splash it on every sky. "Then again, everybody was manufactured to a certain point," he continued. "Paul Anka's manager was with the Ringling Brothers. Here's a guy who was running a circus! Presley's guy sold Hadacol — he sold this snake oil medicine. So give me a break. It's just that I came from nowhere, didn't have a background in singing. So I got murdered."

"Was there a down period —"

"There were many down periods," he interrupted. "My career was over when I was twenty-one. Then I brought it back up again, and it was over again. I've been through it so many times, it's like a yo-yo."

"Was that hard on your self-esteem?"

"The down moments? God, yeah."

Oscar was gone. He'd tactfully slipped away. "What did you think when girls started screaming?" I asked.

"I thought it was *nuts*," he said. "I couldn't imagine what was going on. I learned quickly that that was the barometer of your success. They told me, 'You're successful when those girls scream at you.' I wanted to be a success, so I felt good about that. But I did feel awkward. It's not a natural thing."

I found myself speaking up for all those girls. "It seems to me that if they were screaming, they must have had some anxiety that they were releasing."

But they didn't need me to defend them. "What guys like me represented was a fantasy boyfriend," he said. "That's how they would deal with, maybe, a boyfriend they did not have, or one they thought they wanted. I thought it was — I don't want to use the word *healthy,* because I'm not really sure. But it was an outlet, and maybe in a sense it was a healthy outlet."

"Did you realize they were projecting something onto you?" I said.

"Yeah," he answered. "I went out of my way to talk to them. They would express that they're not doing much in their lives, and talk about how their mothers treated them, or a boyfriend treated them. A lot of them didn't like the way they were being treated. They would express all this to a guy like me, because that's the way they envisioned their life — wanting to be with someone like that. But they were probably the best conversations I had, because that was my only chance to relate to kids my own age. Never got a chance to do it with many guys, because I don't think the guys wanted to talk to me as much. But those girls — I truly, in my own way, loved them. They were my pseudo-friends, my pseudo-normalcy. They would bring me back to reality. Like when the manager would say, 'That's enough time, they've got to leave the room,' I would say, 'Stay and talk a while.' Now, don't get me wrong — some of them I wanted to date. But not all. That was a very good side of those days."

I was getting all mushy and shy. "I think that girl stuff is very important," I muttered. "I had crushes on singers."

"Of course you did," he said tenderly.

"So I know how much that meant. You gave them a great gift."

Fabian took a deep breath. "I loved it," he said in a faraway voice. "The girl in the red dress. I don't remember her name, but it was in Corpus Christi. We sat and talked, after the show, for maybe four hours. In front of my room — not in my room. And I'll never forget it. It was a wonderful experience. We talked about — whatever. Families, brothers, school — you know. And I fell in love with her. I did. She probably doesn't even know that." He sighed. "I did kiss her good night, though. Ha!" He slapped the table with a wolfish chuckle.

I looked at him in wonder. My own twisted dream was coming true. I was living things vicariously that I could never live for real. I'd kissed him without ever touching him.

Later, back at home, I happened to be sitting around one day thinking about my mushy, quasi-sexy moment with Fabian. I was turning the incident over in my mind, trying to understand it, curious about why it occurred. It was only the latest in my long history of falling in love during interviews. I thought back on my experiences as a journalist. Without coming up with an official tally, I'd have to say that during those hours facing people across hotel room coffee tables, driving next to them in cars on their way to some appointment, joining them in skeevy club dressing rooms after shows, sitting down with them in expensive restaurants as waiters flitted discreetly, catching a few minutes with them in movie trailers or — that prize of all prizes — crossing the threshhold into their very own homes, I fell in love more often than not.

There were a few extreme cases. I interviewed Johnny Depp over three consecutive days for *Newsweek*. We were getting along so well that on the third day he invited me to his *Edward Scissorhands*-like mansion in the Hollywood Hills, on the condition that I not describe it in the magazine. When we said good-bye he gave me a T-shirt from the set of his movie, *The Brave*, and kissed me on the cheek; the emotional intensity was so great that I had to close my eyes and pretend it wasn't happening. I remembered winging along L.A. roads on the back of Dwight Yoakam's Harley-Davidson. At a stop sign he glanced over his shoulder and told me to move my arms lower on his hips. "That's where my center of gravity is," he said, and I had to bite my lip to keep from exploding. I trailed Jon Bon Jovi from Sweden to Italy as he promoted his hit song "Blaze of Glory." All day he greeted fans and signed autographs, in record stores, in airports, in fancy restaurants. At one o'clock in the morning we went to the Spanish Steps in Rome for some one-on-one time, but some kids with guitars spotted him and he spent several minutes talking with them. When they finally left, I lost it. I was exhausted myself, and I couldn't stand the degree to which he gave himself up. I started crying — the umpteenth female who had dissolved on him that day. "What are you crying for?" he said, dismayed, hugging me, trying to cheer me up.

It wasn't just men. I fell in love with women, too. I loved Patti Smith and Sheryl Crow and Amy Ray from Indigo Girls. Once I went to Texas on an assignment for the *New York Times*. I was dating a guy down there who was a manager, and he introduced me to a female poet named Jo Carol Pierce. Oh, man, I *whomped*. Later, my boyfriend and I were mingling at a party and someone asked me what I would remember from my trip. "I fell in love in Texas," I trumpeted, and my date brightened. I looked at him sideways. "With Jo Carol Pierce," I amended, and his face fell. But there was something special about the boys. A lot of times the infatuation was in my own mind, but every now and then I realized it went both ways. I interviewed Billy Bob Thornton when he was still sort of innocent and unknown, on the eve of his breakthrough movie, *Sling Blade*. He told me there were three kinds of females: women, girls, and gals. I was a gal. "I'm half in love with you already," he said, throwing back another gin and tonic. But nothing ever came of these encounters. The interview would end, and I'd go away, and sometimes there would be a phone call, but that would be it. I'd harbor my little crushes, trying to exorcise them in the words of the articles I wrote; sometimes that wasn't enough, and I'd pine for days, weeks. The best cure was doing another interview. I'd fall in love again, and the cycle would play itself out in endless repetition.

It was only after meeting Fabian that I began to put it all together. Falling in love with a pop song, falling in love with a musician or actor in an interview: they were the same thing. Both provided the thrill of suspended romance, the ecstasy of connecting nonphysically with another person. This kind of love transports you, takes you away from yourself, allows you to escape the confines of the everyday; it's the soul of entertainment. It's a joyous, wonderful thing, but it has its down side, because it's not real. It's fake. It's nothing like the kind of love you have with another person. That love is painful and messy and difficult to sustain. It can involve fighting and misunderstanding and suffering. But fake love, pop-song love, teen-idol love, is perfect and forever. It's a first blush that never develops into anything more. It's an eternal falling that never hits the ground. It's addictive and obsessive, because it has to be constantly replenished. Nothing in the world is quite like that spike of joy, that illusion of intimacy, because it can't be spoiled or ruined by the intrusion of reality. Real love is overripe and malodorous by comparison. But fake love, for all its grandeur, is perversely unfulfilling. You have to make it happen over and over again, like a drug that needs to be constantly reinjected to supply the same short-lived high. You need a new song on the radio, a new interviewee across the table a month or two later, so you can feel that feeling all over again.

At first, as I thought about all this, I was sort of horrified at myself for indulging in such an excessive, hedonistic pastime. For all my pretenses of being a critic, I had really, in an unconscious way throughout my career, played out this fantasy week after week, job after job, article after article. But then I decided to go a bit easier on myself. In a way, I was proud of my entrepreneurial ingenuity. As a kid, I'd fallen in love with pop music; then I'd found a way to turn that experience into a career, and a lucrative one at that. Besides, that element of fake love, and the fact that it motivated me, didn't take away from my abilities to think about music in an objective way, too. Maybe my awareness of the fake-love element could even inform my thinking in a useful way.

I'd come into the Fabian interview with an image of him as a sort of rock-and-roll villain: the first manufactured star, a purveyor of crap flogged into success by savvy marketers. But where did I get this idea? From critics. But which critics? What specifically did they say? I flipped through my Guralnick, Tosches, and Palmer books, but none of them mentioned him. *The Virgin Encyclopedia of Fifties Music*, edited by Colin Larkin, began its entry this way: "Fabian, almost despite himself, was among the more endurable products of the late 50s when the North American charts were infested with a turnover of vapid boys-next-door — all hair spray, doe eyes and coy half-smiles — groomed for fleeting stardom." Donald Clarke, in *The Rise and Fall of Popular Music*, referred to Fabian and his Chancellor Records labelmate, Frankie Avalon, as "two oafs." In *Rock of Ages*, author Ed Ward linked the popularity of Fabian and other teen idols to a cyclical malaise in rock and roll. They had stepped into the void created when Elvis joined the army, Little Richard left rock and roll for the church, Jerry Lee Lewis married his thirteen-year-old cousin, and Buddy Holly died in a plane crash. "Music was coming down with a case of the creeping blands," he wrote. "With the rise of the likes of Frankie Avalon and Fabian, the idea of finding a pretty face and seeing if it could sing had taken hold. Week after week, the fan and trade press was filled with smiling young men with perfect teeth, conservatively greased hair, and instantly forgettable names, served forth in hopes that the girls would swoon."

Gee. Pretty convincing. No wonder I'd developed a career-long insecurity of being just a hormone-driven maniac crashing a party of towering, unassailable male minds. Apparently my worries had a good grounding in reality. Male critics — some of them, at least — viewed us girls as a stupidity club, wreaking mediocrity on the charts and swaying popular tastes with our sinister and unreliable crushes. But those worries were behind me now, and when I read those passages I just chuckled. Then my eye fell on another book: *The Billboard Pop Charts 1955–1959*. On a whim, I decided to see what this malaise looked like in print. So I found the pop singles chart for the week of February 9, 1959, which happened to be the week that Fabian's first hit, "I'm a Man," peaked at Number 31. I guess I expected to see ninety-nine other duds listed there. What I found instead amazed me. The Number 1 single for the week of February 9, 1959, was "Stagger Lee," by Lloyd Price. Number 2 was "Sixteen Candles" by the Crests. "Donna" by Ritchie Valens was Number 3, and "Smoke Gets in Your Eyes" by the Platters was Number 4. Classics, every one — the kind of songs you heard throughout the film *American Graffiti*, the kind of songs that still get played on oldies radio today. "Lonely Teardrops" by Jackie Wilson sat at Number 7. "I Cried a Tear" by LaVern Baker held Number 12. Scattered throughout the Top 40 were "Peter Gunn Theme" by Ray Anthony, "Charlie Brown" by the Coasters, and "Don't Take Your Guns to Town" by Johnny Cash. "Lonesome Town" by Ricky Nelson and "C'Mon Everybody" by Eddie Cochran were winding down in the upper reaches after lengthy, successful runs. "Sea Cruise" by Frankie Ford made its debut that week at Number 89.

What the hell kind of a lull was that? I scanned the rest of the chart, taking in the awesome breadth of music available. There was rock and roll, R&B, blues, and doo-wop. There were novelties: "The Children's Marching Song" by Mitch Miller, "The Chipmunk Song" by David Seville and the Chipmunks. There were topical songs: "Little Space Girl" by Jesse Lee Turner, "Jupiter-C" by Pat and the Satellites. There were folk songs ("Tom Dooley" by the Kingston Trio), country songs ("The Story of My Love" by Conway Twitty), and girl group anthems ("To Know Him Is to Love Him" by the Teddy Bears). And there was lots of pop, sung by two competing but somehow sympathetic generations. "My Happiness" by Connie Francis, "The Diary" by Neil Sedaka, "With the Wind and the Rain in Your Hair" by Pat Boone, and "Tall Paul" by Annette Funicello represented the young guard. The old-timers held steady too: "Trust in Me" by Patti Page, "There Must Be a Way" by Joni James, "My Man" by Peggy Lee, and "Give Me Your Love" by Nat "King" Cole. And I was just reading words on a page; imagine what it was like hearing all these songs coming out of the same radio. Then I thought about "I'm a Man," and it made perfect sense within the context. Fabian had his place. The threads of these different influences converged in him, and then continued in other directions, all part of the same fabric.

There was no lull. It was a myth, one that critics perpetrated so successfully, for so long, that no one even questioned it anymore. How did they get away with it? It dawned on me that rock history is different from other histories — say, the history of World War II — in that it's written by critics, not historians. A few of the great writers, like Palmer and Guralnick, functioned as both, but for the most part the people telling the story were basing their definitions of greatness on their own opinions, not fact or collective consensus. So we've wound up with a narrative of rock history that places enormous emphasis on bands like the Velvet Underground, who never had a single Top 40 hit, and denigrates Pat Boone, who had dozens. Of course I liked the Velvet Underground. They were amazing. They were dark and inventive and they challenged prevailing opinions on how rock songs could be constructed and they influenced generations of other bands, like R.E.M. and Sonic Youth. But a history of rock that systematically highlights the edgy and obscure to the neglect of what was popular and important to large swatches of people is lopsided at best. Objective! The story of rock was anything but. It was subjective to the core. The irony of it slayed me. For all these years I'd thought these guys were so much brainier than me. But most of them were just working out their own fantasies, whatever those were. They were creating a universe in which the imprecise, unpredictable, and impenetrable crushes of girls could be obliterated and wiped from the record. They were leaving out the music that they deemed "bad," because to them those songs seemed shallow and fleeting and romantic. But those songs were *our* history, the secretly significant history, the overlooked history of a million screaming girls.

I knew of not a single history of rock that gave the girls in the audience any credibility whatsoever. Our tastes always needed to be expurged or overcome. Yet we were driving the mystery train. More than the guys, we were deciding who'd make it to the top, who'd stay there. From Sinatra to Elvis to the Beatles to the Backstreet Boys, we were the voting bloc that swayed every election of heroes. Without us, the music never would have existed. History never would have come to pass.

★ ★ ★

Fabiano Forte was born February 6, 1943, the oldest of three boys. His father, Domenic, was a cop; his mother, Josephine, a homemaker. The family's roots were in Italy. "Naples and Abruzzi," he said. "My grandfather, Fabiano, was a shoemaker. He was the only guy in the family with blue eyes. So I got named Fabian."

His early life, as he recalls it now, was blissfully normal. "I loved being a student, enjoyed my summers in Philadelphia," he said. "The stoops, the concrete — very neighborhoody. Going to the fireplug, dating, eating pizza with the guys, playing cards with the guys, playing football and soccer. I was having a real good adolescence. We didn't have anything, but I was starting to blossom into a human being. One straight direction. It really felt good. Until I met this guy. Then my world was turned around, and it took me many years to get that all back."

This guy was Robert Marcucci, the president of a local independent label, Chancellor Records. In 1958 Chancellor was having its first big success with Frankie Avalon, a former jazz trumpet prodigy who had performed on radio and TV with Paul Whiteman and Ray Anthony before turning, at Marcucci's behest, to teen pop. Frankie's breakthrough, "Dede Dinah," a gimmicky, R&B-inspired blowout with a nasally vocal and a two-ton backbeat, cracked the Top 10 in February 1958. After that he mellowed into a mild-mannered crooner whose trademark was a superhuman level of patience in sexual matters. He was constantly reassuring girls that they didn't have to give it away. "I'll wait for you," he promised in one song. "Bobby Sox to Stockings" reduced the mind-bending hormonal ravages of female adolescence to an innocent change of legwear. "Venus" was a stunningly unerotic depiction of the goddess of love — Doris Day riding a halfshell. The song stuck at Number 1 for five weeks; it's still listed as one of the top hits of the rock era.

Marcucci's discovery of Fabian is legendary. One night, driving home through the neighborhood, Marcucci saw an ambulance in front of a neighbor's house and pulled over to see what had happened. Dominic Forte had suffered a heart attack, and Fabian stood glumly on the stoop. Noting his resemblance to Elvis and Ricky Nelson, Marcucci asked if he could sing, and Fabian said no. Marcucci left, but couldn't forget him. He came back at the family again and again until Fabian agreed to give it a try. "My dad was sick, he couldn't work anymore," Fabian said. "We were broke. I was working for six dollars a week plus change as a delivery boy. I said, 'Can I make any money?' And that's how I got into the business."

Marcucci controlled virtually every aspect of his charge's career: he served as manager, label executive, marketing expert, clothing consultant, groomer, and hair stylist. He also cowrote some songs and dictated the choice of material, although recording sessions were produced by his partner, Pete DeAngelis. For a while, Fabian went along with whatever he was told. When I asked if he resented that his looks were so much of the focus, he shrugged and said, "I guess at times I did. I don't think it was a big deal, though. I mean, I was proud of my genes." Did he like posing with a stuffed tiger? "I thought it was cute. Those days were so fast and furious. We were doing stuff like that all the time." Marcucci's methods had a swift payoff. Fabian's first two singles sank, but with the help of *American Bandstand* "I'm a Man" took off. Within a week of its chart peak, Marcucci had negotiated a deal with Twentieth Century-Fox, earning Fabian $35,000 to star in his film debut, *Hound Dog Man*. (The director would be Don Siegel, of future *Dirty Harry* fame.) Fabian's earnings that year would top $150,000. In July, he touched down in Los Angeles to begin film production, and fans swarmed him at the airport. "I got glass in my eye," he said. "They broke a window trying to get in at me. That stuff happened maybe four, five, six times. I got scratched, they cut off my hair with scissors. I think sometimes the promoters liked that. They wouldn't give you enough security, so it would make the papers."

But the rush evaporated quickly. Fabian began to get hip to his "Tuneless Tiger" image in the mainstream press. It's bad enough to be a puppet; it's even worse to have everyone know it, from booking agents to Mom-and-Pop readers of *Time* magazine. He now believes that his lack of singing talent wouldn't have been such an issue if Marcucci hadn't relentlessly milked it as a publicity gimmick. "He was an egomaniac," Fabian said. "He had to let everybody know he was responsible for my success. And it hurt me."

He took solace in acting. "Loved the acting," he said. "*Loved* it! And fell right into it, kind of natural." He studied on the Fox lot with renowned acting coach Sanford Meisner, and in 1960 signed a seven-year nonexclusive contract with the studio. By then, his music career was sputtering, and his relationship with Bob became impossibly strained. Within another year, he bought out his Chancellor contracts and quit singing to concentrate on movies. He landed some good roles: in 1961, the year of his high school graduation, he played a jive-talking, scripture-spouting juvenile psychopath on an episode of the ABC-TV series *Bus Stop*, directed by Robert Altman. Fabian's character escaped without punishment, and the display of nihilism caused sponsors to withdraw in protest. The ratings jumped, but reviews were stinko. *Newsweek* referred to the *Bus Stop* episode as "Fabian's cynical, perverted and flacked-up opus." (Months after my interview, dying of curiosity, I tracked down a grainy VHS dub of this opus and watched it myself. "Good" might be too strong a word, but it did reaffirm my notion of Fabian as a primordial punk-rocker: he giddily played up his character's loathesomeness, doling out greasy charm as he gunned down an elderly shopkeeper and stabbed the defense attorney who'd just gotten him off. It was as if he were revelling in the real-life ill will he caused people — hurling it back at them, even. You don't like me? No problem. Just stand still while I kill you.)

Bus Stop notwithstanding, Fabian's image wasn't easy to transcend, and after a while he gave up trying. He fell into the teen exploitation racket with films like *Ride the Wild Surf* in 1964 and *Thunder Alley* in 1967. A particular low point was *Dr. Goldfoot and the Girl Bombs*, a 1966 sci-fi bimbo exercise with Vincent Price. "That was a favor," Fabian said. "Frankie Avalon's wife was pregnant and he couldn't go, so he begged me to make this piece of shit. Vincent Price was great, though. We used to get drunk every day at lunch." I remarked that it must have been a low-budget production. "Low budget?" he yelled. "We were supposed to do a cloudy sky one day, right? The director comes in with a clear plate glass with cotton balls all over it. And he shot me and the cotton balls! Oh, you had to live through it. I think one of the first scenes I did, they wrapped me up in toilet paper to tie me up. And I would say, 'I'm going to kill fucking Frankie Avalon.' I used to call him every third day and threaten his life."

In the mid-sixties, Fabian married model Kathleen Regan, and they eventually had two kids. In the mid-seventies, they divorced. I asked him if it was true that he threw a bottle at his mother-in-law. "Yeah, definitely," he said wearily. "And punched her. I was arrested, definitely. One night I had an extra bottle of wine in me, and I was looking at my kids, and I got overwhelmed by the fact that this would end: this marriage, and my kids. And I went bananas. It wasn't a very pleasant thing. We all make mistakes." He tried to revive his music career, releasing a disco song, "Ease on In (Into My Life)," in 1977, and hitting the casino circuit. Self-loathing got the best of him, and he quit again. Then, in 1980, the indignities of his past were rehashed in *The Idolmaker*, a fictionalized film biography of Marcucci, with characters based on Frankie and Fabian. Fabian sued Marcucci, who had served as a consultant on the film, for defamation of character, and won. "His seven-and-a-half percent, I own now," Fabian said. "I made money, but it was a moral victory. They didn't think I was going to stand up for my rights."

To this day, Fabian blames Marcucci for ruining his life. (He remained closer to DeAngelis, who died in 1982.) He calls Marcucci "that prick" and "a sick man." "He was a frustrated performer who tried to have other people live his life for him," he said. "Frankie got it a little bit, and then he found me — forget it, it was over. That's where he got his jollies. I have to live with that my whole life."

For all my infatuation with Fabian, something about his assessment of Bob Marcucci didn't quite add up. If he resented Bob for taking 100 percent of the credit for his success, then how could he hold Bob 100 percent responsible for his failure? And why the vehemence of his anger? Fabian's tirade continued. "About six months ago I was in a restaurant on the Strip," he said, "and he came walking in. He wanted to say hello, and what I actually said was, 'Get lost.' So I'm leaving, and this guy goes, 'Hey, Fabian, meet the *new* Fabian.' Marcucci was there interviewing young guys. I said, 'Be careful, man. Be careful.' And walked away. I know the guy. He's still trying today."

I listened sympathetically. I wanted to be on his side. But I couldn't help feeling weirdly sorry for Bob. Could he really be as bad as Fabian said? I decided that, like Bob Rael, he deserved to give his side. So I looked for him. It turned out that he lived and worked in nearby Westwood, and was willing to talk. A few days later, I went over there. I dreaded going. I pulled my rental car up in front of a tidy suburban-style house, and almost couldn't drag my feet to the door. I felt like I was walking into a pit of lechery. And I was, sort of. Of course I was.

"Bob, Manfred Hampton from Power Rangers."

The voice sizzled out of a speaker phone in

the middle of a dining room table. Bob and I were doing our interview, but he looked at me guiltily and said, "Do you mind?"

"No, go ahead," I said.

He jumped on the line to hustle.

Bob was a busy guy. His home buzzed. Assistants wandered in and out from unseen rooms of the house, shuffling papers, brewing pots of coffee. Phone lines blinked. A TV crackled in the corner. Bob blurted out lines about his current clients: so-and-so had a commercial on the *American Music Awards*, stuff like that. "We manage actors and actresses now," he told me. Chancellor was no longer an active label, but he controlled the catalog. "We lease records to the discount places that put out oldie-but-goodie records, like K-Tel and Reader's Digest." His home was not showy. There was a galley kitchen with a linoleum floor, a sunken living room with deep-pile carpeting and loud furniture. He was divorced, with two grown sons. "None of them are going to be in the business," he said, a little disappointed.

Bob was tall and softspoken, with a thick mustache. He was in a permanent state of agitation, as if he were perpetually twenty minutes late to a meeting across town. Yet he loved talking about the music business, about the fifties. He was generous and anxious to help. When I told him I hadn't seen *The Idolmaker*, he hollered to the next room, and ordered a gopher to bring me a copy to keep. Still, something about him made me uneasy. The whole place seemed creepy, like that house in *Poltergeist* that was built on top of an Indian burial ground. I had the nonsensical fear that a science-fiction monster could explode from under the olive-green shag and devour us all for our sins. And Bob himself had a tragic aura. He seemed haunted by his past. "*The Idolmaker* isn't one hundred percent true," he said, as the gopher trotted in with the video. "They had Frank and Fabe hating each other — that wasn't true at all. But they captured the essence of what I was — a driving, pushy man. The actor [Ray Sharkey] played me very classless. He had the right to do it. He played it the way he saw it."

Twelve years older than Fabian, Bob also grew up blue collar in Philadelphia. His father ran the hotel and restaurant union. "He looked like he could have been Al Capone," he said. "He was tough. He knew all the Mafia people — sure. They made him very Mafia in the movie, and it wasn't fair. He wasn't Mafia at all. He was a very interesting man, a loving father." From an early age, Bob was enthralled with entertainment; he sang, did Al Jolson impersonations. He also had a knack for promotion. "In high school, they did a play called *The Man Who Came to Dinner,*" he said. "I promoted it like mad and did crazy things. I got a room service table from my father, and attached it to my car. I put a sign on it, *The Man Who Came to Dinner,* and drove around with it. The show became one of the biggest at South Philadelphia High."

But his father wanted him to be a doctor. Bob dutifully complied, enrolling in a college pre-med program. "I couldn't stand blood," he said. "I didn't want to go and cut people." Fate got him off the hook: during his first year of college, his father and mother split up. "I was told to make a choice: either I go to college, or he supports my mother," Bob said. "So I chose my mother." For the next ten years, Bob took whatever jobs came his way: he waited tables, worked for a stationery company, worked for a suit company. In 1956, his father, from whom he'd become estranged, offered him ten thousand dollars in seed money to start a business. "I said, 'Do you think ten thousand dollars is going to buy my love? A thousand bucks a year for ten years? You're crazy.' You would never talk to my father that way — never." Still, Bob took the money.

Chancellor's initial releases were Sinatra-style pop, but Bob quickly realized he couldn't compete against the powerful major labels. And he was savvy to changing trends within the music business, particularly in Philadelphia; *American Bandstand*, a rock-and-roll dance show hosted by local broadcaster Dick Clark, was becoming one of the most influential promotional outlets in the business. "I said to Pete, 'We need idols,'" Bob recalled. " 'It's all idols out there, like Elvis. And ours have to be different and adorable.'" He signed Frankie Avalon, and talked his way into better distribution through a deal with ABC-Paramount. Frankie's first two singles bombed, and Bob was down to his last dollar when "Dede Dinah" started to break in December 1957. "We sold three hundred thousand copies in five days," he said. "Which was unheard of. Me, Frank, and Pete went to New York City and got ourselves advance checks, like a thousand dollars each. We went home and had a great Christmas."

But Bob's father, who had seeded the enterprise, was less than impressed. "He said, 'If you do it one time, that's great. If you do it two times, that's even better. The third time we'll really know that you've got it.'" Bob's desperation to please his father made the pressure to find Star Number 2 intense. "I had a lot to prove," Bob admitted. "I wanted his acceptance."

That's when he laid eyes on Fabian. Bob remembered the moment. Yes, he was driving home through the neighborhood. Yes, he saw the ambulance, and pulled over. "And out walked Fabian in his jeans, with his hair mussed up, and he had *the look*," Bob said. "I asked if he could sing and he said, 'God, no.' So I kept looking elsewhere. I had contest after contest. And every time I'd drive by I'd see him on the corner. Finally I just went knocking on his door and said, 'Come on, I want to see if you can do it.'"

Pete, the more musical of the partners, was appalled by Bob's plan. "Pete went nuts," Bob said. "He didn't want any part of it. ABC-Paramount thought I should be committed. But they couldn't say no to me at that time, because we were making so much money for them hand over fist with Frankie." Even Dick Clark disapproved. "He thought I was insane," Bob said. "But he put him on television. And the one time he put him on television, the whole place went nuts." What Bob understood, even more than his colleagues, was that quality is not always the deciding factor in pop music. "Fabian had something that the public liked," he said. "Why should we disagree with that? Everything can't be *La Bohème* and jazz. It's a big, wide open world with people who have all kinds of tastes and dislikes."

Bob catered to the audience's fantasies without apology. "I did a lot of marketing for the albums," he said. "I made sure they had pictures. The front cover was nothing but a picture of Fabe or Frank, almost a whole face shot. On the back we'd put more pictures, and then we'd say things about Frank and Fabe and what they did at home." He put fold-out posters inside. "Kids were in love with Fabe and Frank as people. So the more pictures they could get, the more albums they would buy." When they went out in public, Bob coordinated their look right down to their socks. "These boys had the best of everything," he said. "I owned the label and I owned the publishing and I owned a piece of them, so I would never be cheap. I bought nothing but the best clothes for them. Elegant. I still have clothes that I bought myself and gave to Frankie — alpaca sweaters and everything else. Fabe I copied more of the Belafonte look, which I thought was a heavier, sexier look. They were the two best-dressed kids in that era."

At this point, I finally let it drop that I had already interviewed Fabian. Bob hung his head. "I'm sure he said nothing nice about me, because we're not friends," he said. "No. I guess I was a little smothering with him. I was maybe a little controlling. It was difficult for him, definitely. I don't hate him. I don't have any ill feelings toward him."

I tried to paraphrase Fabian's resentment. "He felt that you took credit for who he was, instead of allowing him to be his own person," I said.

At that Bob bristled. "I didn't do anything to hurt him," he said. "I was constantly rooting for him. I felt every pain that he had. When they used to cut him up and knock him down, I felt all that for him. I'm not an unfeeling person."

Then his tone softened, and, at last, he laid out his cards. "It was my lifetime dream to be Leslie Howard in a movie called *Pygmalion*," he said. "That was my lifetime dream. But that wasn't his lifetime dream. So if he feels that way, that's okay. There's nothing wrong with that. His feelings could be very right."

At that moment a curvy blonde walked into the room. Bob looked at her, distracted, and then mumbled an introduction: "This is one of my clients, Shannon."

"Hi, Shannon," I said.

She looked furious. "Linda," she corrected, with a sour pinch of her lips.

"Not Shannon, *Linda*," Bob said, rubbing his forehead. "I'm sorry. I'm in the middle of an interview. Your stuff's right there, darling," he added, pointing to a stack of files.

I wanted to loathe Bob, but I couldn't condemn him without condemning myself. We were too much alike. I wasn't alone in my misdirected love. Even so, I could understand why Fabian felt the way he did. It's one thing to see helpless adoration in the face of a pretty girl from Corpus Christi, another to witness it in the visage of a powerful older guy. But inside, we were all the same. Me, Bob, my mom, the millions of screaming teenage girls: our insatiable desire for fake love was the axis upon which the music industry turned.

Fabian, to his credit, seemed to have come to terms with all this. At some point after the lawsuit, he accepted his status as the Singer Who Couldn't Sing. In 1985, he teamed with Frankie Avalon and another Philly heartthrob, Bobby Rydell, to form a package tour called the "Golden Boys of Bandstand"; they still perform dozens of concerts a year. He also produces "Fabian's Good Time Rock and Roll Show," a revue that features acts like Lou Christie, Tommy Roe, Bobby Vee, and the Drifters. "I do my

hits and some old rock and roll tunes —
'Johnny B. Goode,' two Presley things, 'Sea
Cruise,' stuff like that," Fabian said. "That's
what our audience comes to see. A few guys
have tried to put in newer, original material.
The audience doesn't come to see that. And
that's fine. It doesn't bother me."

He's now married for the third time. He
spends a lot of time in Los Angeles, but also
has a home near Philly. His son, Christian
Forte, is a screenwriter whose film *Albino
Alligator* was directed by Kevin Spacey. His
daughter, Julie, is an animator and artist.
"They're great people," Fabian said. "We get
along wonderfully, thank God."

Sometimes he even appreciates the public
Fabian. In 1998, he had a guest spot on the
TV show *Murphy Brown*: "It was her fiftieth
birthday on the show, and I was her present."
In 2001, he got a star on the Hollywood
Walk of Fame. All in all, he said, the balance
has tipped in his favor. "Once you have a
major success in this business, people will always remember you as that success," he said.
"There's nothing you can do about that. So
now I make the best of it. I've found, I'd say,
seventy-five percent peace with that."

As for the other 25 percent, it keeps things
interesting. "Every now and then the rebel
comes out in me, and I'm saying 'Fuck you'

to the wrong guy," he said. "It's inadvertent. I just do it. And the guys I work with know that about me. They know I'm not interested in the business, and they let me be. Because they *love* the business. They've always had this burning desire to be in the business, since they were babies. Bobby Rydell was a drummer when he was six or seven years old. Frankie was a trumpet player when he was a kid. They love it! When I see them being a little too slick, I laugh. And they're cool about it."

Fabian was so nice when the interview ended. "I enjoyed talkin'," he said, and told me to call him if I needed anything else. A couple of months later, the Golden Boys played near my home in New Jersey. A girl-friend and I put on summer dresses and went to see them. Fabian was great. His voice was a manly grunt, and his charisma jolted every girl in the place. Frankie and Bobby were good, too, but more professional and somehow less fun. I liked Fabian's on-the-ledge-ness. He sang like he needed us to catch him, and audiences love that — it makes us feel special, like we're doing more than sitting there clapping.

Afterward I went backstage to say hello. Middle-aged ladies waited outside the door, clasping vintage paraphernalia for him to sign. Inside, Fabian was sitting quietly, going over his schedule with his agent. He said hello, and I got the sense that he hadn't totally forgotten who I was. He seemed to associate me with something vaguely positive, like he didn't need to tell me to fuck off. Still, he seemed a little confused as to what I was doing there, so after a few minutes I left. I felt sort of sad that our special moment was gone. But not too sad. Experience told me that a new crush would be waiting right around the corner.

Ten
CONNIE

... The pressure of staying on top has already opened little cracks here and there. Three years ago Connie suffered from skin trouble, which, she says, was the result of overwork. "Everybody was saying it was my diet," she explains, "and they were suggesting all sorts of cures. Actually it was just nervous tension."

The facial blemishes disappeared in time, but Connie still breaks out in a rash occasionally — it is now confined to her back — especially on opening nights. She carries a little bottle of pills prescribed by her physician; taking two of them clears up her skin in an hour or two. "I'm never nervous onstage," she says defensively. "People pay to see me, and they must like me or they'd go down the street to see somebody else."

The professional rat race has also aggravated what Connie herself calls "a very bad temper." If anger flares, she is apt to slam doors, throw books, or vent her fury on friends or associates. When she first played the Copacabana in New York and a photographer came to take pictures for album covers, the club owner, Jules Podell, ordered him out of the place. Connie said furiously, "If the photographer doesn't stay, I won't go on." She actually refused to sing, and Podell had to get Sammy Davis Jr. as an emergency replacement. Another time, recording a new song in M-G-M's New York studio, Connie complained about the arrangement and the musicians. At 2:30 a.m., she suddenly walked out into the cold winter night with no coat or hat and spent an hour dissipating her black mood by trudging up and down the deserted streets, aimless and solitary.

— *"Girl on the Glamour-Go-Round" by Dean Jennings,* The Saturday Evening Post, *September 23, 1961*

Connie Francis was the big kahuna. She was my obsession of obsessions, my Helen of Troy, the face that had launched my book. I was nervous about trying for an interview with her. What if she said no? The book would fall apart. My mother would never love me again. But after I returned from the West Coast, I felt strong enough to try. I called up an old friend at PolyGram Records, and he told me he'd handled publicity for the box set. "Do you need an interview?" he said. "I can hook you up, definitely."

"Wow gee thanks that's so great," I babbled. But his promise turned out to be slightly exaggerated. Over lunch at a Chelsea bistro, he brushed off my questions about Connie's health. "Call me later, at my office," he said. Then it took me a couple of days to get him on the phone. When I did he rattled off a phone number in Florida. Connie had recently moved there full-time after spending her life in New Jersey. "Don't speak directly with Connie," he cautioned me. "Ask for her assistant, Terry."

I gulped. I had hoped *he* would set up the interview. "What if I —"

"Terry'll take care of you," he said.

"But —"

"Gotta run!" he said. "Good luck." Click.

I was petrified. For weeks I stared at the phone number on my desk. Finally one day, hands shaking, I picked up the phone and dialed. A sad, craggy voice said, "Hello?"

"Could I please speak to Terry?" I said.

"Who is this?" the voice demanded.

It was Connie! Help! I explained that I was a writer working on a book. "Oh," she said tiredly. "I'll put Terry on."

Terry was extremely nice. We chatted about Connie's doings, and she said that Connie would soon fly to Italy to tape a live performance for Italian television. I described the book and said that I was a fan. Then I blurted, "Connie reminds me of my mother."

There was an awkward pause. "Why don't you send us some clips, and we'll get back to you," she said.

I sent a package by FedEx and heard nothing. Each day was agony. Finally I called again, and to my surprise Terry said that Connie would be happy to grant an interview. "How about next week?" she asked.

"Um, how about the end of the month?" I said. "I need a couple of weeks to make flight arrangements."

Terry was silent again. "You want to fly all the way to Florida for an interview?" she said. "Wouldn't it be easier to do it on the phone?"

She was going to think I was a stalker. I had to improvise something, quick. "Oh, well, my dad lives in Florida and I was hoping to visit him as well," I said.

This was a total lie. I had no intention of visiting my father in Florida, ever. But it worked for Terry. She put me on hold for a few minutes, then came back on and said that Connie had agreed. We picked a date. "See you then," she said.

We hung up, and instead of feeling excitement I was overwhelmed with dread.

What had I done? Now I actually had to go visit my father and his wife. In the seventeen years since the divorce I hadn't slept under his roof. And worse than staying there would be the act of telling my mother. She'd think I was a traitor. Here I was, trying to make up to her, and she was going to be more furious than ever.

I called Dad, and he seemed surprised and pleased. Connie lived near Fort Lauderdale, on the east coast, and we agreed that I'd spend the two nights beforehand at his place in Naples, on the Gulf. Then I called Mom. It was worse than I had imagined. Our conversations were already strained, and she greeted the news with icy silence. Then she suggested that my father and stepmother wanted to exploit the rift in our relationship in order to further turn me against her.

I sat quietly on the phone, feeling awful, not knowing what to say. The fact that I was interviewing Connie Francis didn't interest her in the least.

I prepared. I learned a lot about Connie. She was born Concetta Maria Franconero on December 12 — that's Frank Sinatra's birthday — in 1938. Her parents were living in Brooklyn, but her mother, Ida, wanted to go dancing in Newark, New Jersey; she got labor pains on the dance floor and barely made it to a hospital. George Franconero shoveled coal in the Brooklyn Navy Yard. When Connie was a year and a half old, shortly after the arrival of a younger brother, Georgie, her father had an accident on the job and couldn't work, so the Franconeros moved in with family in Newark. George was proud and ambitious, undereducated and highly intelligent. He doted on his little daughter. Music was a family passion — his own father had emigrated from Italy in 1905 with little in his possession but a concertina — and he noticed early talent in Connie. When she was three he set her up with lessons at Teresa Masciola's Accordion School. Every time he had thirty-five cents to spare, he'd buy her a new piece of sheet music.

Connie basked in her father's adoration. Her 1984 autobiography, *Who's Sorry Now?*, opens with a scene of her at age four, playing the accordion at an amusement park in Irvington, New Jersey, as her father hovered in the wings. "I knew from the gleam in my father's eye that I'd made him very proud of me," she writes. "And *nothing* was ever more important to me than that! I was clearly the apple of Daddy's eye, and I was always made to feel very safe, very loved, very protected, and very, very special." Music became the focus of her life. By the age of ten she was performing in contests and touring the last vestiges of the vaudeville circuit with talent revues. In 1950 she sang "Daddy's Little Girl" on *Arthur Godfrey's Talent Scouts*; it was Godfrey who suggested she dump her cumbersome last name in favor of something easier, like Francis. "My father will have kittens," Connie whispered in horror, but Francis it was. She spent four years as a regular on a New York TV show called *Startime Kids*, and sang demonstration records for music publishers. When *Startime Kids* went off the air, its producer, George Scheck, became her manager, and he shopped her to major labels. One of her demos, a song called "Freddy," appealed to the president of MGM. He had a son named Freddy, and decided to release the song as a birthday present. At the age of sixteen, Connie had a record deal.

But her first several singles bombed. MGM was on the verge of dropping her when her father intervened. He didn't like the material the label chose for her and suggested she try a song that was already a proven success: "Who's Sorry Now," a million-seller from 1923. "Why don't you sing it just like any regular ballad, but add rock and roll triplets behind it?" he said, according to

Who's Sorry Now? "It'll be a new song to the kids — they'll wanna dance to it. And the grown-ups — they've already made the song a standard." Connie hated the song — "It's so square, it's pitiful" — but she was not in the habit of disobeying her father. Franconero's formula for bridging the generation gap worked. Dick Clark debuted "Who's Sorry Now" on *American Bandstand* on January 1, 1958, and it went to Number 4 on the pop charts. From that point on, she would never seriously challenge her father on a decision related to her career. If he didn't think a song was right for her, she didn't record it. " 'Who's Sorry Now' wouldn't be the only hit my father would pick for me — he went on to select a whole bunch of them," she wrote in her autobiography. "He had the uncanny knack of knowing just what the public would or would not accept from me. He taught me never to appeal to esoteric tastes or to the critics — only to the people. 'Those other jerks, they don't buy your records, anyhow. The hell with 'em!'"

Her reliance on her father's instincts paid off. Between 1958 and 1963, Connie was the leading female pop singer in the world. She placed thirty-five songs on The Top 40, including three that went to Number 1. Some of her hits, like "Stupid Cupid" (written by Neil Sedaka and Howard Greenfield), had rock and roll arrangements that established her with teenagers; others, like "My Happiness," were updates of Tin Pan Alley oldies. By 1960 her palette was broadening. Guided by her father, she recorded an album of Italian ballads, *Connie Francis Sings Italian Favorites*; it went to Number 4 on the charts, the biggest-selling album of her career. A throw-down performance of the hit "Mama" on *The Perry Como Show* helped her sell out Carnegie Hall and brought her to nightclubs like the Copa. Other ethnic-themed albums followed: *Connie Francis Sings Spanish and Latin American Favorites*, *Connie Francis Sings Jewish Favorites*, *Connie Francis Sings Irish Favorites*, *Connie Francis Sings German Favorites*. She also worked out a dreamy country-pop hybrid in hits like "Everybody's Somebody's Fool" and "My Heart Has a Mind of Its Own," back-to-back Number 1 hits in 1960. Based on her singles chart success, Connie was the most popular female singer of the rock era until the advent of Aretha Franklin in the late sixties. She remained the Number 2 singer well into the nineties, when Madonna finally surpassed her. To this day she ranks Number 3: ahead of Whitney Houston, Mariah Carey, and Barbra Streisand. Ahead of Carly Simon, Linda

Ronstadt, and Tina Turner. Ahead of Janis Joplin, Joni Mitchell, Carole King, Gladys Knight, Dionne Warwick, Donna Summer, Stevie Nicks, Annie Lennox, Cyndi Lauper, Sarah McLachlan, Alanis Morissette, Janet Jackson, and Bonnie Raitt.

But the rigid control exerted by her father had a downside. George Franconero wanted nothing coming between him and his daughter. He discouraged anything that would distract her from her music career, including beaus. In the year before "Who's Sorry Now" hit, Connie met a hustling performer and songwriter, Bobby Darin. He had cowritten a song called "My First Real Love" that Connie recorded; it was one of her bombs, but she and Darin, equally ambitious and obsessed with music, connected. Darin wanted to elope, but out of fear of her father Connie put him off. When Darin showed up at a taping of *The Jackie Gleason Show* where Connie was scheduled to perform, Franconero chased him out of the building with a gun, and the romance officially ended. Connie was distraught. She claims in her autobiography that she never got over Darin. (He married actress Sandra Dee in 1961, and died of complications from a lifelong heart ailment in 1974, at the age of thirty-seven.) Franconero was constantly "protecting" his daughter from seamier show-biz elements. Backstage at a rock-and-roll show, Connie munched an apple and was approached by a musician, who asked for a bite, wink wink. Her father sprang from the shadows and ground the apple into the young man's face. Connie's response? She quit playing rock-and-roll shows. "Anyway, I'd always enjoyed working for grown-ups in nightclubs better," she rationalized.

And if her father taught her not to cater to critics, the strategy worked. Despite her enormous achievements, Connie's critical profile today is nil. *Rock of Ages*, a 649-page treatise written by Ed Ward, Ken Tucker, and Geoffrey Stokes, gives her two sentences. Even Fabian gets more ink. In *The Rise and Fall of Popular Music*, Donald Clarke grouses, "Francis has to be mentioned here somewhere, for she had over fifty *Billboard* Hot 100 entries in ten years and represented a transition from the period of early 1950s jingle-pop" into rock and roll. Then he calls her music "junk." Even histories of women in rock shortchange her. In *We Gotta Get Out of This Place*, Gerri Hirshey adopts the old party line about namby-pamby boys like Frankie Avalon taking over the pop charts, then dismisses Connie as part of a coterie of female counterparts. "The hit parade embraced angoraed Daddy's girls and primly permed teen angels: Brenda Lee, Connie Francis, Shelley Fabares, Lesley Gore and that Mouseketeer-grown-into-a-C-cup, Annette Funicello." *The Rolling Stone Book of Women in Rock* devotes whole chapters to Liz Phair and Polly Jean Harvey, but Connie, who defined female stardom in the early rock era, who set the standard for a generation of singers to follow, from girl groups like the Teddy Bears to pop divas like Dusty Springfield, barely merits a passing reference.

The arrival of the Beatles in early 1964 hit Connie harder than most other singers. Her career simply died; not one of her singles would crack the Top 40 after May 1964. Groomed for stardom since she was a child, she had nothing to fall back on. Unlike Paul Anka, she didn't write songs; though she costarred in the 1960 movie *Where the Boys Are* and three other teen-oriented pictures, she didn't feel comfortable acting. And she had no personal life outside of her work. Most of her dates had been photo ops staged for fan magazines. In August 1964, she married Richard Kanellis, a public-relations man for a Las Vegas casino; they divorced five months later. Her second marriage, in 1971, ended almost as quickly. Her third marriage, to Joseph Garzilli, a tourism executive, got off to a rocky start when Connie suffered a miscarriage. The couple made plans to adopt a child, and Garzilli encouraged Connie to attempt a comeback. In the fall of 1974, she began a U.S. tour at Westbury Music Fair, a theater-in-the-round in suburban Long Island.

Then, in the early-morning hours of November 8, 1974, after her performance at Westbury, Connie was raped at knife point in a Howard Johnson's motel room. The assailant was never caught, and a police officer leaked her identity to the press. Later that day, her father pinched her chin and told her not to worry. "It won't be so bad," he said. "You're lucky Joe's the kind of guy he is." The arrival of an adopted baby boy could not stop Connie from descending into a lengthy depression. In 1976, she sued Howard Johnson's for providing inadequate security. The trial, in a Brooklyn federal court, became a media circus. "Connie: Rape Opened Door on Sex Blahs," screeched the *Daily News*. Her lawyers tried to bar the press from the proceedings, but in a landmark First Amendment case an appeals court allowed the press entry. Connie eventually won $1.5 million from the hotel chain. But her life was in shambles. In 1977, she lost her voice after nasal surgery. In 1978, she and Garzilli split up. And in 1981, her brother, George, was shot to death in the driveway of his New Jersey home. An attorney, George had pleaded guilty in 1978 to bank fraud charges, and was convicted in 1980 on land fraud. He had twice testified for state and federal investigations into organized crime.

The eighties were her darkest decade. A diagnosed manic-depressive, she spent years in and out of mental hospitals. She was involuntarily committed by her father in 1982 and in 1983. A court battle to gain her release in 1983 found its way to the tabloids. In 1984, she was rushed to a hospital in a coma after an overdose of sleeping pills. She was back in the news a few months later with the publication of *Who's Sorry Now?*, and briefly remarried in 1985. In December of that year she was arrested for refusing to put out a cigarette on an airplane. She was hospitalized again in early 1986, and given shock treatments for her depression in 1988. But the nineties were better. Her illness stabilized and she resumed a limited performance schedule. Her voice was a shadow of itself, but fans seemed thrilled just to see her on a stage again.

But when George Franconero died in 1996, Connie decided to break with the past.

She sold off stage gowns and memorabilia at an auction in Newark and left New Jersey for good. She'd long held a condo in Florida, but she bought a big new house with room for her mother, Ida, who was alone after sixty-two years of marriage. This was the house I would be visiting. Three days before I was supposed to leave, Connie left me a rambling message saying that she wasn't feeling well and needed to reschedule. I was afraid she was going to blow me off entirely, but we picked a new date and I alerted my dad.

During those weeks of delay, my research grew cold. As the new date grew closer, I called Terry to confirm and she said everything was set. I packed my research materials into a work bag, figuring I'd have time for a refresher in Florida. To be honest, I was so preoccupied by family drama that Connie had fallen a bit into the background. I was miserable about the state of my relationship with my mom. And I felt guilty as hell for visiting my dad — the person my mother hated the most. Everything I was trying to do to win her back was playing out all wrong.

The visit with my dad went off surprisingly well. He and his wife gave me the prodigal treatment. They squired me to department stores in downtown Naples, lunched me at frouffy Italian bistros, showed off their high-end hurricane shutters, and put me up in their building's "guest condo," a room of seashell motifs in peach and taupe, with its own phone line, temperature controls, and cable TV. The lifestyle was foreign to me, but I eased into it pretty quickly. The day before the interview, my stepmother bowed out of a scheduled beach excursion so that Dad and I could bond. We rode a little golf cart along a plank walkway through the mangrove swamps and opened folding chairs on the beach. It was only the second instance of major quality time I could recall since the divorce. The first was when I was a sophomore in college, a few months before he remarried; he attended parents' weekend and we shared a pitcher of beer at a deli. I remember thinking, Gee, he's not so bad. I had the same feeling that day on the beach. Like, how did our acrimony get blown so far out of proportion? We'd never had much in common, conversationally — I didn't follow the stock market, he'd plead ignorant about alternative rock — but suddenly, as he was explaining Gulf storm patterns, I realized that my mom wasn't the only parent who'd been around in the fifties. So I asked him what he remembered about the music of his youth.

Dad lit up. He told me he loved "Diana," by Paul Anka, and remembered driving around in the summer of '57 with it blaring from his car radio. He poked amicable fun at Pat Boone, mock-crooning a few bars of "Love Letters in the Sand." He said that he had programmed the local oldies station as the number one button in his Mercedes, and that his wife, a crucial six years younger than he and a Rolling Stones fan, teased him when he sang along to sock-hop standards. I was about to ask him about Connie Francis, but then I found myself cutting to the chase. I asked him what my mom was like when they met. Dad grew misty and looked at the sea. "A lot of laughs," he said. "We were at a debutante party at a country club. We both had other dates, but we ended up at a table together. I had some alcohol. My father was a member at the club, so the waiters knew me and looked the other way. I remember we were dancing and your mother kicked off her shoes. She said something like, 'I don't need these.' And she used four-letter words. That impressed me, because back then women didn't do that." That summer, Dad left town to be a camp counselor and wrote to the postmaster in Mom's hometown, asking for her address. "Back then they had these double postcards," he said. "You could write on one half, and the person could tear off the other half and send it back to you. I wanted the postmaster to write down her address and send it to me, but somehow he forwarded the whole thing to your mother. I got back the other half: 'I've heard a lot of lines in my life, but this one . . .'"

By the time Dad went to college Mom was dating someone else, but a year or two later she ended up at his school for a function, and that was that. "I don't regret the way we did things — having kids so early," he said. "But it put a lot of pressure on us. Took away a lot of the fun times."

"Mom won't talk about the past," I complained.

He gave me this look, like, You think I'm going to explain her? "I like remembering the good times," he said. "The good times were good."

That night in my room I pondered these revelations. Dad seemed so much *healthier* than my mom. Nostalgia held no threat; he could incorporate it into his current life. Mom wanted to close off the past, blot it out. What the hell was her problem? How did she get so neurotic?

I sank into my seashell-print bed and eyed my work bag in a corner. I should refresh my memory about Connie's background information, get my thoughts straight for the interview. Oh, hell — I could wing it. I blew off work and flipped on the TV.

The next morning I woke with an uneasy feeling in my gut. I met my dad and his wife for breakfast at a French pastry shop in a highway strip mall, and Dad pulled out a map to help me with my route. I had to drive two and a half hours across the state to Parkland, a dot near Fort Lauderdale. Dad told me to take I-75, better known as Alligator Alley, a highway that stretched like a snap-line through the Everglades, with nary a hill nor a bend to break the monotony. He and his wife issued hysterical warnings. "Don't go too fast! Check your mirrors before changing lanes! Cars come up out of nowhere! Drivers fall asleep and end up in the swamps! Watch for alligators — they crawl up and sun themselves on the pavement!" I looked at them, like, are you people nuts? It's a road, not a fifties science-fiction movie. I was already nervous about the interview — I didn't need them getting me more wound up. With a hasty good-bye, I trundled into my rental car and sped off.

On the highway, my nervousness ballooned into panic. Why hadn't I spent time the night before going over facts about

Connie's career? I began to obsess about the holes in my knowledge. The only one of her four films I'd seen was *Where the Boys Are*. I'd taped *Follow the Boys* on TCM but hadn't gotten around to watching it; I'd read blurbs about *When the Boys Meet the Girls* and knew it featured incongruous guest appearances by Louis Armstrong and Liberace. And while I'd accumulated close to twenty of her vintage LPs, I hadn't bothered to listen to most of them — there might be some jewel on her duet album with Hank Williams Jr. that would have provided a thoughtful and provoking interview angle. And her autobiography — I'd skimmed it, at least the early chapters. But now, things I once knew seemed to fly from my mind. What was the name of her pre-school accordion teacher? My brain was a bouffant: frizzed and frazzled, with teetering domes of thought held together by frail bobby pins of logic.

My work bag sat on the floor of the passenger side. I decided to do some cramming while I drove. With one hand on the wheel, I fumbled through the bag and located my portable CD player, then dumped a pile of CDs onto the seat. The first thing I grabbed was *On Guard with Connie Francis: National Guard Radio Shows with Mitchell Ayres Orchestra and Bob Crosby and His Bobcats.*

With a roll of my eyes I threw it back on the floor. What the hell did I bring that for? If I didn't care about armed forces radio transcripts with Bing Crosby's brother, it was safe to assume no one else would. I rifled through the pile again and got my hands on disc number two from the *Souvenirs* box set. This would help: it was the CD that had triggered my fascination two years ago at *Newsweek*, launching me on this manic odyssey. I loaded it into the player and propped the liner notes on the steering wheel so that I could read along. But the music just made me more confused. Each song was a different style. "Among My Souvenirs" was sudsy pop, a 1927 relic Connie had remade with a gentle rock-and-roll beat. Irving Berlin's "God Bless America" was ceremonial pomp sung with shrill earnestness. "Mama" was a grandiose old-country hanky-wringer, sung partially in Italian. "Teddy," written by Paul Anka, was pre-Spectoresque teen melodrama. "Valentino" — an Iberian castanet-clacker, simply awful. "Everybody's Somebody's Fool" — her first Number 1 hit, a pop-country concoction with banjo and hurdy-gurdy organ; cute, but hardly awesome. I was starting to despair. How was I supposed to make sense of someone who dabbled in so many different genres? Everything sounded rarefied, a little contrived. Connie didn't bring herself to different styles, filling in their distinctive and intriguing corners; she brought the styles closer to her, subjugating them under a mantle of pop broadness and generality. Why would I defend someone who specialized in watering down ethnic styles for mass consumption? How did I get myself into this ridiculous situation to begin with?

A car was in front of me in the cruising lane, and without thinking I swerved to pass it. Another car honked, and I belatedly checked my rearview mirror — whoops, there was someone behind me, too. Rattled, I slid back into the cruising lane. No need to get into an actual wreck — my mind was racing badly enough. I tried to calm down and refocus on the music. I needed to remember what I loved best about Connie: her voice. I skipped to "My Heart Has a Mind of Its Own," her second Number 1 hit. This was more like it: a languorous country song embellished with the unexpected touch of mariachi horns. Connie sang it in Patti Page–style double-tracked harmony, but her voice was different than Patti's; it had more angst, more urgency. She was telling the story of a lover who dumped her as if she were barely keeping it together, as if these were her last breaths before dissolving into total hysterics.

There was something else about her voice, though, something I'd never noticed before. An element of high-pitched plaintiveness; an immaturity. I thought, as I had in the past, of Patsy Cline. Their voices were actually quite similar: both had immense power in the upper ranges, a forcefulness that could cascade into abject vulnerability in the space of a measure. And they were peers: like Connie, Patsy's peak years were 1957 to 1963, a time in which country evolved from a small-band acoustic format into the orchestrated sophistication of the Nashville Sound. Patsy and Connie even overlapped with material. Connie covered Patsy's hit "I Fall to Pieces" on her 1962 album *Country Music Connie Style*, while Patsy sang a sassy version of Connie's breakthrough, "Stupid Cupid," during a 1960 army radio show. Yet today Patsy is hailed as one of the great icons of country music; her music remains relevant, constantly repackaged and reconsidered by critics. Connie's reputation, on the other hand, founders. She sounds hopelessly dated, a prisoner of some repressed bygone era. What separated them? Why did fame cling to one, and ignominy to the other?

As if to address my question, "Where the Boys Are" came into my headphones. The music splashed and clamored: ray-thin violins and shimmering cymbals, booming kettle drums and pounding piano. Connie's voice pierced the gloom, effortless and true. For a few seconds I forgot my worries as the song swept me along. I loved it just as much as ever. No one could sing this but Connie. No one could tie together longing and innocence in quite the same way. Someday the knowledge of love would come to her, but until then she was content to wait, content to remain pure and untouched, wrapped in the mantles of mystery.

And that was when it hit me. The thought arrived in my head like a transmission from another dimension. The words couldn't have been clearer if they'd been written on a road sign.

She hadn't had sex yet.

I knew with absolute certainty that Connie was a virgin when she sang these songs. Her first marriage wasn't until 1964, a date that eerily coincided with her fall off the charts; the hits I was listening to were all recorded before then. I could hear it in her voice. *That* was why she sounded immature; *that* was why the performances seemed strange, a little off. *That* was what separated her from Patsy Cline — sexy, feisty, husband-busting, mother-of-two Patsy Cline. No one talks about Connie today because no one relates to her virginity-rock. Her stiffness and formality irk us, the way the abject suffering of old blues records sometimes irks African Americans who feel as though they've moved past it. Of course she carries no cachet in postfeminist times. Her aura of compliance is too vivid a reminder of everything women have tried to leave behind.

No sex.

It was the key to Connie. It explained everything. And I had the sense that it explained even more — about my mother, about my attraction to this music, about myself. A memory came to me as I was driving, something that had happened to me a few years back. It was a painful, shameful memory. I didn't want it coming back to me, but it did.

"Do you mind if I get drunk?"

It was 1992. I was sitting in a bar on New York's Upper West Side, across from a singer whose band had just performed in front of three thousand people. I loved the group's new album. I was obsessed with it. I played it all the time. I was especially obsessed with the singer, his voice, his words. I wanted to meet him, talk to him. I wanted to feed my unhealthy thing. So I arranged an interview. It only took one phone call. At the time I was a journalist with the *New York Times*, and I could interview pretty much any rock singer in the world. No one questioned me. No one said I was just some wacko with a crush.

I knew this singer liked to drink, and that was all the excuse I needed. The waitress came to our table, and I ordered a tequila and a beer. Then I said to him, "Do you mind if I get drunk?"

The tape recorder was rolling. He looked at it curiously. Then he said, in a low, deliberate voice, "I don't have a problem with that."

We talked about his album, his band. We ordered another round, maybe two. "Your album has all these references to heaven," I said. I wasn't asking a question. I was just laying him out on the line. "You use the word in three or four different songs. What's that about?"

At this he got fed up. He knew the conventions of mainstream rock journalism, and my methods did not fit them. He knew that I was just supposed to write a boilerplate piece about the latest cool band trying for a commercial breakthrough. "Why are you asking me about this?" he demanded. "You can't write about this in the *New York Times*!"

I was defensive. "I can too write about this in the *New York Times*! This is what matters to me!"

But he refused to answer. We ordered another round. At some point the tape ran out, and I didn't bother to flip it. We were off the map now. We finished our drinks and took a cab downtown to another bar. We drank more. We danced to Frank Sinatra's "Summer Wind" on the jukebox, hanging on each other. The world blurred. I was supposed to deliver him to a nearby restaurant, where his manager was waiting. Somehow we got ourselves back on the street.

"I really like you," he said.

We were crossing Eighth Avenue, hand in hand. The neon light in the restaurant's window loomed in the wee-hours darkness. I was wasted, yet suddenly the world was clear again. And I knew, in my horrible, instant sobriety, that I could not make it real. It would ruin my career, my reputation. My interviews had become decadent courtships that I was not allowed to consummate. NO SEX. It was my drumbeat, my unconscious mantra. "I'm a lousy pick-up," I told him.

He protested, and I insisted. We arrived in front of the restaurant. The magic haze of the evening had evaporated. I walked him into the bistro, enduring a stern glance from his manager. Hanger-on types gathered at the table. I waved good-bye to the singer, but I wasn't sure if he saw me.

The next morning, my head in a hangover vise, I faced my deadline. I wanted to express what the music meant to me, and in some way I wanted to write about those squishy things that were happening between my subjects and me, yet at the same time I was terrified to reveal myself. If I wrote honestly, I would be seen as some girl with a crush who didn't deserve to be a professional. So I tried to pull off a half-and-half thing, banging out a rambling piece about the band, bars, and heaven.

Usually my pieces went in clean, but this time an editor from the Arts desk called. He was confused. The piece didn't make sense. He wanted a rewrite. My paranoia kicked in. It was as if this editor *knew*. He had seen me drunk at 3 a.m. He had seen through me; I'd get my walking papers any second. I'd be back in my room, daydreaming about rock stars instead of actually meeting and talking to them. I rushed him a revamped boilerplate about the latest cool band trying for a commercial breakthrough. That version went into the paper, no questions asked.

Darkness fell outside my apartment window as the piece finally closed. My hangover hadn't receded. In the aftermath I felt scared, like a burglar who had almost tripped an alarm. I lectured myself. You must not have feelings for the people you interview. And if you do, under no circumstances can you be foolish enough to write about them.

So much for lectures. Here I was, years later, creeping around Parkland, Florida, obsessed as ever. I'd gotten there quickly, flying along the highway, so I had time to kill before the interview. Exhausted yet weirdly exuberant, I coasted through the neighborhood, looking at house numbers. Parkland was odd. Only one side of Connie's road was developed. Sullen, fancy homes sat on mounds of dirt that had filled in the swampland that used to be here. I found Connie's place and, skulking past it like a prowler, trying to distinguish characteristics inside just by the glaze of its windows and the cut of its flagstones, got a shivery thrill. The intimacy was unbearable, almost pornographic. I wanted to remember every detail. I flipped open my notebook and described what I thought would be the view from her front step. *Bulldozer tearing up a field across street. Everglades in the distance. Overcast sky.* In my excitement I forgot to write down a single notation about the house itself. Was it white with dual-story columns and Palladian windows? Did lilies and bougainvillea bloom in the manicured gardens? I'll never remember.

Then I thought, what if she looks out a window and sees me idling here and ogling her? I sped away and headed back to the highway interchange. I stopped at a quickie-mart for a drink, then decided to check out the town. Heading away from Connie's neighborhood, the road arced smoothly to the right. The pavement was new and unblemished; I saw one other car. I passed a not-yet-rented strip mall, its sand-colored, cheap-construction shell hulking roadside like a newborn ghost. Then civilization, such as it was, petered out. There *was* no town. Parkland did not actually exist; it was a still-forming figment in a developer's imagination, a pioneer outpost, a stake against future real-estate encroachment. The uneasy feeling returned to my gut. Who would live here, in a town anchored by a quickie-mart and populated by bulldozers? I felt unmoored myself, adrift in someone else's unfinished dream.

I turned back to Connie's house, and even though I was still early I pulled into the driveway. Here goes. I threw my bag over my shoulder and got out of the car. Fat drops of rain fell on my head. My hair's gonna frizz, I thought sadly. I walked to the door and rang the bell.

My first few minutes inside were a blur. Probably Terry showed me in. The atmosphere in the house felt like the backstage area at Carnegie Hall after a sold-out show. People buzzed about, some without discernible purpose. Assistants manhandled paperwork and ferried items between rooms. A host of workmen hung around the dining area, futzing with furniture and unrolling a floor-length carpet. I caught a glimpse of Connie's mom: she was cheerful and petite, wearing a rose-colored shirt and lilac-colored shorts. For a while I was neglected, and I stood around like a movie extra waiting for a camera call. I floated between rooms, finding the lay of the land: an open kitchen-living area, the dining room, the foyer. Everything was spanking new. At some point I ducked into a bathroom and scribbled notes about the décor: "Living room a riot of zebra print and silver. Large black wall unit loaded with big-screen TV and high-end stereo equipment. Elongated animal tchotchkes on shelves. Gold records stacked against wall in front hall, waiting to be mounted. Settee with embroidered pillows bearing mottos: SO MANY MEN, SO LITTLE TIME and ITALIAN AMERICAN PRINCESS."

Then I was seated on the zebra-print sectional, and Connie was next to me. She wore a cream-colored blouse with lots of decorative, intentionally nonmatching buttons sewn on the pocket, and a matching broad-brimmed hat decorated with the same nonmatching buttons. Her hair was dyed red and pulled back into a long ponytail. Her eyes were large and brown and unbearably gentle. There was something youthful and vulnerable about her: forever teen. She won't hurt me, I thought. She'll give me what I need. I can pull this off.

We exchanged pleasantries, and I set up my portable tape recorder. As I drew in my breath to formulate my first question, she fired one at me instead. "Karen, what is your book going to be about?"

I was getting used to this. I gave what seemed to me a clear, concise reply. "It's about pop singers in the fifties, and how rock and roll affected the course of pop music."

"Mmm-hmm, mmm-hmm," she said, unconvinced.

I ratcheted up the flattery. "I just thought there should be a book that I could pick up that would tell me about you or Tommy Sands or Pat Boone," I said. "I was getting interested in the era, and I wanted to learn more about it."

She clapped her hands impatiently on her knees. "Well, Dick Clark has a number of books on the era. You might want to call his office in Burbank. Ask for Amy Schroeder

— she's the executive secretary. Tell her I suggested that you call, and ask if there's any informative books that she could recommend or send you."

Great — she was giving me library tips. "Yes, I'm familiar with his books," I said. "I was also hoping to write from a younger person's perspective —"

She took off the hat and patted down her hair. "I just brought my mother from the doctor's, and I got caught in the rain," she said.

That one threw me. I decided to start over. "Connie, thank you so much for seeing me," I said. "It's such a thrill to meet you."

"Thank you, thank you," she said, Gloria Swanson-like.

"You were such a pioneer," I gushed. "For a woman to get into the pop music field when you did —"

"It was almost unheard of, because it was a totally male-dominated market," she said. "The majority of the people who bought records were girls. And their idols were boys. So they bought records by boys. I was really a fluke. And then, of course, I think it was 1960 that Brenda Lee had her first hit record. I remember listening for the first time to 'Sweet Nuthins.' I sent a telegram to her and said, 'Now I know who my competition is.'"

"There was Brenda, and Annette had a few records, and Patti Page —"

"The whole demarcation line was Presley," she cut in. "Everything prior to Presley was not considered rock and roll, and it *wasn't* rock and roll. By and large, the advent of Elvis and Fats Domino and those people on the charts — *that* was the beginning of rock and roll, and that was about 1957."

I didn't agree with her — I found the lines between rock and roll and what came before much blurrier than that, and, moreover, Elvis wasn't the beginning, he was just the guy mass audiences latched onto — but I didn't want to turn the interview into a semantics battle about the origins of rock and roll. "I think you fit into that demarcation line in an interesting way," I said. "You were influenced by older music, but you fit right in with rock and roll."

"The first time I saw the inside of a recording studio I was fourteen years old," she said. "I was making demonstration records for all the big publishers. When they had a song, they wanted me to sing it in the style of the particular artist that they hoped would do the song. So they would say, 'This song is called "Blah Blah Blah." Connie, give us some of that great Patti Page.' I'd do Patti Page. Next record: 'Come on, give us some of that old Rosemary Clooney sound.' 'Rosemary Clooney, you got it.' 'Connie, this one is for Kay Starr.' 'OK, you got it.' I didn't have a style of my own. I hated 'Who's Sorry Now.' For a year and a half my father was saying, 'Sing this song. This song is going to make you a star.' I'd say, 'Daddy, the kids on *American Bandstand* will laugh me right off the show.' He said, 'Sister, if you don't record this hit, the only way you're going to get on *American Bandstand* is if you sit on top of the TV set.' I hated it so much that I didn't, for a change, try to imitate anybody else, I just sang it in my own natural voice. And that became my style. It was really a fluke."

I wanted to get into the issue of my love for her. "I've been listening to the box set that PolyGram did —"

"Oh, *that*," she said. "They put on all those ridiculous songs! Songs I refused to let them release twenty-five, thirty, thirty-five years ago."

I wasn't sure what she meant. The most ridiculous song I could think of was something called "Baby Roo," a bouncy love song about a fat boy. "Who's got a heart that's as big as a whale?" she sings. "Who draws a crowd when he steps on a scale?" "Like 'Baby Roo?'" I asked.

She looked offended. " 'Baby Roo' was

a Number One hit in Japan and Italy," she said. "I mean stuff that *really* stinks. And as a result, there is no anthology of my music in the stores that is totally representative of what I've done." She grabbed her neck suddenly. "My throat is killing me. I'm going to go take something for it. Turn your machine off." She got up, and returned a few moments later sucking on something.

"So," she continued, "if an anthology was going to be put out, they should have followed the pattern of a German company, Bear Family Records. Terry!" she hollered.

Terry appeared at her elbow.

"Can you bring me the German Bear Family albums that I can show Karen?" Connie asked.

Terry ran off, and reappeared with three box sets containing up to ten CDs each. There was one box set of fifties material, one from the early sixties, and a third from the late sixties. Connie's eyes sparkled. She picked up the fifties box set and caressed it. "They even have me singing 'Daddy's Little Girl' on the *Arthur Godfrey Show* with my accordion when I was eleven," she said. "They accompany each one with photos and candids — I mean, some of these pictures I've never seen before." She opened a booklet, and pored over the photos. " 'With Troy

Donahue backstage during rehearsal . . .'"

I had mightily coveted these box sets. They listed for close to three hundred bucks each. Saliva formed in my mouth. I picked one up and flipped it over and began scanning the titles. When I glanced up, Connie and Terry were both looking at me funny. Like a nabbed thief, I handed the package back to Terry, and she whisked the box sets away.

"You know, Karen," Connie said, "there's an outstanding article that was written about me. It would take me three hours to go over all the information with you."

"Was it a *Goldmine* piece?" I asked. *Goldmine* is a record collectors' journal. Each issue features a career retrospective story with an extensive interview and discography.

"*Goldmine*, yes," she said. "I'm surprised you haven't seen it. Turn off your little machine. *Terry!*"

Terry trotted back into the room. Connie instructed her to make a photocopy of the *Goldmine* article, and Terry returned with a fat sheath of 11 x 17 paper. "It's such an extensive piece, like twelve pages long," Connie said. "Karen, anything you want to know after you've read *Goldmine*, you can call and ask me over the phone." Then she stood up and left the room.

I stared at the *Goldmine* cover picture. It was a vintage shot of Connie wearing a smocked blue dress. Miniature Gold records dangled from a charm bracelet on her wrist. She was smiling that tight, frozen smile. One hand held a spiky set of kitchen shears, and the other held a paper heart that she had presumably just cut out. Her lengthy manicured nails ripped the air like talons. The picture depressed me. I couldn't help identifying with the heart, shorn and pierced by this cheerful demon. And as I stared, it slowly dawned on me that Connie thought the interview was over. She was finished with me. It was time for me to go back to New Jersey. I had been at the house for under half an hour.

At that moment Terry showed up and tried to pry me off the couch. And that's when I lost it. I don't remember exactly what I said, but smoke billowed from my ears and hot lava bubbled from my eye sockets. I communicated to Terry that she would have a basket case on her hands if she didn't fetch her boss immediately.

Terry looked at me with surprise and, I think, a flicker of respect. She was clearly familiar with the procedure for handling women on the edge. She patted me soothingly, eased me back onto the couch, and promised to bring Connie back.

Connie sat down again, and we resumed the interview as if nothing had happened. "Did you prefer singing big-band stuff?" I said.

She nodded. "I liked the challenge. Dick Wess was a great arranger. He did —"

"A lot of Bobby Darin's hits," I finished.

"That's right," Connie said. "Bobby called me and said, 'I'm sending you my new album, *That's All*. Listen to this arranger.' And so I used Dick Wess after that." A phone rang so loudly it could have been amplified through the house on a P.A. Terry crept in and whispered in Connie's ear. "Excuse me," Connie said, and went to take the call. She came back a moment later and said it was her friend Ronnie, a Bobby Darin impersonator. "He has *BD* written on his robes, and he does this show — a very, very good show. He's very talented. He does Bobby from beginning to end, he knows everything Bobby recorded." Ronnie wanted to drop by. "He said, 'I'm in the neighborhood.'" Connie scrunched up her face girlishly and leaned toward me. "It would take him forty-five minutes from where he lives to be in this neighborhood! Nobody comes to Parkland unless they know where they're going."

"It's right when we were talking about

315

Bobby, too," I said.

She giggled. "This is so funny, Karen, that Ronnie is 'in the neighborhood.' I mean, you come up here to see *cows?* Horses? A couple of stray alligators were found last week on a neighbor's lawn. And they were telling everybody, 'Take your children and keep them in the house while we wrap up these alligators.' That's how funny 'I was just in the neighborhood' sounds. Nobody ever comes here. Originally I wanted to live in Boca. I told my real estate agent that I wanted to live in Boca, and he said OK. I didn't really know where we were going. The first house I saw, I said, 'I like it, I'm going to take it.' He said, 'Wait a minute, look at other houses first.' I wasn't paying attention to directions. I'm a lousy driver and terrible with directions. He said, 'There's another house I'd like you to see, and you might like it better.' So he drove and we were talking and finally we got up to this house, and as soon as we saw it I said, 'This is the house I want. I don't want to see any other house.' I didn't realize I was thirty minutes away from Boca! I had no idea I was this far west. I never looked at a map to see where Parkland was. So here I am."

I asked when she moved in. "About six months ago," she said. "But I had an interior designer come in, and she took almost a year to do it. When I was able to be comfortable in it — when the couches were in and the TV was in and my bedroom was finished — then I moved in and let them work around me."

"This must be the first time in your life that you haven't had a house in New Jersey," I said. "Do you ever miss it?"

"Not even a little bit," she said. "I go into a cold sweat when I don't see palm trees."

Ida puttered around the kitchen. "She looks great," I whispered.

"Doesn't she?" Connie whispered back. "She's eighty-seven years old."

"Was she born in this country?"

"There were sixteen children, and fifteen were born in Italy. My mother was the last one, and she was born here."

Things were warming up. I was so relieved. "Connie, I know you were working very hard on your music from a very young age. How did you get so driven to pursue your goal?"

"They say that if you want to be a success, find the work that's play, and then play very hard," she said. "That's what I was doing. I was playing. If I didn't have a show to do, I was depressed. I wanted all the time to be working and playing. I was driven, but nobody was driving me to do this. I was driven in a happy way. My father would say, 'Take it easy already. Even a train stops.'"

"A lot of articles from that time portrayed you with a sort of wistfulness," I said. "Like, 'She's got success, but —'"

"But she's not happy," she finished.

"Right. Or, 'She's not dating.'"

Connie snorted. "They should have a dime for every date I had. And not only dates in the United States, but dates with the top singer in Germany, the top singer in Italy, the top singer in France. I was dating all the swingers of the world. And then the *Photoplay* magazines and the fan magazines would have these arranged dates. They would set up these ridiculous liaisons for me. One of the first was with Tony Perkins. His office called my office and we made an appointment to meet in Central Park. Tony showed up with his manager and a photographer, and I showed up with my manager and my father — what else is new. They took a thousand pictures of us in twelve minutes. Tony and I shook hands, we wished each other luck in our careers, and the next time I saw the guy was in *Psycho*.

"That was the tip of the iceberg. It was George Hamilton, it was Edd 'Kookie' Byrnes, it was Troy Donahue — I could go on and on with these fake romances and fake dates. But there was never anything serious. I was going to be a virgin when I got married, there was no question about it, and I told them that right off the bat."

Bingo.

"Then you'd pick up another fan magazine and it would say, 'Poor Connie Francis. She doesn't date, she doesn't go out,'" she continued. "There were so many stories like that: 'Connie's married to her business, it's all work, work, work,' this kind of stuff. No, I would say that they were the most fun days of my life. I could never have that again, for so many reasons. They were really great, fun-filled days. My manager's wife said, 'You've got to have a fur coat.' I said, 'I don't like fur coats, I don't want to wear a fur coat.' 'But you have to have an image, you have to have a fur coat.' So reluctantly I let the furrier in one afternoon. And I bought a leopard, a Tourmaline mink, and an ermine floor-length coat — *that day.* Then my friend Charlotte would say, 'Enough already with the Monet jewelry! You have to have the real thing.' So we'd go shopping. I saw a beautiful fourteen-carat emerald diamond ring. I said, 'Oh, that's nice.' She said, 'Tonight at the Copa, when you're doing your show, have a terrible headache through the whole show. Brush your hands across your forehead and show that ring.'

"It was like living a Cinderella world until I got married for the first time. Every marriage was a disaster, but the first time that I got married the real world set in. Because he was an alcoholic and he was a wife-abuser. He hit me twice really badly. The first time I went home and said to my mother and father, 'I'm leaving him. Just look at me.' My father and mother said, 'Connie, you're a good Catholic girl. You've been married two months. How can you possibly get a divorce? You'll lose every Catholic fan in the United States.' My mother said, 'They'll take away your Entertainer of the Year award from Seton Hall University.' I said, 'Oh, Ma, do me a favor. You get beat up.' The second time it happened, that was the end of the relationship. Frankly, I see no humor at all in the subject of marriage, believe me. And I vow that I will never get married again, unless of course Al Pacino decides to accept my proposal."

"Was the sex disappointing when you got married?" I asked.

"No, that was the best part," she said. "But that didn't even last a week, because I saw what kind of a man he was. Sex can only be as good in bed as it is out of bed."

Ida had worked her way toward the living room. She was poking around the book-shelves as if she were looking for something, or maybe catching up on her dusting.

"You remind me of my nana," I called to her. My mother's mother.

"Oh, yeah?" Ida said with a wink. "Poor Nana."

She ambled toward the couch.

"Do you like living here?" I asked.

"No," Ida frowned.

"You don't?"

Her frown lengthened. "I don't like the weather. Never did."

Passive-aggressive and critical of her daughter — that reminded me of my nana, too. "You don't like Florida?" I asked again.

"All my friends are back home," she complained. "I have nobody here. Well, I have my niece here, thank God. She's young. She has a booth in one of the flea markets. She sells this kind of stuff — all expensive stuff. No junk."

Connie glared at her. Ida rolled her eyes and sashayed off.

When she was out of earshot, Connie resumed. "Sex is only as good in bed as it is out of bed. If you're having conflict and turmoil and your husband drinks a bottle of Jack Daniel's on his wedding night and you have to take the second bottle, which he's about to open, and crack it over a sink and break it, which is what happened to me —"

"Your wedding night?" I repeated, aghast.

"The second night," she said shiftily. "Now, that marriage had no shot at all. My father interfered terribly in my relationships before I got married. That's one of the reasons I got married, is to get my father off my back. The thing I did, which was totally my fault, was, if I wanted to hire a designer, an attorney, a physician, I would do more research than I did on any of the people I married. Hire a detective. Get his real background. Find out what all his past mistakes were. My first husband told me he'd been married once — he'd been married twice. There were a lot of things that I could have found out with one phone call. Is he a drinker? Yes. Is he a wife abuser? You can find that out through an investigator real easily."

"What did you like about him?" I asked.

"He was very handsome, which wasn't my first criterion," Connie said. "There had to be chemistry. I had known Dick for four years. He was the public relations director for the Sahara Hotel, and I started working the Sahara Hotel when I was twenty, twenty-one years old. So every time I came into town, we would have lunch and go see all the disc jockeys and go to the local newspapers and magazines. So I knew him, but in a superficial way. I didn't ever check into his private life. That was my mistake and my fault. I made all the wrong choices for all the wrong reasons. There's a book called *Loving Men for All the Right Reasons*. After I read it, I realized why I made so many mistakes. One of them was that, in a relationship you can't —"

A crash of dishware arose from the kitchen. "Who's that?" called Connie angrily.

Ida poked her head above a counter. "It's me," she said innocently.

Connie seethed. "I'm sorry, Karen," she said. "I'll tell you this story in a minute." She told me to follow her to her bedroom, where eavesdropping mothers were apparently not allowed.

We had barely gone two steps through the kitchen when a new commotion broke out. Ronnie arrived. He sailed into the kitchen, practically carried aloft by Terry and a second personal assistant of Connie's, who squealed over him as if he were a genuine idol — Darin himself alighting from heaven. Ida, en route to banishment, found an excuse to linger. Connie threw her arms around him.

Ronnie greeted me warmly, all charm. He did resemble the real Darin, with a round face and medium-brown sideswept hair. Ronnie stepped over to Ida and laid a kiss on her cheek. "Hello there, little girl," he cooed, as if this were the Copa.

Ida was still smarting from Connie's anger, but she managed an eye flutter and a wounded "Hi."

Ronnie eyeballed the current state of the renovation. "Well, the house is shaping up. It really looks great. I haven't been here since you moved the stuff in."

"And the bedroom —" Connie said.

"I didn't see it yet," said Ronnie.

"I'll show it to you," said Connie. "Come on in."

Oh, great, I thought.

We headed through the dining area, and Connie stopped to check on the progress of the carpet installation. Several workmen were in the process of lifting a heavyweight dining room table and chairs into position. A lead contractor stood to one side, holding a clipboard and coaching the movers on the exact placement of the furniture on the rug's complex pattern.

Connie surveyed the scene. "Oh, isn't that gorgeous," she said. "I think it looks gorgeous."

"Beautiful!" seconded Ronnie.

I was craning my neck, trying to see over the gallery of heads. I had fallen to the back of a rather large entourage. The lead workman beamed.

"Oh, I love it," Connie continued. "The only thing is, it's too close to the wall."

The lead workman's face fell. The movers stopped in their tracks. The lead workman consulted his clipboard, which apparently contained instructions from an interior designer. "According to Eli, it's supposed to be a foot away from the wall. And when you measure that —" He whipped out a tape measure and marked the distance between the edge of the rug and the wall. "Connie, it's actually got to go a little bit closer."

"It can go *closer?*" said Connie, displeased.

"If you want it to stay there, it can stay there," the lead workman placated.

"Terry!" Connie called. "Terry, next to my bed there's a drawing of the room that shows how the furniture is supposed to be placed on the rug." Terry sprinted off.

When she returned, Connie studied the drawing. A bead of sweat appeared on the lead workman's brow. "Personally, I think it's too close," he ventured.

"It's too close," Connie concluded.

The movers hoisted the table and chairs off the rug, and the lead workman got down on his hands and knees, finagling the rug an inch further from the wall.

He straightened up and examined the new

layout. "Right here, it's a decent amount away," he said.

"I wouldn't want it further away than that," Connie agreed.

The movers lugged the table and chairs back into position on the rug. "Oh, that looks great," Connie said. The movers exchanged relieved glances. Suddenly, concern flashed on Connie's face. "Can the chairs be pulled in and out without leaving the rug?"

"Absolutely," the lead workman said.

"Let me see," Connie said.

A subordinate pulled out a side chair, sat down and pulled the chair back to a comfortable seating position. "Oh, I see," Connie said. "I thought the chair was going to be outside. Okay."

"No, no, no," the lead workman said. "At no time will the chair be on the outside."

"Fine, fine." Connie marched onward. "Ronnie, where are you?" she called.

The entourage had thinned by the time we made it to the bedroom — just Connie, Ronnie, Terry, and me. But in the bedroom, we were joined by a housekeeper, who blasted a high-powered vacuum over the din of daytime television.

"Oh, this is beautiful, Connie!" Ronnie yelled over the noise. "Wow, it really turned out great!"

"It's not easy being a princess," Connie said, giggling.

The walls were flanked with rows of custom armoires. Ronnie ran his hands over one of them. "These units are huge!" he said. "This is a big, big room. It seems cozy now."

I had never seen so much built-in closet space. "Are your show clothes in these?" I asked naively.

"Oh, no," said Connie. "They're in the garage."

Ronnie burst out laughing. "She needs a house just for show clothes," he said. He peered around the room. "I like the venetian blinds. They really softened things up."

My attention had shifted to the bed. It was a massive, canopied affair dressed in high feminine style: multiple shammed pillows, layers of floral quilts, sheets in mauve and seafoam green. It was unmade. Behind the bed, a picture window overlooked the street, the dug-up field, and the distant, rain-shrouded Everglades.

"The bed is so pretty, too," I murmured.

"It's, you know, Deco," said Connie.

Terry called Connie aside. Ronnie and I drifted together. He told me that he had been Connie's personal assistant before Terry. "I've known her all my life," he said. "My parents lived across the street from Connie's parents in Newark. But we've been close about fifteen years now. I've been through the good, the bad, and the ugly."

The vacuum cut off, and Connie shooed the housekeeper out of the room so we could talk without distractions. Ronnie gave me a wink, like, *Batter up*. Then he and Terry filed out.

Connie fluffed a few pillows and flopped on the bed. "Have a seat, Karen," she said, snuggling into a quilt.

I knew instinctively that this was it. The big moment had come. We were finally alone together. Connie patted a spot on the bed next to her, a naked patch of mauve fitted sheet. Wow. It was a little *too* perfect. She wanted me in bed with her. Talk about literal. My mind flickered back to the memory that had come to me while I was driving that morning. What was really going on? What game was I playing? What game was she playing?

Deep inside I knew that something was really, really off about this whole scenario. My insane fixation, my misdirected passion, were signs of my own mental instability. But then I brusquely pushed all thoughts of subtext out of my mind. I told myself that what I really wanted from Connie was quite innocent: I wanted a connection. She seemed to like me, after all; I could ask her anything. I wanted a revelation that I could take away with me and hold dear. I wanted that thrill of fake love — and maybe that was fine. I kicked off my shoes and climbed in bed with her.

My mind became almost greedy. Surely a revelation was owed to me. I deserved it. "Connie," I said tenderly, "you were working before women's lib, before culture and society changed. I think what you achieved is significant, because women weren't encouraged to work. They were supposed to marry and have children."

Her expression became thoughtful and earnest, as if she were moved by the sincerity of my sentiment. "We're fifty-two percent of the population," she said. "We're fifty-three percent of the workforce. It's a whole different story now. I'm so glad they're bringing out tough harassment laws, because so many women have been victims. You know, I wasn't going to sue Howard Johnson's. It wasn't a thing I did for money. To expose my personal life, and the events of that night — I said, 'I'm not putting Joe through this,' which was my husband. 'I'm not putting myself through this, I'm not going to expose our sex life.' And then six months after the rape, our lawyer, who was also a good, good friend, went in with a court order, and examined a percentage of the rooms there with an engineer, a photographer, and litigators from Howard Johnson's. They found that in fifty percent of the rooms that they examined, when the balcony door was in a locked position, with a little jiggling it could be opened from the outside. And the slash in the screen door of my window was still there, and the lock had never been fixed. I thought of all of the women who had stayed in that place since then, and I got so riled up about it. I was so angry that I said, 'Okay, go ahead, sue.' That was a big deal. It made a big difference. A lot of women who had been vacillating about whether or not they should pursue a rapist or go to court or to the police — it gave them courage to do it. So I think it was very important."

"I think it was very brave of you," I said. "I know it took a tremendous toll."

"I was such a hermit after that," she said. "When I walked into the courtroom that first day, there were lines of people asking for autographs, and it was alien for me. It was alien for me to do the thing I'd done my whole life, and that was to be surrounded by people and smile at them. It was just so strange all of a sudden. And then the judge barred the press from the courtroom for a couple of days, but the ACLU and the New York Press Club got his decision overturned. So it was a carnival, it really was. It eroded my marriage really badly."

"Look at the way the media is now," I said. "Now you'd expect it to be a carnival, a celebrity situation like that. But back then, who would have known?"

Her eyes were brown and unbearably soft. "No Hollywood writer could dream it up, Karen," she said. "Some of the things that occurred . . . And my experiences in mental institutions. I was in the hospital having electroshock treatments for depression. I got out and I felt a little better from them. They were very helpful to me. That was in 1988. In '89, my friends and I went to see Wayne Newton appearing during the Orange Bowl Parade. My friend Beverly said, 'You have to be on that stage.' So March 6, 1989, I went out and did my show after four years of not performing, just being in mental institutions — in and out and in and out and in and out. I haven't had any problems, thank God, since 1991. I haven't had any hospitalizations. And I've been fine. I've been very even, which is not even a part of my personality to begin with. It's either all or nothing at all. I feel great. Nothing really can get me that angry or that excited. I don't know if that's good or not. It's great to be on a high, but it's better being sane."

"Have you got medication that helps you?"

"I take lithium," she said. "And I've got my assistant, Terry. She was a fan. I was appearing at the Garden State Arts Center in New Jersey, and she came with her son, Allen. She said her favorite singers were Elvis and myself. And then Terry and I became very close, and when I was in the hospital she would come to visit me every day with Allen. After I came out of the hospital in '91, I asked her to be my secretary, and she was so good that secretary didn't fit any more and I call her my assistant. Terry is really great, because she can say, 'You're overdoing it, you're talking too much, you're buying too many things'. She can recognize all the signs of manic depression. She has sat with me at every meeting with my psychiatrist, because I'll ask her, 'How did it happen, what is your opinion,' that kind of thing. That's how close we are."

I moved in a little closer. "Sometimes, in your autobiography, it sounds like your dad didn't encourage you enough. Or you wanted his approval and never quite had it."

"Exactly," she said. "It was always very important to me what Daddy thought of a record, or what Daddy thought of something I wore, or what Daddy thought of anything that was important. My father was a very talented, very smart man. He would read the newspapers from cover to cover every day. He knew about any political subject, any scientific subject. If an issue came up in the news — like, say, the Iranian hostages — I would say, 'What is this all about, Daddy?' And in one or two sentences he would give me the whole picture. He had a fabulous mind. He only went through fifth or sixth grade, and then he had to quit and skin pigs and split rails on the railroad, because there were thirteen children in his family and they lived in two rooms — a real shack on Astor Street in Newark. If he had had the benefit of a college education, his life would have been completely different. I don't think he would have been as forceful and as strict with me. I have a lot of regrets in my life. There were a lot of mistakes, but one of the biggest ones was allowing my father to exert as much influence over my personal life."

My thoughts flashed, for some reason, to my mother: my strained relationship with her, the push and pull of love and resentment. Connie was opening herself to me; I wanted to open myself to her. We would confide in one another, relieve our burdens, share our pain. This was it: the moment I'd been waiting for.

"I know just how you feel," I said softly.

Connie was looking at me intensely, her eyes scanning my face. She could see through me; she knew how I felt, too.

"My mother —" I began.

She leaned close to me, her hand almost touching mine on the sheets. And then, before I could finish the thought, she spoke.

"I'd love to do your hair and makeup," she said.

What? I mustn't have heard right. This wasn't how it was supposed to be. *I'd love to do your hair and makeup.* What was she talking about? Was she criticizing me? I never wear makeup. A few early experiments with Maybelline frosted blue eyeshadow in high school, and then I gave up. My mom never wore it either, so she never taught me. And my hair — I had rushed out the door this morning, so preoccupied — and the rain —

My hands self-consciously went to my head, trying to smooth flyaways. I felt so small. She had found me lacking in some way; now it seemed that she didn't like me. "I have very frizzy hair today," I said, my voice whispery with shame. "It's not even brushed."

Connie leaned back and pursed her lips in

a tsking way. "First of all, you can't go gray, because you're too young. You've got to keep your hair colored, definitely. *Definitely.* You know, even when I'm in my coffin I don't want gray hair."

I looked at her in shock. So it was my premature gray she was carping about! Another hand-me-down from my mother — we had both started going gray at thirty. The whole time I was growing up, my mother used to talk about coloring her hair, and my brother and I would always forbid it. We loved her gray hair, we thought it was cool. I would never color my hair! It was my legacy. I couldn't believe Connie was lecturing me about it.

"It's not a question of too young or too old," she chattered on. "It's that your face is so absolutely great. I know I could do a job and you'd look like a different person with makeup. You'd look great. You have such good features! I wish there were time today, because I love to do that with people."

My fractured mind was trying to put a positive spin on this. Okay, she'd do a job on me and I'd look like a total nightmare, but it would make good copy for the book. Before I could formulate a reply, Terry knocked on the door.

"Come in!" shouted Connie gaily.

"Girls, I hate to rush you," Terry said, "but Connie, you have to have that conference call soon."

"Okay, okay!" She couldn't have been more overjoyed if she were getting out of prison. "Karen, if you have any questions, you can record it on the phone. You do have one of those attachments, don't you?"

The phone rang. Terry hustled me out of the room. I tried to resist. "But —"

Connie was already yakking it up with someone else.

"It's a very hectic day," said Terry firmly, and the door slammed shut behind me.

I had lost it with Terry once already. My chips were spent. "But, but!" I wailed. "She wanted to do my hair and makeup!"

"There just isn't time," she said.

I was desperate. Even my fake love hadn't been consummated this time. My body throbbed with frustration. I couldn't leave. "Terry, please!"

Terry deposited me in the living room next to my work bag.

"What about tomorrow?" I begged. "I could change my plane ticket. Couldn't I come back for just a little while?"

She gave me a look, as if *she* might lose it. "Tomorrow's just as busy," she said. "I'm sorry." And she disappeared.

Tears were springing to my eyes. Embarrassed over the scene I was making, I ran through the kitchen and into the foyer, past the not-yet-hung Gold and Platinum records, and found the door to the guest bathroom. With my eyes almost blinded, I slammed the door and flipped on the light.

Then I sat on the toilet and just sobbed. It was the little nervous breakdown I'd been building up to for so long. My limbs quaked, my breath heaved. I could hear the vacuum cleaner running in the hallway nearby. Good, I thought through my stupor. No one will hear me.

I was wrung out. I didn't have a shred of dignity left. After a few minutes, the sobbing started to work itself out. My breathing calmed. I took a fistful of tissues and wiped my eyes. Then I stood up, turned on the faucet, leaned down, and splashed some water on my face.

With my eyes squeezed shut I felt for a towel. Then I dried off my face, straightened up, and looked in the mirror.

What I saw was the same face I always saw. Brown hair (turning gray), brown eyes, long chin. I felt the same slight sense of dismay I always felt looking at myself, as if the good features — the warmth in my eyes, the pleasant curve of my mouth — might have added up to real prettiness if only a few things had been different: if my cheekbones had been more distinct, or my eyes not so close together, or the skin around my jaw not so chubby. The crying, the flushed color, the puffiness made the effect that much worse. As I beheld myself and experienced that familiar disappointment, something else came to the surface, an emotion I lived with every day but was loathe to acknowledge: a longing to be loved. Fulfilling that longing was my endless quest. And my inability to see and understand it was taking me on some awfully strange detours.

In that moment I came, at last, to an agonizing awareness of what this whole strange journey had been about. I understood why this music had drawn me in. I loved it because I related to it. Not because it was kitschy or corny — that was just a way to express interest without committing myself. And not even because it was my parents' music, although that was certainly a part of it. I loved it because it was mine. The pop music of the fifties had called out to me, playing notes in my unconscious mind, resonating within me. It pinpointed feelings that had no outlet, desires I was too embarrassed to admit to, fantasies that rumbled around in me despite my best efforts to suppress them. This is pop music at its finest; this is its artistry. Its pull is irrational, unideological, inexplicable. Pop music lays its finger on our breast; we can't see it but we feel it, and our blood starts pumping a little faster and our toes wiggle and we respond, without knowing why. It can be artless in every sense of technique and skill, it can *suck* in all the logical ways, but if that mystical element of soul has gone into it, something in us responds.

My life to that point had been a ballad of repression. I had tried for over a decade, as I matured and learned rock history, to be someone else — to hear music the way the critics I admired heard it, and to respond as they had responded. But it had never quite worked. What I heard and how I felt when I listened to music were different from what they had heard and felt, from the time I was fourteen and drowning my jilted sorrow in Bruce Springsteen, or from even further back, hurling myself at age nine upon the altar of Morris Albert's "Feelings." I could intellectualize music until the cows came home, I could revere Sonic Youth for their miasmic, psychedelic grind, but at the end of the day it was always a brokenhearted love song that got me in the gut. Springsteen and his highway-loner epics had rescued me after my first breakup, and from that moment on I was hooked. Pop music became my preferred partner. It was safer, lovelier, and more perfect than any romance I could drum up on my own.

We had a good, long run, pop music and me. Throughout my twenties, I flourished professionally as a rock critic. I kept writing for bigger and bigger publications, for more and more money. I was hard-working, motivated, in demand. But in order to protect my career, there was one thing I had to avoid at all costs, and that was sex. I could get close to musicians, I could ride around on the bus, even sleep in those weird, lateral mobile bunks. I could get drunk in bars and backstages, I could elicit people's innermost secrets and dreams and sometimes share my own, I could stand in the wings while great performers played, but I told myself I must never, ever cross that line into physical contact. Otherwise I would become the dreaded *g* word: a groupie. I avoided the *g* word with a studiousness bordering on paranoia. If I got saddled with the *g* word, no one would ever take me seriously again. I was acutely conscious of that. As a woman writing about rock and roll, I rarely felt that opportunities weren't open to me because of my gender. But I did feel the inequality of the *g* word, a pitfall that would never apply to a straight white male writer. So I played the game on male terms, trying to conduct myself without acknowledging the squishy stuff. I tried to write precisely and analytically. I tried to be objective and discern good music from bad.

This weird habit of staying above it all spilled over into my personal life. I tried, apart from work, to date normal people, and once or twice a year I'd embark on a relationship with some nice non-musician, albeit someone who usually shared my rabid fandom (a manager, a record company guy, a semi-famous musician's friend). But I was ill at ease in relationships. Consciously or not, I knew that the hurts associated with real intimacy were even worse than the dreamy emptiness following a spectacular interview. And sex, even with a non-musician, felt risky to me. The most important value my mother had handed down to me — the brick at the foundation of fifties values — was to avoid sex. She was incredibly successful at instilling in me a fear of sex. *Don't sleep with him.* I can remember her instructing me when I was seventeen and had a new serious boyfriend: *Once you sleep with them, there's nothing left for them to pursue.* She taught me above all to contain and protect my sexuality, because once I gave that away a guy would dump me by the side of the road like a used rag, undesirable to the next happy hunter, too. Granted, I didn't always follow her advice. I had sex on occasion, and I wildly enjoyed it, but I never got over that feeling of danger, that fear of recklessly spending what I had, that sense that ruin lurked just around the corner. So I had sex extremely judiciously and discreetly. The no's far outnumbered the yeses, and there were plenty of times that I got right to the brink (shades of being fourteen with Jeff) and then zipped up my pants and went home.

And, as I said, never, ever with a musician I interviewed. That was my ultimate taboo. But for all my obsessive caution, what had happened? I was a groupie in every sense but sex. I was a just-say-no Pamela Des Barres. I'd cried on Jon Bon Jovi's shoulder, zoomed around on Dwight Yoakam's Harley, delicately held out my cheek for Johnny Depp's kiss, and then wound up in bed alone, again and again. Rock and roll, that alleged liberator, was the vehicle for my repression. The codes and aphorisms of rock music — sex, drugs, indulgence, freedom, revolution — never applied to me. From where I stood, Woodstock-generation values were just snake oil, and I wasn't buying it.

Until my work on the book, I'd had no frame of reference for understanding any of this. I had no models for my behavior, no female rock journalists who'd laid out the pitfalls in a tell-all memoir. But meeting these fifties singers — bonding with Patti Page and Georgia Gibbs, crushing on Pat Boone and Fabian, feeling for Tommy Sands, and now cracking up over Connie — had given me perspective. There in the bathroom, I understood my interview rigamarole in a new light. I thrived in interviews because I knew I'd never have to sustain anything or cope with the inevitable ups and downs that occur in real relationships. I soared on the emotions of pop music, because it was a way to feel without danger. In pop music, especially the pop music of the fifties, love and romance remained unsullied, abstract, uncomplicated. It's so much easier to experience love that way. One can connect with a song, and never have to worry about that song connecting back.

I realized that writing about music, for me, was basically a way to avoid myself, and the emptiness I encountered when I looked in the mirror. It had always been a point of pride with me: I was all about the music. I could celebrate a song, celebrate a celebrity, and never have to use the word *I* if I didn't want to. I could live vicariously through the accomplishments of others, and never be forced to confront my own failings. I could ignore my inability to connect, live a bizarre sort of semi-chastity. Eventually, though, I became unsatisfied living that way. And right around that same time, I met Dave. Finally I found someone that I could risk being with — someone who wouldn't hurt me. And it was such a relief. We had a great time together, we acted irresponsibly, and, yay, I was getting properly laid, without guilt. But then what happened? My mother, my very own George Franconero and Jack Rael and Bob Marcucci, did everything she could to stop me. She punished me for having a relationship; she made me feel I had to choose her or my husband. But I soldiered on, exploring real love for the first time.

Amazingly, once I was away from my mother, I gave myself permission to look in the dark, off-limits corners of my own mind. I looked at my relationship with pop music for the first time. I wanted to cop to the wounded little girl inside. I wanted to acknowledge those seemingly inappropriate feelings from that botched, drunken, late-night interview-romance back in 1992; even more, I wanted to write about them. Because this was the heart of what had brought me to pop music. I wanted to bring that part of myself into the light.

Standing in the bathroom, I splashed my face with water one last time, dried myself off, and straightened up again. I looked around Connie's magical Italian princess bathroom, feeling purged and miraculously unburdened. Then I turned the knob and opened the door. What a beautiful irony, I thought. I've spent my entire adult life in the chains of rock and roll, and now this repressed, uptight music has set me free.

The living room was empty. As I walked toward the couch, I happened to look through the sliding glass doors toward the back patio. Yet another workman was out there. A pool guy. He lumbered around, then stopped and picked up a garden hose. A tiny spurt of water trickled out. He wore a satisfied expression, like, Yeah, I'm on the payroll and doing absolutely nothing. Something about him cheered me up even more. He wasn't letting the craziness of the universe get to him. He was poking around, doing his own thing. I laughed a little. Then he turned in my direction, and caught my eye through the glass. We smiled at each other, and waved.

As I gathered up my things, Ronnie came back into the living room. "How'd it go?" he said.

I shrugged. "Not so good," I said cheerfully. "But that's okay."

He sat down next to me on the couch, and his eyes had a faraway look. "I remember seeing her when *Follow the Boys* was released," he said. "She came to the Loews State Theatre in Newark. They showed her movie, and then she came running down the aisle, and it was like, wooowww! The place just went bananas." He shook his head. "If she was healthy — I always tell her that. 'Connie, if you had your health, nothing could have stopped you.' Because if you look at her past, you can see. She was a vibrant little thing who knew what she wanted and how to get it. If she didn't get sick, she would be Streisand. Or competing with her."

I was touched by his insight. A question occurred to me. It wasn't the exact question I had been about to ask Connie on the bed, but it was related — maybe even more to the point. "Do you think her dad wanted what was best for her?"

Ronnie looked startled. "Are you kidding?" he said. "Her father loved her."

Somehow that was all I wanted to hear. I shook Ronnie's hand.

"Good luck with your book," he said, with another wink.

"Thanks," I said. And then, with my bag

over my shoulder and my head up, I walked out into the rain, got into my little rental car, and drove away.

Afterword

March 2005

Seven years ago, when I started work on this book, if someone had remarked to me, "The music of the fifties is rife with undercurrents of sexual anxiety," I would have said, "Well, yeah, duh." I mean, everyone knows that fifties culture was all about the suppression of sex. The stiff skirts. The starched smiles. The lacquered hairdos and the knotted neckties. A single hair springing uncontrollably out of place could be a telltale sign of an id run amok. Then rock and roll came along, sexuality reared its head in popular culture, and everyone finally loosened up . . . the familiar story. What I wouldn't have believed was the notion that four decades later, this anxiety was alive and well — in *me*. I assumed I had benefited from cultural changes. Come on — what about the sixties? Sexual freedom, social revolution. What about the seventies? Marijuana, long-haired girls in skin-tight bellbottoms. So much had come to pass since those repressive fifties, so much that affected me personally: women's liberation, feminism, and even, when I think of my mother, the right to divorce and the idea that women deserve personal fulfillment, even at the cost of the nuclear family. From the time I was in my teens, my mother had trained me to be independent, self-sufficient, professionally ambitious. Me, repressed? Pshaw!

And yet, inside I was buttoned up tighter than a debutante with an 8 p.m. curfew. A part of me believed all that garbage my mom taught me: that dressing provocatively was bad, that drawing attention to my own sexuality was asking for trouble, that having sex with too many people would ultimately land me, husbandless and shamed, in a nunnery. And I don't think I'm alone. On the surface, popular culture seems more permissive than ever: reality TV is a roulette wheel of deadly sins, porn-star memoirs make the best-seller list, and a former teen-pop star like Britney Spears, marketed just a season or two ago to prepubescent girls, mock-humps a male dancer onstage. But the messages are mixed. Do we relish Paris Hilton for her bodacious nonchalance, or burn her in hell for her Internet sex video? And if we're all so sexually liberated, why are celebrity weddings and actress moms the biggest things in tabloids? *Wife* and *mother* are apparently the most plumb offscreen roles a glamorous

woman can aspire to. The cheerful slutti-
ness of pop culture is matched only by its
gagworthy Disneyfication. Whose mind *isn't*
a confused swirl of conflicting images and
shaky moral boundaries?

I think it's actually a little dangerous to
place too much stock in what the media tells
us about ourselves. Out there in red-state
America, media images carry less weight
than we coastal snobs think they do. I think
a lot of women grow up, go to church, read
the Bible, date, get married, start a family,
and hold down a part-time job to make ends
meet; their choices are not that complicated.
People are still careful about sex. The sixties
didn't lead to rampant fucking in the streets,
Madonna videos notwithstanding. The fifties
may have cast puritanism in a particularly
prim, perky light, but postwar Americans
didn't invent sexual repression — and the
baby boomers who followed them didn't kill
it, either. That puritanical ethic continues
to manifest itself, whether in anti-abortion
rallies or no-gay-marriage referendums. One
thing I learned during the writing of this
book is that the fifties didn't have a lock
on the idealization of marriage. Over the
past several years I've had to confront my
own high expectations, and reconcile my romantic fantasies with the day-to-day reality

of making a long-term relationship work. I thought that because I married for love, because I waited until I was thirty to tie the knot, and because I'd learned firsthand from my mother's mistakes, I'd have a great marriage and cruise through life on a bed of sexual fulfillment and romantic bliss. Not the case. Dave and I have simmering, weeks-long arguments over the other person's way of hanging up a coat. In nine years of marriage, there have been plenty of times when the thought has occurred to me, If I weren't married to this nightmare, I'd be so out of here. Again, I don't think I'm alone. On Valentine's Day 2005, the *New York Times* ran dueling Op-Ed pieces about love. The first suggested that, culturally speaking, it's a relatively new idea — and perhaps a mistaken one — for partners to look for passion in marriage; a mere two hundred years ago, folks were wise enough to realize it was a contract about property. The second pointed out that the new Supermom and Superdad syndrome — attachment parenting, family beds, putting the children first — is draining intimacy from marriage, and pressuring couples to remain in flawed relationships out of a desire to protect their kids; these young parents lived through *their* parents' divorces, and can't bear to inflict it on another generation. Stay tuned for the postwar years all over again, where spouses bicker into their nineties. I'm not sure which trauma is worse.

And thinking about it all, I feel such warmth and respect for the fifties singers I interviewed. In the music of Connie Francis, Patti Page, Pat Boone, and the rest, these subterranean wishes and dreams rose right to the surface, and the stickiness and complexity of sex sank without a trace. Betrothal solved everything. Love would endure forever, unchanging, unimpeded, a Platonic ideal, an impervious force. These singers sounded so sure of themselves. I envy that conviction — it's what we've lost. In the past four and a half decades, plenty of singers have hawked eternal love, from Barry Manilow to Michael Bolton, from Whitney Houston to Celine Dion, from the Bee Gees to Billy Joel. New generations of teen idols have come and gone: Donny Osmond and Shawn Cassidy, Debbie Gibson and Tiffany, Britney Spears and N'Sync. But these come-latelys all feel half-baked to me. That combination of rock energy and pop ideals, that peculiar sense of junior adults dressed in gowns and tuxedos, that strange, sexless sophistication, hasn't existed since Tommy Sands and Connie Francis conjured that world in their songs. Listeners and musicians alike are too informed now, too ambivalent, too self-conscious to re-create what the fifties projected. The fifties offered a particular bliss of ignorance, and we can't have that back.

By the time this book went to press it had been several years since my interviews with the singers, so I looked in to see how everybody was doing.

When I called Patti Page to see what she'd been up to, she quipped, "More of the same." That was just her being modest. She's actually kept up a busy recording schedule, releasing four new albums since 1998. *Live at Carnegie Hall* won a Grammy Award in 1999 for Best Traditional Pop Vocal performance; *Brand New Tennessee Waltz* featured guest appearances by Emmylou Harris, Kathy Mattea, Trisha Yearwood, and Alison Krauss. She also recorded a new Christmas collection, *Sweet Sounds of Christmas*, and a children's album, *Child of Mine*, which included a new version of "Doggie in the Window," zested up with carnival organ and a shuffle rhythm. In 2004 she was inducted into the Casino Legends Hall of Fame; she also received the Licia Albanese-Puccini Foundation's Baccarat Award in recognition of achievement in the arts. She and husband Jerry still sell Patti Page Maple Products (although their syrup is now certified organic, and the old-timey graphics that I loved have been updated). They continue to spend summers at Hilltop Farm, although the property has been on the market for several years, with an asking price of $1.9 million. "We're not being too aggressive about it," Patti said cheerfully. Her next project: a gospel album, which she planned to record in Nashville in 2005. Visit www.misspattipage.com for more info.

Frankie Laine, now ninety-two, had a node removed from his vocal cords and no longer performs in public. But he continues to reshuffle and repackage his old material: CDs for sale on his Web site include *Together Again*, *My Buddy* (patriotic favorites), *She World* (women in song), and *Teach Me to Pray* (inspirational songs; liner notes by Pat Boone), all combining material from as early as the forties and as late as the nineties. A 2003 documentary bio, *An American Dreamer*, produced by Frankie's comanager Jimmy Marino, is available on DVD. Bear Family, the German reissue label, now has three box sets devoted to Frankie: *Rawhide* (nine CDs), *I Believe* (six CDs), and *That Lucky Old Sun* (six CDs) offer an astounding survey of his career. In 2000 the Western Music Association inducted him into its

Hall of Fame; he also received a Golden Boot award from the Motion Picture and Television Fund, a charity organization supporting performers and technicians who contributed to Hollywood Westerns. My favorite obscure Frankie nugget is a rock-and-roll song, "Don't Make My Baby Blue," that surfaced on a 2005 compilation called *Hearing Is Believing: The Jack Nitzsche Story 1962–1979*, released by Ace Records. Nitzsche, a stellar producer and arranger who worked with Phil Spector, Neil Young, and the Rolling Stones, recorded this unexpected teen-angst gem in 1963. With fuzz guitar blaring, tom-toms pounding, and chick singers ahhhing and ohhhing, Frankie unleashes a vocal that balances vulnerability and nonchalance, adolescent naiveté and hard-won maturity. It's exquisite. Frankie's Web site is www.frankielaine.com.

Pat Boone did not retire when he turned sixty-five, as he promised Shirley. He continues to record, tour, and irk rock's liberal establishment with his Ivy League–level conservatism. The year 2005 marked his fiftieth anniversary in show business, and he planned to whoop it up big. Charlie, his office assistant, told me that an album of R&B duets, intended as a genre-busting follow-up to Pat's 1997 heavy-metal album and featuring such guests as James Brown, Smokey Robinson, and Earth, Wind and Fire, was scheduled for release, as well as a country album, *Ready to Rock*, with appearances by former Eagle Timothy B. Schmit and famed session guitarist James Burton. A gospel collection, *Glory Train: The Lost Tapes*, was recorded in the seventies but never issued, and its release was now planned for 2006. A career-retrospective coffee-table book will offer photos of him with Joe DiMaggio, Mohammed Ali, Rocky Marciano, and every president since Truman. Pat's hipness factor got a boost when he became known as Ozzy Osbourne's beloved next-door neighbor on the MTV series *The Osbournes*. "People think Pat Boone's a nerd, and I must confess I was in that category for a while until I met him," slurred heavy-metal's most put-upon dad, and then praised Boone's endless tolerance for Osbourne family shenanigans. Still, Pat keeps the hard-right flames burning: a 2004 interview with the *Washington Times* bore the headline "Censorship in arts 'healthy,' Boone says." His patriotic post-9/11 album, *American Glory*, contained a new song, "Under God," that defended the use of those words in the Pledge of Allegiance. Those who want to learn more about his views can visit his Web site, www.patboone.com, and click on "Pat's Blog."

Georgia Gibbs is still trying to sell her life story. She has a 230-page "synopsis," based on her own transcribed remembrances, which she's trying to shop around Hollywood through someone she knows. Georgia described him as a well-known screenwriter. "He wrote a Tom Hanks movie," she bragged. "Tom Hanks is no chicken liver!" I asked her to tell me his name. "Oh, I'd rather not," she answered suspiciously. When I asked her what else she was up to, she snapped, "I'm saving it for my own book."

I tried several times to line up a follow-up interview with Tommy Sands, with no success. Alan Eichler, his publicist, said in a brief e-mail that Tommy now lives in the Toluca Lake area of Los Angeles and performs occasionally in clubs around the U.S., the U.K., and Japan; Eichler then stopped answering my messages. In 2000, a Web site called www.redhot-n-rockin.co.uk reviewed his show at the Townhouse in Enfield, England. The site said that Tommy had been mugged before leaving for England, and that the club had posted a disclaimer outside the door saying he was in poor health. Still, the Web site called it "a very good, entertaining night" and praised Tommy's versions of "Maybellene" and his own "The Worryin'

Kind." The TV movie about Tommy's life was never made.

Fabian married his third wife, Andrea Patrick, in the fall of 1998. Their wedding was featured in *People* magazine's "Weddings of the Year." The couple built a home in western Pennsylvania; they have twenty acres and a lake, where Fabian enjoys fishing. He continues to perform with Golden Boys Frankie Avalon and Bobby Rydell, and his latest tour package is called "The True Legends of Pop," featuring Bobby Vee, Tommy Roe, and the Chiffons. It was nice to chat again with Oscar Arslanian, his manager. We instantly re-bonded in our mutual adoration of the former idol, and I told him it was my life's dream to see Fabian perform with a punk rock band. "You know, it's funny you say that," Oscar replied. "You've heard of this band Supergrass? They're young guys, English guys. They called me and said they had a song they were releasing, and they wanted to use Fabian's image in the video. They sent me a rough cut, and I listened to the singer, and goddamn, he was like Fabian! The way he phrases — I couldn't believe it. He really reminded me of Fabe." For news, discography, picture sleeves, and a slew of old fan magazine covers, visit www.fabian-forte.com.

Connie Francis still lives in Parkland, and gives occasional concert performances. Her mother, Ida Franconero, died in early 2000 at the age of eighty-eight. The pop singer Gloria Estefan purchased the rights to *Who's Sorry Now?* and she and Connie are writing a film script together. According to Terry, they want Danny De Vito in the role of Connie's father and Olympia Dukakis as her mother; Gloria would star as Connie. In 2005, Connie recorded a disco version of "Who's Sorry Now" in five languages, and Terry said they were looking for a label to release it.

And me? I'm a mom now. My daughter, Loretta, was born at 3:51 a.m. on the morning of January 1, 2000 — a millennium baby. In the summer of 2004 we moved to a beautiful, rickety old house in upstate New York. There's a yard for Loretta, a workshop for Dave, and a writing room for me. After seventeen years spent within a mile or two of the Jersey Turnpike, I felt weird leaving my adoptive home state. I'm all for cows, cornfields, and cleaner air, but sometimes I yearn for the ugly, mythical landscape of my youthful dreams, the Springsteenish refineries and radio towers, the brown fields and blighted streets. It's like some industrial-wasteland version of *Out of Africa*, when Meryl Streep goes back to Europe at the end but can't forget her years struggling in Kenya. Do you think those Jersey highways miss the way Dave and I used to cruise along in a beat-up Japanese car, Dave at the wheel and my knees on the dash, a Sonic Youth song blaring on the stereo as pollution tinted the sunset a flaming red? Do you think there's a tread in the pavement that matches my tire, and does the sour summer rain pool in it in a slightly different way because of me?

As for my relationship with my mom, well, our fingers may be white from the effort, but we continue to cling to our love for each other. We've had more rough times since I started writing this book in 1998, squabbling over sins and slights both real and imagined, not the least of which was her discovery, through channels other than me, that my long-awaited book, which supposedly chronicled singers of the fifties, had another bizarre dark heroine: herself. I was on vacation at the Jersey Shore with my family — my new family, my Dave-Loretta family — when I got a call from her on my cell phone. My brother had told her about an item on the Internet that said the book was about her. She had no idea. Why hadn't I told her? I had betrayed her. I got that old, shivery feeling as we talked. I still freeze up inside when she yells at me. As she went on and on listing her grievances against me, I started to believe what she was saying. Then a rational thought thawed the ice in my brain. "Mom," I interrupted, "the book isn't about you. It's about me."

See, I worry a lot that my life and my marriage and my friendships and relationships aren't more perfect. I'm always noticing the flaws, and it makes me feel as though I've failed in some way, and I keep trying to make things better. I should get along better with my mom, I should try not to fight with my husband, I should be a better mother, yada yada. But lately it's dawned on me that maybe *this* is the true nature of love: the acknowledgment that the people in our lives aren't perfect, and we aren't perfect, and so we forgive and love onward. It's a small realization. Maybe it's even a platitude. But I know I wouldn't have come to it if I hadn't spent a year traipsing from place to place, meeting singers and talking to them and trying to figure them, and myself, out. It's almost as if, by spending so much time listening to and thinking about music that espouses perfect, impossible love, I was finally able to forge something viable for myself: an imperfect love, the kind that hurts and breaks but withstands the pain and survives.

So I'm moving on from fifties pop, and trying to live by this new concept. I hope it has a good sound track.

Bibliography

Anderson, John. "Rock 'n' Roll's Great White Buck." *Rolling Stone*, January 29, 1976: 26–31.

Brooks, Tim, and Earle Marsh. *The Complete Directory to Prime Time Network TV Shows 1946–Present.* 3rd ed. New York: Ballantine Books, 1985.

Bufwack, Mary A., and Robert K. Oermann. *Finding Her Voice: The Saga of Women in Country Music.* New York: Crown Publishers, 1993.

Clarke, Donald. *The Rise and Fall of Popular Music.* New York: St. Martin's Griffin, 1995.

DeCurtis, Anthony, and James Henke with Holly George-Warren. *The Rolling Stone Illustrated History of Rock & Roll.* New York: Random House, 1992.

Escott, Colin, ed. *All Roots Lead to Rock: Legends of Early Rock and Roll.* New York: Schirmer Books, 1999.

Ewen, David. *American Popular Songs: From*

the Revolutionary War to the Present. New York: Random House, 1966.

Francis, Connie. *Who's Sorry Now?* New York: St. Martin's Press, 1984.

Friedwald, Will. *Sinatra! The Song Is You: A Singer's Art.* New York: Scribner, 1995.

Gillett, Charlie. *The Sound of the City: The Rise of Rock and Roll.* 2nd ed. New York: Da Capo Press, 1996.

Guralnick, Peter. *Last Train to Memphis: The Rise of Elvis Presley.* Boston: Little, Brown and Company, 1994.

Harrison, Nigel. *Songwriters: A Biographical Dictionary with Discographies.* Jefferson, NC: McFarland & Company, 1998.

Jennings, Dean. "The Case of the Screaming Troubadour." *Saturday Evening Post,* December 11, 1954: 18+.

— — — . "Girl on the Glamour-Go-Round." *Saturday Evening Post,* September 23, 1961: 38+.

Laine, Frankie, and Joseph Laredo. *That Lucky Old Son: The Autobiography of Frankie Laine.* Ventura, Ca.: Pathfinder Publishing, 1993.

Shaw, Arnold. *The Rockin' '50s.* New York: Hawthorn Books, 1974.

Ward, Ed, Geoffrey Stokes, and Ken Tucker. *Rock of Ages*. New York: Rolling Stone Press/ Summit Books, 1986.

Whitburn, Joel. *The Billboard Pop Charts 1955–1959*. Menomonee Falls, Wis.: Record Research, 1992.

— — — . *Pop Memories 1894–1954: The History of American Popular Music.* Menomonee Falls, Wis.: Record Research, 1986.

— — — . *Top Pop Singles 1955–1993*. 7th ed. Menomonee Falls, Wis.: Record Research, 1994.

— — — . *Top R&B Singles 1942–1999*. 4th ed. Menomonee Falls, Wis.: Record Research, 2000.

Acknowledgments

Thank you to the singers who generously gave their time and reminiscences to this project: Patti Page, Frankie Laine, Pat Boone, Georgia Gibbs, Tommy Sands, Fabian Forte, and Connie Francis. Thank you, also, to those who granted interviews but whose stories didn't end up in the book: Paul Anka, Ann-Margret, Harry Belafonte, Teresa Brewer, James Darren, Shelley Fabares, Eydie Gorme, Tab Hunter, Joni James, Julius La Rosa, Steve Lawrence, Brenda Lee, Johnny Mathis, Neil Sedaka, Keely Smith, Kay Starr, Connie Stevens, Johnny Tillotson, and Bobby Vee.

Thank you to the publicists, agents, managers, assistants, and friends who facilitated the interviews: Michael Glynn, Eileen Cleary, Mary-Jo Coombs, Susan Clary, Alan Eichler, Oscar Arslanian, Steve Karas, Terry Hall, Kim Jackworth, Alan Margulies, Patricia Story, Dennis Sopko, Bob Golden, Rob Wilcox, Carol Getko, Alan Glasser, Robert Nicolas, Jimmy DiMarzo, Judy Tannen, Debbie Much, Bob Borum, Kris Ferraro, Robert Scott, Ruth Gillis, Leslie

Kitay, Henry Miller, and Kevin Sasaki.

Thank you to the executives, writers, deejays, producers, relatives, and other shrewd observers who helped get me up to speed on the music industry in the fifties and early sixties: Berle Adams, Lou Adler, Freddie Bienstock, Steve Blauner, Jimmy Bowen, Dodd Darin, Joe Delany, Steve Greenberg, Ren Grevatt, Art Laboe, David Leaf, Cary Mansfield, Bob Marcucci, Jeannie Martin, Frank Military, Mitch Miller, Ruth Roberts, Jerry Schilling, Jonathan Schwartz, and Harriet Wasser.

Thank you to the friends and associates who supported this project in its infancy: Gina Arnold, Sally Henry, Russ Galen, and Jim Fitzgerald. Thank you to the writers who inspired and goaded me: Nick Tosches, Peter Guralnick, Greil Marcus, and Dave Marsh. Thank you to my *Newsweek* guidance counselors: Jeff Giles, David Gates, Cathleen McGuigan, and many other friends on the editorial staff. Thank you to Ruth Tennenbaum for research assistance. A special thank you to John Leland for his invaluable kindness.

Thank you to the Starbucks gang who kept me company in my early-morning writing hours: Ramon, Sandy, Elsie, and Chet. Thank you to my wonderful babysitters:

Dorien, Naneen, Isatou, Khady, Margaret, and Jen. Thank you to the moms in the 'hood: Stephanie, Ruth, Robin, Karen, Paula, and Patti. And to a dad, Mark, who always cheered me up when the business side of life got me down.

Thank you to the loyal friends who provided encouragement, editorial advice, crisis management, and the occasional Bobby Darin CD or Ann-Margret fan book: Cheryl and Todd Abramson, Rich Schultz and Barb Smalls, Otis Ball, and Karen Durbin.

An especially heartfelt thank you to Robert Lloyd and Sarah Folger, who tended so conscientiously to me in L.A. I couldn't have done this without them.

An especially hyperbolic thank you to Wylie O'Sullivan, the most talented, sympathetic, insightful, poetic, and all-around fabulous editor on the planet. Thank you also to Dominick Anfuso, Martha Levin, Jennifer Weidman, Edith Lewis, Dana Sloan, Katie Adams, Nicole Kalian, Gail Anderson, and Eric Fuentecilla at Free Press.

Thank you to my agent, Dave Dunton, who rode in on a white horse and single-handedly rescued this project from oblivion. He believed in me when I didn't believe in myself. I am eternally grateful.

Thank you to the Salzbergs for their

endless repository of humor and good will. Thank you to my extended former nuclear family: Mom, Dad, Doug, Maureen, Eno, and Marie. Thank you, most of all, to Dave, for expanding my definition of love and showing me the value of a journey, and to Loretta, for shining like the sun.

In Memoriam

Julie London, Bobby Troup,
George Sidney, Jack Kroll

About the Author

Karen Schoemer was born in White Plains, New York, and grew up in New Canaan, Connecticut, the town portrayed in the film *The Ice Storm*. Her father was an accountant, her mother an antiques dealer. She graduated from the College of William and Mary, where she majored in philosophy and worked as a deejay and station manager at WCWM, the campus radio station. Schoemer has written about pop music for fanzines such as *The Bob* and *Option*, as well as major publications like *Rolling Stone*, *Blender*, *Mademoiselle*, and *O: The Oprah Magazine*. She was the first woman to serve as a pop stringer at the *New York Times* and the first female chief pop critic at *Newsweek*. Her work has appeared in the anthologies *Rock She Wrote: Women Write About Rock, Pop, and Rap*; *Trouble Girls: The Rolling Stone Book of Women in Rock*; *Da Capo Best Music Writing 2000*; and *Innocent When You Dream: The Tom Waits Reader*. Married, with a six-year-old daughter, she currently resides in upstate New York.